THE COMING WORLD LEADER

Understanding the Book of Revelation

DAVID HOCKING

MULTNOMAH · PRESS

Portland, Oregon 97266

"MAJESTY" - Jack W. Hayford
© 1981 Rocksmith Music c/o Trust Music Management
6255 Sunset Blvd. Suite 705, Hollywood, CA 90028
Used by permission. All rights reserved.

Unless otherwise indicated, all Scripture references are from the Holy
Bible, New King James Version, © 1982 by Thomas Nelson, Inc.

Cover design by Killion McCabe & Associates

THE COMING WORLD LEADER
© 1988 by Calvary Communications, Inc.
Published by Multnomah Press
Portland, Oregon 97266

Multnomah Press is a ministry of Multnomah School of the Bible, 8435
Northeast Glisan Street, Portland, Oregon 97220.

Printed in the United States of America.

Library of Congress Cataloging-in-Publication Data

Hocking, David L.
   The coming world leader/David L. Hocking.
      p. cm.
   Bibliography: p.
   ISBN 0-88070-219-2 (pbk.)
   1. Bible. N.T. Revelation—Commentaries. 2. Second Advent-Biblical
teaching.   I. Title.
BS2825.3.H63   1988
228'.077—dc19

88 89 90 91 92 93 94 95 – 10 9 8 7 6 5 4

Contents

Prelude

Students of world history are keenly aware that the nations of the world are facing enormous challenges and difficulties that were simply unknown in the past. The age of nuclear power has brought with it some frightening possibilities and realities.

Many sociologists and scientists are now speaking of the terrifying prospect of nuclear war and the end of human civilization as we know it. Movies, magazines, and television have pictured and described a holocaust of destruction and devastation previously thought impossible. Today it is a reality facing us all. The cries for world peace have become stronger with each passing decade.

In the midst of all these terrifying realities stands a problem for which there does not seem to be an answer. It is the problem of leadership—some would call it a crisis. Leaders have failed us. Politicians have lied to us. No matter who is elected or comes to power by force, the world situation rarely changes. It seems that world history is out of control. Is there anyone who can bring world peace?

Various religious groups, past and present, have challenged us with the need for a world leader, someone who can bring peace to planet earth. There have been many suggestions and attempts to bring such a leader to the world's attention and support. The cry for leadership continues, and the world seems ready, if not desperate, for it.

One of the most remarkable books in all of literature is found in the Bible. The last book of the New Testament, "the book of Revelation," contains an amazing look at the future, and speaks powerfully about a coming world leader who can bring peace to a troubled globe, order to the chaos and confusion that now plague this planet.

Prelude

This world leader is described as the "King of kings, and Lord of lords." According to the predictions of the book of Revelation, this coming world leader has been on this planet before, living among us, urging us to put our faith and trust in Him. He was rejected, criticized, and crucified by the Roman authorities of His time, but the memory of what He did and said lives on in the hearts of millions.

World history has been profoundly affected by His life and teachings. He was a Jew, born in the little village of Bethlehem and raised in the small town of Nazareth. For about three years He traveled throughout the land of Israel as an itinerant preacher. He was crucified just outside the city walls of ancient Jerusalem about forty years before the Roman invasion and destruction of that city in A.D. 70.

The New Testament records the events and teachings of this remarkable Person, and gives us information about the people who followed Him and continued His work and influence. One of His closest friends and associates was responsible for the book of Revelation which tells about Him as no other book does. According to this book of predictions about the future, this Man, called Jesus of Nazareth, is still alive! He arose from the dead three days after His execution and is coming back to this earth to rule and establish peace forever. He is the promised Messiah of the Jewish people, the only hope for the entire world.

Before you reject the possibility of the return of Jesus Christ to this planet, consider this fact: *Over three hundred prophecies about a coming world leader were fulfilled by Jesus of Nazareth during His lifetime on earth over nineteen hundred years ago.* The chance of this happening by coincidence or even the deliberate planning of a deceived group of followers is extremely slim, if not impossible.

The book of Revelation will astound you as it unfolds the future, both in the accuracy of its assessments of coming world events as well as in its predictions of how world problems will be solved. Its predictions no longer appear to be fanciful or unlikely. They are as current as the front pages of our newspapers.

The world cries for leadership, and the book of Revelation reveals the answer. There is a world leader coming who will bring peace forever to this planet. That's what this book is all about, and you owe it to yourself to read it and draw your own conclusions.

Introduction

The book of Revelation is prophecy, the majority of its teachings yet unfulfilled. It has a long history of differing interpretations and while fascinating to read, it remains a mystery to the average person.

Understanding the Book of Revelation

Is It Possible to Understand this Book?

Some people give you the impression that you need a Ph.D. or a working knowledge of Hebrew and Greek in order to understand the Bible, much less the book of Revelation. But while such credentials might be helpful, they are certainly not essential. The Bible is meant for everyone, not just a select group. Before you get started, consider some of these basic prerequisites for interpreting and understanding the Bible:

Faith. If you approach the Bible with preconceived ideas about its accuracy or reliability, doubting that it is the Word of God, your chances of understanding its message are extremely limited. Hebrews 11:3 tells us it is "by faith we understand." Verse 6 adds, "without faith it is impossible to please Him, for he who comes to God must believe that He is, and that He is a rewarder of those who diligently seek Him." That's pretty clear. We need faith in order to understand the Bible and please the God of the Bible.

It is faith that causes a person to pray to God and ask for His help in understanding the Bible. God wants you to know the message of Revelation more than you personally want to understand it. Psalm

119:18 says, "Open my eyes, that I may see / Wondrous things from Your law." Is that your desire? A strong appeal for understanding is given in Psalm 119:169: "Let my cry come before You, O LORD; / Give me understanding according to Your word."

A clean life. This may be a bit surprising, but the ability to understand the Bible is related to moral purity. Psalm 66:18 says, "If I regard iniquity in my heart, / The Lord will not hear." Such teaching is implied in 1 Peter 2:1-3: "Therefore, laying aside all malice, all guile, hypocrisy, envy, and all evil speaking, as newborn babes, desire the pure milk of the word, that you may grow thereby, if indeed you have tasted that the Lord is gracious."

James 3:17 states "But the wisdom that is from above is first pure." Purity is essential for knowing the wisdom of God and being able to understand the Scriptures. When there is sin in our hearts that remains unconfessed and unforsaken, it is a barrier to our ability to interpret the Bible.

Obedience. Those who obey the teachings of the Bible have a better understanding of the Bible than those who do not. Psalm 119:100 says, "I understand more than the ancients, / Because I keep Your precepts." Jesus taught us, "If anyone wants to do His will, he shall know concerning the doctrine, whether it is from God or whether I speak on My own authority (John 7:17)."

Study. It takes time, patience, and effort, but there is no substitute for it. Acts 17:11 commends the believers at Berea: "These were more fair-minded than those in Thessalonica, in that they received the word with all readiness, and searched the Scriptures daily to find out whether these things were so."

Most people do not take the time to search the Scriptures. We simply accept what some "authority" told us. Paul instructed Timothy (2 Timothy 2:15): "Be diligent to present yourself approved to God, a worker who does not need to be ashamed, rightly dividing the word of truth." Correct interpretation is based on careful study, being diligent, and working at it.

The reason this is so important in understanding the book of Revelation can be easily seen when we learn that this book quotes from the Old Testament over two hundred times. Unless we take the time to study the background behind these quotations, we will probably come to inaccurate conclusions or inadequate observations.

How Should We Interpret the Events Described in this Book?

This is a crucial issue. Revelation is filled with events and facts that must be interpreted due to the highly involved symbolism found in the book. Any person who reads the book for the first time is immediately aware of the presence of symbolic language. How should we interpret these things? Church history has given us at least four approaches to this problem.

Historical view. This viewpoint sees the book as a series of events that have already taken place, but serve as an example to believers in the future, especially those who find themselves alive at the second coming of Christ.

Symbolical view. This is also referred to as the allegorical view. It sees the book as an expression of great spiritual truth in symbolical language. The events are not to be taken as literal history, but as illustrations of spiritual principles and insights.

Spiritual view. Closely related to the second view, this approach sees the events in Revelation as descriptive of the conflict between Christianity and paganism. It is sometimes called the Preterist View.

Futuristic view. Combining some aspects of the historical view, this look at Revelation sees most of the book as future or unfulfilled prophecy. Most of the proponents of this view understand the contents from chapter 4 through the end of the book as being future events. Some prefer to call this the literal view. Those who hold to it speak of its events and details as being literally fulfilled one day.

.

Which View Is Correct?

Naturally, the one you believe! Perhaps it is best if we argue for reading the book as you would any other book. Apply the same principles of context, language, culture, and history that you would use with any other historical document.

A simple axiom for all Bible study is that if words do not mean what they say, then no one can say what they mean. Take the words literally unless there is clear indication in the text that the words are symbolic or figurative.

A common clue in the book of Revelation that something is to be taken symbolically is the appearance of the word "as" or "like." Such expressions help us to understand that the words are expressing like-ness or similarity in external form or appearance, but are not to be taken literally.

When Will Jesus Christ Come Again?

The answer to that is a part of the problem we all have in trying to understand the book of Revelation. Chapter 20 mentions a period of a thousand years, commonly referred to as the *millennium* (Latin word for "one thousand"). Is Jesus Christ coming again before or after that time? Or is the thousand years to be taken literally? These questions deal with three major viewpoints about the millennium:

Amillennialism—the belief that the reference to a thousand years should be taken symbolically and not literally.

Postmillennialism—the belief that Jesus Christ will return after the thousand years are over. This view stresses the impact of the gospel in this present age.

Premillennialism—the belief that the thousand years are to be taken literally, beginning after Jesus Christ returns to the earth to set up His kingdom and reign as King.

One of the fascinating things about these viewpoints is how they affect a person's understanding of Old Testament promises given to the nation of Israel. Amillennialists see these promises as fulfilled in the church, while premillennialists see the church age as a "parenthesis" in history, after which God will again work directly with the nation of Israel and fulfill all His promises to her. Naturally, events in the land of Israel today are interpreted quite differently by these two viewpoints.

The Rapture Question

The second coming of Christ is referred to in the New Testament by different Greek words. A simple look at the potential problem this creates can be seen by the following:

Parousia—a word emphasizing the presence or arrival of someone (cf. 1 Thessalonians 4:15; 2 Thessalonians 2:1).

Epiphaneia—a word meaning "to shine forth" or "to appear upon." In Greek literature it is used of the appearance of a god to men (cf. 1 Timothy 6:14; 2 Timothy 4:1, 8; Titus 2:13).

Apokalupsis—a word meaning "to uncover" or "unveil." It is the word in the title of this book—Revelation (cf. 2 Thessalonians 1:7; 1 Peter 4:13).

Each is important in describing the second coming of Christ. Some Bible teachers have tried to show a distinction between the words, believing that *parousia* refers to the rapture, a secret coming of Christ for church-age believers mentioned in 1 Thessalonians 4:13-18, and *apokalupsis* to the public appearance and return of Jesus Christ to the earth at the end of the tribulation period.

Are There Two Second Comings?

The word *rapture* is not found in the Bible. It comes from a Latin word used to translate a Greek word in 1 Thessalonians 4:17, where it says believers will be "caught up" to meet the Lord when He comes. A distinction is made by many Bible teachers today between the event described in 1 Thessalonians 4:13-18 and the event in Revelation 19. They see the second coming of Christ as happening in two phases. One will occur in the air and involve only church-age believers: this is called the rapture. The second phase will be the coming of Jesus Christ to the earth and involve the whole world: this is called the revelation.

Is the rapture the same as the revelation? Some believe it is; others disagree. Your view does affect the way you interpret the book of Revelation. Actually, there are at least five views of the rapture. They are associated with the tribulation period, the time of God's judgment being poured out on the earth, described in the book of Revelation.

A-Tribulational view—the belief that there is no literal period of time yet future known as the tribulation period.

Post-Tribulational view—the belief that the rapture and the revelation are one and the same event. This is the dominant view of church history until the twentieth century.

Mid-Tribulational view—the belief that Jesus Christ will return for church-age believers in the middle of a seven-year tribulation period. The two witnesses of Revelation 11 are seen as types of church-age believers.

Partial Rapture view—the belief that only Spirit-filled believers will be raptured by Jesus Christ before the tribulation period. Carnal believers will have to go through the tribulation period. This view is similar to the concept of purgatory, where believers are supposedly purged of their sinful attitudes and practices.

Pre-Tribulational view—the belief that Jesus Christ will come for His church before the tribulation period begins, and that He will return to the earth after the tribulation to set up His kingdom for a thousand years.

Introduction

Which View Is Correct?

Bible teachers disagree, but that does not diminish our confidence in the authority and accuracy of the Bible. There is only one correct interpretation of the Bible, and that's the one which God intended when it was first written.

Our problem is that we are limited in our knowledge and experience and subject to human weakness and opinion. We will one day have these matters cleared up by the Lord Himself, but until that time, we struggle the best we can with the resources available to us.

The viewpoint of this book is that the events of Revelation should be taken literally unless symbolical language is employed that would indicate otherwise. From this perspective, the events from chapter 4 to the end of the book are still future.

A Possible Outline of the Book

The key verse is Revelation 1:19 where the apostle John is told: "Write the things which you have seen, and the things which are, and the things which will take place after this [or, 'after these things']." John thus organizes the book into three parts:

The things which you have seen—the vision of Jesus Christ in chapter 1 (everything preceding verse 19) which pictures Him after His resurrection.

The things which are—messages to the seven churches recorded in chapters 2 and 3. According to Revelation 1:20, "the seven stars *are* the angels of the seven churches, and the seven lampstands which you saw *are* the seven churches."

The things which will take place after this —everything after chapter 4, which begins with the phrase "after these things," the same phrase from Revelation 1:19.

The messages to the churches are for all of us who live between the time of the resurrection of Jesus Christ and the time of the Great Tribulation, described in chapters 6-18. The return of Jesus Christ to this earth is found in chapter 19, and events which follow are presented in the final three chapters of the book where we learn about the heavenly city with streets of gold.

The book of Revelation centers on the Person and Majesty of Jesus Christ the coming King and sovereign Lord. To help emphasize that central focus in our study of the book, we have organized it in three parts:

Part 1—Lord of the Churches
(Revelation 1:1-5:14)

Part 2—Lion over the Nations
(Revelation 6:1-20:15)

Part 3—Lamb among God's Servants
(Revelation 21:1-22:21)

Background Information for the Book of Revelation

Who Wrote the Book and When Was It Written?

Revelation 1:1, 4, 9, and 21:2 tell us the apostle John, one of the original twelve disciples of Jesus, wrote the book. He likewise claims to be an eyewitness of these events and descriptions: "Now I, John, saw and heard these things" (22:8).

Verse 9 of chapter 1 indicates that John is on the island called Patmos, having been exiled there by the Roman emperor Domitian. Various Greek cruises will take you to this island today and you will see why it was used as a place of exile in ancient times. It is a desolate place, surrounded by water.

Irenaeus, one of the early Christian leaders in the second century A.D., tells us that the book was written during the reign of Domitian (A.D. 81-96), and claims to have had direct contact with John through his disciple and friend, Polycarp, bishop of Smyrna (a major city on the western shore of Turkey).

John states in 1:9 that he "was" on the island called Patmos. Though it appears the vision of this book came to him while on the island, that remark indicates that he was, in fact, released. Tradition tells us he died and was buried in Ephesus. It may have been there where the book was put into its final form and distributed among the churches. According to tradition, he was released under the Emperor Nerva and returned to Ephesus.

John's lifespan covers the first century A.D. He was a disciple of Jesus at a young age, and was the disciple whom Jesus loved (John 21:20). He was entrusted with the care of Jesus' mother, Mary (John 19:25-27), and tradition tells us that she is buried in Ephesus along with John. John was the only disciple who did not die as a martyr for his faith. He wrote the Gospel of John, the three short epistles of John and the book of Revelation.

Introduction

To Whom Was the Book Written?

The opening chapter (1:4, 11) reveals that the immediate destination of this book was the seven churches in Asia (a Roman province covering the western side of present-day Turkey) or Asia Minor. This fact is repeated in 2:1, 8, 12, 18; 3:1, 7, 14; and 22:16.

The opening verse says that God gave this to "His servants." In addition to the specific intent of giving this message to the seven churches of Asia, we must also insist that it was intended for all of God's servants. In several places, we encounter the phrase "he who has an ear, let him hear what the Spirit says to the churches" (2:7, 11, 17, 29; 3:6, 13, and 22). That obviously applies to all who will listen to what is being said to those seven churches. The message is for all of us.

Inspired by the words of Revelation 1:3, let's begin the exciting adventure of studying the book of Revelation!

> Blessed is he who reads and those who hear the words of
> this prophecy, and keep those things which are written in
> it; for the time is near.

Chapter 1

A Book about Jesus Christ

(1:1-3)

A father was trying to read his morning newspaper while his little daughter was asking him all kinds of questions. He decided to give her something to do with her hands that would give him time to finish his reading. He found a map of the world in the paper and tore it out, folded it in several ways, and then cut it into small pieces. He said to his little girl, "Here, honey, is a map of the world. See if you can put the puzzle together." Confident that she didn't know anything about geography, he settled back into his chair and continued to read.

In a matter of minutes the little girl had it all put together on the floor. The surprised father said, "How did you do that so fast?" She replied, "Well, I found a picture of Jesus on the other side, and I knew when I had Him in the right place, the whole world would be all right!"

As the title reveals—"The Revelation of Jesus Christ"—here is a book about the Savior. This book unveils His person like nothing else you will ever read! A "revelation" indicates that something not known in the past is now being understood. This revelation of Jesus Christ can refer to the following three things:

1. Things to know about Jesus Christ Himself;
2. The event in which He comes to this earth;
3. The information He gives to John and to us about what is going to take place in the future.

The prophecy of Daniel is closely related to the events of Revelation. In Daniel 12:8-9 we read:

Although I heard, I did not understand. Then I said, "My lord, what shall be the end of these things?" And he said,

17

> "Go your way, Daniel, for the words are closed up and sealed till the time of the end."

However, in Revelation 22:10 we read:

> And he said to me, "Do not seal the words of the prophecy of this book, for the time is at hand."

In Daniel, the words are sealed; in Revelation, they are opened for all to see and understand. In Daniel, they are sealed until the "time of the end"; in Revelation, "the time is at hand." As each day passes, we draw that much closer to the events described in this marvelous book of Revelation. Christians speak of the second coming of Jesus Christ as their "blessed hope."

The Titles Given to Jesus Christ

To emphasize why this book is an unveiling of the person of Jesus Christ like no other book in the Bible, consider all the various titles and descriptive phrases given to Him in this book:

1. The faithful witness (1:5)
2. The firstborn from the dead (1:5)
3. The ruler over the kings of the earth (1:5)
4. The Alpha and the Omega (1:8)
5. The Beginning and the End (1:8)
6. Who is and who was and who is to come (1:8)
7. The Almighty (1:8)
8. The First and the Last (1:11, 17)
9. The Son of Man (1:13)
10. He who lives (1:18)
11. He who holds the seven stars in His right hand, who walks in the midst of the seven golden lampstands (2:1)
12. He who has the sharp two-edged sword (2:12)
13. Son of God (2:18)
14. He who has eyes like a flame of fire, and His feet like fine brass (2:18)
15. He who has the seven Spirits of God and the seven stars (3:1)
16. He who is holy (3:7)
17. He who is true (3:7)
18. He who has the key of David, He who opens and no one shuts, and shuts and no one opens (3:7)

19. The Amen (3:14)
20. The Faithful and True Witness (3:14)
21. The Beginning of the creation of God (3:14)
22. The Lion of the tribe of Judah (5:5)
23. The Root of David (5:5; 22:16)
24. The Lamb (5:6, 8, 12, 13; 6:1, 16, and elsewhere [28 times])
25. Lord, holy and true (6:10)
26. Lord God Almighty (15:3)
27. King of the saints (15:3)
28. The Word of God (19:13)
29. King of kings and Lord of lords (19:16)
30. The Bright and Morning Star (22:16)
31. Lord Jesus (22:20)
32. Lord Jesus Christ (22:21)

What a testimony to the person and work of Jesus Christ! If you do not see Jesus in this book, you must be blind. He is the focus of it all, the centerpiece of its pages, the reason for its message, the glory of its words.

The Uniqueness of This Book
(1:1-3)

¹The Revelation of Jesus Christ, which God gave Him to show His servants—things which must shortly take place. And He sent and signified it by His angel to His servant John, ²who bore witness to the word of God, and to the testimony of Jesus Christ, and to all things that he saw. ³Blessed is he who reads and those who hear the words of this prophecy, and keep those things which are written in it; for the time is near.

The book of Revelation is unique in at least two ways: (1) It is unique in the *way* it was given (1:1-2); and (2) it is unique in the *worth* of its message (1:3).

How Was this Message Given by God to Us? (1:1-2)

The opening verse tells us immediately that God gave this message to Jesus Christ, who in turn sent it to John by means of an angel.

According to Revelation 22:16, Jesus claims to have sent His angel to give this message to John for the churches. In chapter 1, verse 2,

John is the one "who bore witness to the word of God, and to the testimony of Jesus Christ, and to all things that he saw." The words "I saw" or "I heard" appear over sixty times in the book, some forty-four of those referring to separate or distinct visions given to him.

The message given by God to Jesus Christ and sent to John by the angel was communicated by means of signs or symbols. Verse 1 says it was "signified." We should expect, therefore, to see a great deal of symbolic language in the book.

An important insight is found in Revelation 1:10 concerning the unique way in which this message was given to John. John claims: "I was in the Spirit on the Lord's Day." Some believe this simply means he was filled with the Spirit when he wrote the book and that it happened on Sunday or the Sabbath (Saturday). The "Lord's Day" is referring to the promised "Day of the Lord" which involves the period of time known as the tribulation. It is what we call an *eschatological* term (referring to the study of "last things"). The message of the Revelation is primarily dealing with future events—the Day of the Lord.

John's reference to being "in the Spirit" is most interesting. The New King James text (along with many others) has already interpreted the word *Spirit* as referring to the Holy Spirit by capitalizing it. But does that mean that he was merely Spirit-filled?

It is also possible that John is speaking of the realm of the spirit as opposed to the realm of the flesh. He may have been transferred spiritually to the time of these events and thus actually did see them unfold in front of his eyes. He then tried to explain them in the language of his day and time, some of which seems quite strange to us today.

The following observations lend support to the interpretation that this is what happened to John:

1. The article *the* is not in the Greek text preceding the word *spirit*;
2. The verb translated "I was" (*ginomai*) would be better rendered "I became" indicating a change of condition;
3. Such an experience possibly happened to the apostle Paul (cf. 2 Corinthians 12:1-4);
4. This helps explain the reference in 4:1-2 where John is evidently caught up to heaven and says "I was in the Spirit";
5. It would also explain the experience of Revelation 17:3 and 21:10 where John is "carried away in the Spirit."

If this view is correct, it would appear that John was transported by some spiritual time device that placed him at the time of the future events mentioned in this book. John actually saw them occurring.

How Important Is this Message to Us Today? (1:3a)

The book of Revelation is unique in terms of the blessing it promises (1:3). This promised blessing emphasizes the importance of the book's message. Three kinds of people are mentioned, all of whom are candidates to be blessed:

He who reads. Before the Bible was printed so that we could each have our own copy, an important function of the pastor was to read the Scriptures. Paul told Timothy (1 Timothy 4:13) "Till I come, give attention to reading." The one who read the book would receive a special blessing from the Lord, and that promise is still true today for all who will simply read its message.

Those who hear the words of this prophecy. The change from "he" to "those" indicates that one person read the book in the hearing of others. Those who would listen to the public reading of this book would also receive a blessing from its message.

Those who keep those things which are written in it. This does not refer to keeping the book in a safe place, obviously. It refers to obedience—responding to the message and challenges of this book (and there are quite a few to consider).

How Close Are We to the Events of This Book? (1:3b)

The opening verse states that these events are "things which must shortly take place." Verse 3 adds, "the time is near." How close are we?

The word translated "shortly" is found seven times in the book of Revelation (including 1:1):

> "Repent, or else I will come to you *quickly*" (2:16)
> "Behold, I come *quickly*" (3:11)
> "The third woe is coming *quickly*" (11:14)
> "Behold, I am coming *quickly*" (22:7)
> "And behold, I am coming *quickly*" (22:12)
> "Surely I am coming *quickly*" (22:20)

It seems to indicate the suddenness of what is coming. It would be similar to the idea of being surprised or taken by surprise. It also indicates that the coming will be soon, perhaps at the point when the events of Revelation begin to unfold.

The phrase "the time is near" refers to the season or opportunity for these events to unfold. The specific "time" involved is the time for God's judgment and wrath to be poured out upon this world. If there has been a delay (and there certainly has—for over nineteen hundred years!), it is for the salvation of people:

> The Lord is not slack concerning His promise, as some count slackness, but is longsuffering toward us, not willing that any should perish but that all should come to repentance (2 Peter 3:9).

The disciples of Jesus asked Him this question right before His ascension to heaven: "Lord, will You at this time restore the kingdom to Israel?" (Acts 1:6). Jesus responded with these important words: "It is not for you to know times or seasons which the Father has put in His own authority."

In Matthew 24 Jesus taught: "But of that day and hour no one knows, no, not even the angels of heaven, but My Father only. . . . Watch therefore, for you do not know what hour your Lord is coming. . . . Therefore you also be ready, for the Son of Man is coming at an hour when you do not expect Him" (vv. 36, 42, 44). Chapter 25, verse 13, emphasizes the point again: "Watch therefore, for you know neither the day nor the hour in which the Son of Man is coming."

In the great prophecy of Luke 21:20-28, which speaks of the destruction of Jerusalem (A.D. 70) as well as the coming of the Lord, Jesus made this statement: "And Jerusalem will be trampled by Gentiles until the times of the Gentiles are fulfilled."

Some Bible teachers believe these "times of the Gentiles" are over now that the nation of Israel has control of the city of Jerusalem. They then conclude that "the time of the end" is upon us, and it won't be long before Jesus Christ returns. Other Bible teachers are not sure about the application of this prophecy of Jesus to the present control of Jerusalem by the nation of Israel.

In Romans 11:25, the apostle Paul wrote:

> For I do not desire, brethren, that you should be ignorant of this mystery, lest you should be wise in your own opinion, that hardening in part has happened to Israel *until the fullness of the Gentiles* has come in.

Is the "fullness of the Gentiles" the same as the "times of the Gentiles"? Some believe it is. It speaks of the period of time between the day of Pentecost in Acts 2 and the second coming of Christ when God is pouring out His Holy Spirit upon all nations of the world and bringing a multitude of Gentiles to salvation. He is not through with Israel, however. The nation of Israel, according to Bible prophecy, will turn to the Lord when He comes (Zechariah 12:10; Romans 11:26), and the partial hardening will be removed.

We believe the "times of the Gentiles" refers to Gentile control of Jerusalem. The "fullness of the Gentiles" refers to the salvation of Gentiles during this age (often called "the church age"). It is possible that they are synonymous in terms of time, although referring to different matters during that time period.

So Is This the Time?

Jesus told us to watch and be ready. That should be enough. Too much speculation keeps us from doing what He said to do while we wait. Guessing is a waste of time. We are obviously closer today than we were yesterday.

As we study the book of Revelation, we must always remember that it is not primarily a book telling us how to set dates or develop a chronological table of events, but rather an unveiling of the Person and work of Jesus Christ our Lord in all of His glory. It's a book that ought to give us hope and joy! It should draw us closer to our Savior, inspiring us to love Him more and to anticipate that glorious day when He shall return in power and great glory.

Chapter 2

God's Final Message to the Churches

(1:4-11)

Though written to seven actual churches in the Roman province of Asia Minor (western Turkey), this is God's final message to all churches throughout history. The book of Revelation closes His written revelation to us (cf. Revelation 22:18-19).

The Source of This Final Message
(1:4-6)

⁴John, to the seven churches which are in Asia:

Grace to you and peace from Him who is and who was and who is to come, and from the seven Spirits who are before His throne, ⁵and from Jesus Christ, the faithful witness, the firstborn from the dead, and the ruler over the kings of the earth. To Him who loved us and washed us from our sins in His own blood, ⁶and has made us kings and priests to His God and Father, to Him be glory and dominion forever and ever. Amen.

The Father is described as "Him who is and who was and who is to come." Present, past, and future—the eternal God, no beginning or end—He has always existed. The Bible's opening statement is "In the beginning *God . . .*" No more needs to be said. The Bible does not try to prove the existence of God; it merely assumes it. Nothing has meaning or purpose without it.

The Problem of the Seven Spirits of God (1:4)

These greetings also come from "the seven Spirits who are before the throne." There are two major views regarding the meaning of this phrase.

It refers to the seven angels mentioned in the book. Hebrews 1:14 calls angels "ministering spirits." The fact that this phrase says "the seven Spirits" would be no problem if the reference is to angels. The messages to the seven churches are addressed in each case "to the angel of the church of . . ." Seven angels blow seven trumpets, announcing the judgments of God (cf. Revelation 8:2), and seven angels are involved in pouring out the bowls of the wrath of God (cf. Revelation 16:1).

It refers to the Holy Spirit. Some believe that the number "seven" refers to the description of the Holy Spirit in Isaiah 11:2, "The Spirit of the LORD shall rest upon Him, the Spirit of wisdom and understanding, the Spirit of counsel and might, the Spirit of knowledge and of the fear of the LORD."

If the first statement, "the Spirit of the LORD," counts as one characteristic, then there are seven items mentioned, though interestingly, they are grouped into three categories in the text, noted by the repetition of the words "the Spirit of." More likely, this text lists six characteristics, not seven.

Others believe that the number "seven" speaks of completion or perfection and would refer to the totality of the Spirit's ministry.

We believe the phrase "the seven Spirits of God" as used in the book of Revelation should be connected with the seven angels mentioned frequently in the book. Revelation 8:2 says "And I saw *the* seven angels who stand before God . . ." This seems to imply the special group previously mentioned "who stand before God" and "before His throne" (1:4). The words about these seven angels in chapter 15 and 16 seem to support this view as well.

It's a Word from Jesus Christ

The book is called a "revelation of Jesus Christ," not only in the sense of revealing new truths about His nature and work (which it does), but also in the sense of the content being communicated from Jesus Christ our Lord. That is quite clear in the opening of each letter to the seven churches.

Four things are quickly brought to our attention by this initial greeting: His place of authority, His plan of redemption, His purpose for the believer, and His praise for eternity.

His Place of Authority (1:5a)

Three titles are given to Him initially to remind us of His authority and why we should heed His message:

The faithful witness (establishes His credibility). To Pilate in John 18:37 Jesus said, "You say rightly that I am a king. For this cause I was born, and for this cause I have come into the world, that I should bear witness to the truth. Everyone who is of the truth hears My voice." In Revelation 3:14, this title is repeated with an additional adjective, "the Faithful *and True* Witness."

The firstborn from the dead (establishes His superiority). Colossians 1:18 states: "And He is the head of the body, the church, who is the beginning, the firstborn from the dead, that in all things He may have the preeminence."

"Firstborn" is a word referring to rank or position. Romans 8:29 speaks of the reason why God predestines us to be conformed to His Son "that He might be the firstborn among many brethren." Hebrews 1:6 makes it abundantly clear when it says, "But when He again brings the firstborn into the world, He says: 'Let all the angels of God worship Him.'" The Firstborn Son of God is to be worshiped!

The ruler over the kings of the earth (establishes His sovereignty). No book proclaims His authority and sovereignty like the book of Revelation. At the sounding of the seventh trumpet, loud voices proclaim, "The kingdoms of this world have become the kingdoms of our Lord and of His Christ, and He shall reign forever and ever." Revelation 19:16 says, "And He has on His robe and on His thigh a name written: KING OF KINGS AND LORD OF LORDS."

His Plan of Redemption (1:5b)

The past tense of the verbs *loved* and *washed* reminds us of the day Jesus died on the cross for our sins. It was that moment in history when God demonstrated His love for us (John 3:16; 1 John 4:9, 10) and settled forever the problem of our sins.

When the text says *washed* it uses the Greek word *to loose* and refreshes our minds with the great truth that we have been released from the slavery of sin, set free by the purchase price of the blood of Jesus Christ (1 Corinthians 6:20; 1 Peter 1:18-19). It was not the blood of an animal that atoned for our sins (Hebrews 10:4) but it was "his *own* blood" that provided our redemption and salvation.

Redemption is a primary theme of the book of Revelation and the description of Jesus which continually emphasizes that fact is that He is "the Lamb" (mentioned 28 times).

27

His Purpose for the Believer (1:6a)

What wonderful words of blessing! The Lord intends believers to be both "kings" and "priests," and the goal of such authority and ministry is the Lord Himself—"to His God and Father." Notice carefully the statement repeated often in the New Testament that the Father is the God and Father of our Lord Jesus Christ—a mystery to us how God could be manifested as both Father and Son, yet maintain a blessed relationship and distinction between one another so that the Son can refer to the Father as "His God and Father."

Some translations read that He has made us to be a "kingdom" rather than "kings." It is by spiritual birth that we enter that kingdom (John 3:3, 5), having been translated into it by the work of Jesus Christ (Colossians 1:13).

Peter makes it quite clear in 1 Peter 2:9 that all believers are priests. He calls us "a royal priesthood," designed by God to proclaim His praise. We must always remember that the purpose of our priestly ministry and worship is to praise and worship the Lord, not ourselves.

His Praise for Eternity (1:6b)

The book of Revelation, God's final message to the churches, is intended to show us the ultimate objective of God in creating the world and mankind—that everything might praise and worship Him! This is a book about worship. Often in the book you will read of creatures that God has made (both men and angels) falling down and worshiping Him. The scene of heaven itself throughout the book is one where the worship of God is the primary activity.

The "Amen" at the end of this section does not mean the end of what he has to say; it is a word of agreement, an outburst of praise (in a sense), proclaiming our joy at what was just said.

A Summary of This Final Message
(1:7-8)

> [7]*Behold, He is coming with clouds, and every eye will see Him, and they also who pierced Him. And all the tribes of the earth will mourn because of Him. Even so, Amen.* [8]*"I am the Alpha and the Omega, the Beginning and the End," says the Lord, "who is and who was and who is to come, the Almighty."*

These two verses give us an overview of the book of Revelation. They reveal that it is a book dealing with the coming of our Lord to this earth, and the character of our Lord Himself. The book unveils the event of His return and the glory of His Person—what it will be like when we see Him.

The Second Coming of Jesus Christ (1:7)

At least three things can be gleaned from this one glorious verse:

The anticipation of the event. Behold, a simple word asking for our attention, is used thirty times in this book. It literally means "look for yourself." It suggests there is a responsibility we all have in anticipating this great event of the return of Jesus Christ. Are you looking for Him to return?

The association of clouds with His coming ("He is coming with clouds"). Similar words are found in Matthew 24:30—"and they will see the Son of Man coming on the clouds of heaven with power and great glory" (cf. Daniel 7:13; Luke 21:27). First Thessalonians 4:17 suggests that believers will be caught up to meet the Lord "in the clouds" and "in the air." When our Lord ascended to heaven (Acts 1:9) we are told that "a cloud received Him out of their sight." Since He is to return "in like manner" (Acts 1:11) we should expect His coming to be associated with clouds.

It was a pillar of cloud that led the children of Israel through the wilderness by day (Exodus 13:21-22), a visible manifestation of the Divine presence. The glory of the Lord appeared "in the cloud" (Exodus 16:10) and "the cloud of the Lord was above the tabernacle by day" (Exodus 40:38).

Perhaps the simplest idea behind His coming "with clouds" is that clouds are associated with the Divine presence of God.

The attitudes expressed when He comes ("And all the tribes of the earth will mourn because of Him. Even so, Amen"). A clear reference to Zechariah 12:10-14 is found in this verse. That prophecy speaks of the day when the inhabitants of Jerusalem will experience the outpouring of the Holy Spirit and "they will look on Me whom they have pierced; they will mourn for Him as one mourns for his only son, and grieve for Him as one grieves for a firstborn."

The whole world will see the Lord return to this earth. This is no secret coming (as 1 Thessalonians 4:16-17 implies) for believers only, but is a world-wide demonstration of the Lord's presence and power. It will not merely be the children of Israel who will mourn, but "all tribes of the earth" will express the heartfelt longing of one who mourns over the loss of his only son. All will recognize clearly that this is the One whom they have ignored, rejected, and hated.

The Glorious Character of the Coming King (1:8)

The eternal character of the coming King is clearly portrayed and identified with the God of the Bible. Isaiah proclaims:

> "Thus says the LORD, the King of Israel,
> And his Redeemer, the LORD of hosts;
> 'I am the First and I am the Last;
> Besides Me there is no God.'"
> . . . .
> Listen to Me, O Jacob,
> And Israel, My called:
> I am He, I am the First,
> I am also the Last"
>
> (Isaiah 44:6; 48:12).

Revelation 22:13 echoes Jesus' claim to be "the Alpha and the Omega, the Beginning and the End, the First and the Last." "Alpha" is the first letter of the Greek alphabet, and "Omega" the last. Our Lord is everything that can be said! He is proclaimed as the eternal God and clearly identified in these titles as Jehovah, the God of Abraham, Isaac, and Jacob. The deity of Jesus Christ is clearly proclaimed in the book of Revelation.

The Situation Behind This Final Message
(1:9-11)

⁹ I, John, both your brother and companion in tribulation, and in the kingdom and patience of Jesus Christ, was on the island that is called Patmos for the word of God and for the testimony of Jesus Christ. ¹⁰I was in the Spirit on the Lord's Day, and I heard behind me a loud voice, as of a trumpet, ¹¹saying, "I am the Alpha and the Omega, the First and the Last," and, "What you see, write in a book and send it to the seven churches which are in Asia: to Ephesus, to Smyrna, to Pergamos, to Thyatira, to Sardis, to Philadelphia, and to Laodicea."

The Person Who Saw the Vision (1:9a)

From 1:1, 4 and 22:8, we are convinced that John was the one who wrote the book and received this wonderful vision of our resurrected Lord Jesus Christ. He describes himself as "your brother," indicating his spiritual relationship and equality with the believers he was writing to in the seven churches of Asia Minor.

He also calls himself "your companion in tribulation, and in the kingdom and patience of Jesus Christ." This seems to indicate the general condition of things at the time he wrote the book. Christians were being persecuted by the emperor Domitian, as they had been under a previous emperor, Nero. John identifies with these fellow believers in their time of suffering and hardship, reminding them that he was experiencing the same things.

The Place Where He Saw the Vision (1:9b)

The first time I saw Patmos, I was impressed with its barrenness. It is an island approximately ten miles long and six miles wide, covered with rocks and very little vegetation. It was obvious to me why the Romans chose this island as a place of exile. There was no escape from it.

One of the early church leaders, Hippolytus, tells us of John's suffering under Domitian. He says that he was first plunged into boiling oil, and then sent to this island exile. Another leader, Victorinus, states that John was forced to labor in the mines located on Patmos. Others, such as Irenaeus, Clement, and Eusebius, say that John returned to Ephesus after his exile, went to the various churches, and appointed leaders and set things in order.

The Persecution that Led to His Exile (1:9c)

John says he was on the island of Patmos "for the word of God and the testimony of Jesus Christ." That indicates he was faithful in proclaiming the gospel of Christ and was not afraid of what might happen to him. In God's wonderful plan, he was arrested and exiled in order to receive this marvelous revelation about the future. It reminds us of Paul's instructions in Philippians 1 not to worry about his imprisonment because God was using him to further the spread of the gospel.

Today, many believers do not enjoy freedom to worship or proclaim the good news of Jesus Christ. Persecution still exists in many parts of the world, and often Christians must meet in secret. It is encouraging to see how God uses those difficult times for His glory. Our role is to trust Him fully and to have no fear of those who oppose our message or hinder our religious freedom. May God give us strength, courage, and wisdom to understand these things when persecution comes, no matter how mild or severe it may be.

His State When He Received this Vision (1:10)

John says he was "in the Spirit on the Lord's Day." As discussed in chapter 1, this is not a reference to being Spirit- filled on Sunday or the Sabbath, but rather a statement about his being transported by the Spirit into the world of prophetic visions where he was allowed to witness a future time of terrible judgment, "the Day of the Lord." John literally saw these events take place. It sounds incredible, but remarks in the book about his position in the grandstands of the future leave us no other choice.

The Purpose Behind This Vision (1:11)

Simply stated, John was to write the vision down and send it to the seven churches of Asia Minor:

Ephesus	Thyatira	Philadelphia
Smyrna	Sardis	Laodicea
Pergamos		

It has been my privilege to visit these sites and to examine the evidence behind their existence in ancient times. These were actual cities, and each has a rich history to study and explore. We will deal with some of that information when we take up the messages that were sent to each of these places.

The "loud voice" is mentioned twenty times in the book, and the single word *loud* (great) occurs eighty-two times. This causes some people to speak of Revelation as the *great* book of the Bible. Everything is presented on a grand scale.

This voice was like the sound of a trumpet, and it is none other than the voice of Jesus Christ. It reminds us of 1 Thessalonians 4:16 where we are told that the return of Jesus Christ for the believers will be accompanied with a "shout . . . and the trumpet of God."

Chapter 3

A Vision of Jesus Christ

(1:12-20)

A noticeable change has taken place from what the four gospels describe when they speak of Jesus Christ. This is a picture of what He is like now that He has risen from the dead. He is not pictured in the robe of humanity, but in the garments of royalty and deity. He is no longer the humble, suffering Servant, willing to endure the agony and death of a Roman cross— He is now the King of kings and Lord of lords! He has risen from the dead, and the glory He had before He came into the world in a manger in Bethlehem is now brilliantly displayed. It is a picture of glory and greatness.

A Vision of Glory and Greatness
(1:12-20)

12 Then I turned to see the voice that spoke with me. And having turned I saw seven golden lampstands, 13 and in the midst of the seven lampstands One like the Son of Man, clothed with a garment down to the feet and girded about the chest with a golden band. 14 His head and His hair were white like wool, as white as snow, and His eyes like a flame of fire; 15 His feet were like fine brass, as if refined in a furnace, and His voice as the sound of many waters; 16 He had in His right hand seven stars, out of His mouth went a sharp two-edged sword, and His countenance was like the sun shining in its strength. 17 And when I saw Him, I fell at His feet as dead. But He laid His right hand on me, saying to me, "Do not be afraid; I am the First and the Last. 18 I am He who lives, and was dead, and behold, I am alive forevermore. Amen. And I have the keys of Hades and of Death. [19] Write the things which you have seen, and the things which are, and the things which will take place after this. [20] The mystery of the seven stars which you saw in My right hand, and the seven golden lampstands: The seven stars are the angels of the seven churches, and the seven lampstands which you saw are the seven churches."

His Exalted Position (1:12)

The "lampstands" represent the churches (1:20) and Jesus is standing in the midst of them. According to Revelation 2:1, He "walks in the midst of the seven golden lampstands."

Matthew 18:20 says, "For where two or three are gathered together in My name, I am there in the midst of them." This verse relates to the authority of two or three witnesses who go to a brother who has sinned against a fellow believer but has refused to acknowledge it. The "two or three" are now to be witnesses to what he says. If they are in agreement, it carries the force of Christ's presence and authority.

To say that Jesus is "in the midst of" the churches is to recognize His central place of authority and to acknowledge His sovereign presence. One of the greatest needs in churches today is to see Jesus Christ in all of His glory and to submit to His presence and authority. Too much attention and honor is paid to human leadership that often robs the Lord Jesus of His central place. He, not a board of elders, or a pastor, or the vote of a congregation, is "the Head of the church."

His Eternal Humanity (1:13a)

He became man for us ("One like the Son of Man") that He might know human life by personal experience. He knows what we are like and has been touched with the feeling of our weakness and need (Hebrews 2:17 and 4:15), and thus is a merciful and faithful High Priest, constantly interceding for us.

"Son of Man" was the favorite title Jesus used of Himself. It has special meaning to students of Bible prophecy. In Daniel 7 there is a picture of God the Father, "the Ancient of Days," seated upon His throne. Before Him stands "One like the Son of Man" who will one day have a kingdom that shall never be destroyed. This is the coming Messiah.

God became man—that's the heart of the gospel message. If Jesus is not God, then He can do nothing to save us from our sins; only God can forgive sins. If He is not man, then there was no genuine death to substitute for us and pay for our sins. But this seeming difficulty is resolved by accepting the Bible's clear statements about Him—He is both God and man.

The fact that He retains His humanity following His resurrection is both a guarantee to all believers of our future bodily resurrection as well as a blessing that we will have an everlasting revelation of God in human form. What an aid to our understanding and need!

His Unique Appearance (1:13b-16)

This is no ordinary look at the man we know from the gospels as Jesus Christ. To say that His appearance is unique is also an understatement; it is supernatural, a glorious description that could be given to God alone.

His majesty ("clothed with a garment down to the feet and girded about the chest with a golden band"). This is not the garment of the average peasant of Middle Eastern culture. It is not the short tunic, but the garment of wealth, high position, and royalty. It is like the garment of the high priest of Exodus 39, and a reminder that Jesus is our High Priest (Hebrews 3:1).

The golden band around the chest pictures His majesty and authority as King of kings. When Isaiah had a vision of the Lord (Isaiah 6:1), He saw the train of His robe filling the temple—a scene of great majesty and dignity.

Jack Hayford has captured the glory of our resurrected Lord in his beautiful song, "Majesty":

> *Majesty, worship his majesty.*
> *Unto Jesus be all glory, power, and praise.*
> *Majesty, kingdom authority*
> *Flow from his throne unto his own,*
> *His anthem raise.*
> *So exalt, lift up on high the name of Jesus.*
> *Magnify, come glorify Christ Jesus the King.*
> *Majesty, worship his majesty.*
> *Unto Jesus be all glory, power, and praise.*
> *Majesty, worship His majesty.*
> *Jesus, who died, now glorified,*
> *King of all kings.*

His purity ("His head and His hair were white like wool, as white as snow"). Isaiah 1:18 makes the phrase "white as snow" and "white like wool" apply to cleansing and purity. It reads:

> "Come now, and let us reason together,"
> Says the LORD,
> "Though your sins are like scarlet,
> They shall be as white as snow;
> Though they are red like crimson,
> They shall be as wool."

The promise of our sins being cleansed is pictured in this passage, and this biblical background urges us to reflect on the absolute purity of the Son of God.

There is no sin in Jesus Christ according to the Bible. Second Corinthians 5:21 says that He "knew no sin," and Hebrews 4:15 states clearly that He was "without sin." Jesus Himself said in John 8:46, "Which of you convicts Me of sin?" No one could. It was Pilate himself who declared "I find no fault in Him" at the time of His trial and crucifixion. Hebrews 7:26 says that Jesus is "holy, harmless [innocent], undefiled, separate from sinners."

His authority ("and His eyes like a flame of fire; His feet were like fine brass, as if refined in a furnace, and His voice as the sound of many waters; He had in His right hand seven stars, out of His mouth went a sharp two-edged sword"). Eyes, feet, voice, hand, and mouth—all speaking of His powerful authority. It's a picture unlike the gospel accounts where the sympathetic Savior is seen as the humble servant of God, loving, healing, forgiving, and so on. This is different! He's in charge now. He is ready to execute judgment upon the world. You are looking at the King of all kings, and the Lord of all lords.

Eyes represent knowledge. He sees everything we do. Hebrews 4:13 states, "And there is no creature hidden from His sight, but all things are naked and open to the eyes of Him to whom we must give account."

The eyes "as a flame of fire" suggest that He is indignant about what He sees; He intends to bring judgment upon what He knows about the world. Fire often represents judgment in the Bible. Hebrews 12:29 says "our God is a consuming fire." Hebrews 10 speaks of a "certain fearful expectation of judgment, and fiery indignation which will devour the adversaries" (v. 27) and adds, "It is a fearful thing to fall into the hands of the living God" (v. 31). This should serve as a good reminder to all of us of our accountability to Jesus Christ as the Judge of all the earth.

The feet also speak of judgment. They are like fine brass that has been refined in a furnace. His feet are described in unusual terms in Revelation 19:15 when it says "He Himself treads the winepress of the fierceness and wrath of Almighty God."

His authority and judgment of the world is being pictured in these phrases, and the reference to His voice only reconfirms that viewpoint. It says that His voice is "as the sound of many waters." Psalm 29:3-4 says:

> The voice of the LORD is over the waters;
> The God of glory thunders;
> The LORD is over many waters.
> The voice of the LORD is powerful;
> The voice of the LORD is full of majesty.

That psalm goes on to add that the voice of the Lord breaks the cedars, divides the flames of fire, shakes the wilderness, and strips the forests bare. Other passages, such as Hebrews 12:25- 26, further emphasize the power and authority of the Lord's voice.

His sovereign authority is again emphasized by the fact that the seven stars (representing the seven angels of God) are in His right hand. The Father's right hand is emphasized frequently throughout Scripture as a place where Jesus is seated (Romans 8:34; Hebrews 1:3). It is also emphasized in Revelation 5:1 as the place where the seven-sealed scroll is kept—"in the right hand of Him who sat on the throne." That scroll contains the message about the judgments of God upon the whole world during the tribulation period. Being in the right hand of God the Father means that He has sovereign control over all these events.

Out of the mouth of Jesus comes a "sharp two-edged sword." This is repeated in Revelation 19:15 with an additional word— "that with it He should strike the nations." The words of His mouth will result in the judging of the nations and the wrath of God poured out on this world. What a picture of the power and authority of Jesus Christ, the One to Whom the Father has committed all judgment. When He speaks, we'd better listen!

His centrality ("and His countenance was like the sun shining in its strength"). Here is a summary statement as to His striking and dazzling appearance, the resurrected Christ in all of His glory! It represents the place He should have in all of our hearts. When you look at the sun shining in all its strength, you will see little else. Jesus Christ is to be the focal point of the universe, the cosmic center.

On the mount of transfiguration, Matthew 17:2 records that "His face shone like the sun." He is "the Light of the world" (John 8:12), the one Malachi 4:2 calls "the Sun of righteousness." The apostle Paul claimed that the vision he had on the Damascus road involved "a light from heaven, brighter than the sun" (Acts 26:13).

Majesty, purity, authority, and *centrality* —what a glorious picture of Jesus Christ, and how wonderfully unique from what we learn about Him in the four Gospels. The glory He had before He came into the world, that glory which He lovingly and willingly set aside so that He might know human life by personal experience and identify with us in our need, has been fully restored. He stands as our King of kings and Lord of lords. The churches may be lampstands and the angels like stars, but Jesus is the *Sun*!

The Impact upon the Apostle John (1:17a)

What an experience John had on that deserted island of Patmos. John had only one response to seeing the glorified Christ—"And when I saw Him, I fell at His feet as dead." John worshiped Him. How significant for all of us. What is our response when faced with the real Jesus Christ?

According to Hebrews 1:6, the Father wants all of the angels to worship His Son, Jesus Christ. And yet, when John fell down at the feet of the angel (Revelation 22:8-9), the angel told him not to do that. He said the only One we are to worship is God. We draw only one conclusion: Jesus Christ is God, otherwise, John would not have been right in worshiping Him, nor would God the Father be right in urging the angels to worship His Son.

The Instruction He Received (1:17b-20)

John received immediate comfort and encouragement from our Lord Jesus Christ. The Lord laid His right hand (symbol of power and authority) on him and said: "Do not be afraid." Naturally John was afraid. Wouldn't you have been at the sight of the Son of God in all of His glory?

The Lord reminded John of His real identity as God in human flesh ("I am the First and the Last"), of His resurrection power ("I am He who lives, and was dead, and behold, I am alive forevermore"), and of His authority ("I have the keys of Hades and of Death"). The devil is not the king of hell, by the way. He is the chief prisoner. He does not hold the keys of Hades and Death—Jesus does. We will learn more about this later.

The Lord instructed John to write what He had just seen, as well as to write about the "things which are" (the seven churches in chapters 2-3), and "the things which will take place after this," words repeated in 4:1.

A final word is given to John to unfold the mystery about the seven stars and seven golden lampstands. They represent the angels of the seven churches and the seven churches themselves.

Something to Think About

If you have read this far, you are already aware that this book of Revelation presents a unique picture of Jesus Christ. He is much more than a mere human being. He is much more than a good person who was executed nineteen hundred years ago by wicked hands. Jesus Christ arose from the dead, ascended to heaven, and now sits at the right hand of the throne of God the Father. The picture we have in Revelation is of a Person with tremendous power and control over all that takes place in heaven and on earth. He is the One Who will come back to this earth and set up a kingdom that shall never end—perfect in every way and filled with every conceivable blessing which a loving God would provide for the creatures He made.

But where do you stand in all of this? Does it seem too incredible? How close or far away are you from allegiance and commitment to Jesus Christ? What do you really understand the Bible to be saying about Him? Do you understand that He deserves your worship and praise? Have you placed your complete faith and confidence in him as your Lord and only Savior from sin? Time is running out. As you continue to read, please evaluate carefully your commitment to Him. Your eternal destiny depends on it.

Chapter 4

Neglected Priorities

(2:1-7)

Jesus Christ is described in the Bible as the Lord of the churches. A particular title is given to Him to impress deeply upon our minds His sovereign authority and power. The church, composed of all believers in this age, is described as the body of Jesus Christ of which He is the *head* (Ephesians 1:22-23; 4:15-16; Colossians 1:18; 1:24; 2:9-10). As head of the church, He has the right to tell us what is wrong and what we should do about it. His headship is clearly depicted as He addresses each of the seven churches portrayed in Revelation, beginning with the church at Ephesus.

What Is the Significance of Seven Churches?

To some, the number "seven" indicates perfection or completed action. Seven churches would, therefore, represent the total church throughout history. While we must remember that there were seven actual churches by these names existing in John's day, what the Lord says to these seven churches is what He would say to any of us living at any period of time.

Many Bible teachers have concluded that all of church history is being pictured between chapter one and chapter four. They relate these churches to the outline which the writer John gave to us in Revelation 1:19:

> "Write the things which you have seen"
>   (Revelation 1)
> "and the things which are" (Revelation 2-3)
> "and the things which will take place after this"
> (Revelation 4-22)

Neglected Priorities

This outline may suggest that the seven churches, while a part of the events of John's day, include everything which characterizes the church age until the future events start unfolding, beginning with Revelation 4. Some teachers have even placed these churches within given historical time periods, such as Sardis representing the period of the Reformation. While interesting, such a formula cannot be conclusive.

Church history has been marked by periods of revival and growth as well as periods of corruption, decline, and apostasy. The lessons of these seven churches in Revelation must be carefully observed by Christians in every age, regardless of the brand name on our church door or the repute of our religious tradition.

What Troubles the Church?

When we examine carefully the churches to which John wrote, we see the following things that can trouble the church:

Ephesus: *neglected priorities*
Smyrna: *satanic opposition*
Pergamos: *religious compromise*
Thyatira: *immoral practices*
Sardis: *spiritual apathy*
Philadelphia: *lost opportunities*
Laodicea: *material prosperity*

These troubles affect all Christians and churches, not only when such matters specifically begin to influence us, but also when a given period of time is generally characterized by these problems.

Neglected Priorities in the Church at Ephesus
(2:1-7)

[1]"To the angel of the church of Ephesus write,

'These things says He who holds the seven stars in His right hand, who walks in the midst of the seven golden lampstands: [2]"I know your works, your labor, your patience, and that you cannot bear those who are evil. And you have tested those who say they are apostles and are not, and have found them liars; [3]and you have persevered and have patience, and have labored for My name's sake and have not become weary. [4]Nevertheless I have this

against you, that you have left your first love. [5]Remember therefore from where you have fallen; repent and do the first works, or else I will come to you quickly and remove your lampstand from its place—unless you repent. [6]But this you have, that you hate the deeds of the Nicolaitans, which I also hate. [7]He who has an ear, let him hear what the Spirit says to the churches. To him who overcomes I will give to eat from the tree of life, which is in the midst of the Paradise of God." '"

Ephesus was "the metropolis of Asia," the center of trade and business. It was a seaport, the capital of the province of Asia Minor and its largest city.

It was a pagan city with idolatry and immorality dominating its religious and social life. One of the seven wonders of the ancient world was in Ephesus—the temple of Artemis (Diana) with its multibreasted colossal statue to a goddess of sex and fertility.

According to one tradition, the apostle John spent his last days there, and his burial spot, along with that of Mary, the mother of Jesus, are found among the artifacts remaining from ancient times.

The uncovered archaeological ruins of ancient Ephesus are amazing to behold. One of the first things that strikes the tourist is the size of the city. This was no small village, but a major metropolitan area with perhaps as many as 500,000 inhabitants. The Roman amphitheater seats 25,000 people with an acoustical design that eliminates the need for microphones. One can imagine it crowded with people shouting "Great is Artemis (Diana) of the Ephesians" as Acts 19 records. Much of the city remains underground waiting the archaeologist's shovel to uncover more that will enhance our knowledge of this remarkable place.

The city was also known for its great library, rivaling those of Rome, Athens, Antioch of Syria, and Alexandria, Egypt. It was a cultural center and a place where one could find people from all over the world, representing every occupation, language, and belief. What an opportunity for the gospel!

The impact of the gospel in Ephesus began with the teaching of an Alexandrian Jew named Apollos, a convert from the ministry of John the Baptist, who later came under the tutelage of Aquila and Priscilla, friends of the apostle Paul. After Apollos had gone to Corinth, Paul came to Ephesus and had an extensive ministry there lasting for more than two years.

Who Is "the Angel" of the Church? (2:1a)

At the beginning of each letter we read "To the angel of the church in _____." Does each church have an angel over it? There are two major viewpoints to consider:

The "angel" is the pastor of the church. The idea here centers on the broad meaning of the word *angel* as "a messenger." According to this view, John was addressing the pastor of each church in order to impress upon them the message that Jesus Christ would have them deliver to the congregation.

The "angel" is a supernatural being, one of the seven angels mentioned throughout Revelation. This appears to be a better answer. Revelation 1:20 says "the seven stars are the angels of the seven churches," and 2:1 begins with Christ holding "the seven stars in His right hand." This view does not require us to interpret symbolically, but literally.

Angels are described in Hebrews 1:14 as "ministering spirits sent forth to minister for those who will inherit salvation." Angels are seeing that God's desires and plans are accomplished. They operate under His direction and control.

A Description of Jesus Christ for the Church in Ephesus (2:1b)

His sovereign control is pictured by the seven stars in His right hand, a symbol of power and authority. The basic message to the church in Ephesus is to remember Who is in charge. It is so easy for a good church to forget that basic truth. We start running things according to our desires and plans, rather than His. Neglected priorities are the result of taking our eyes off the One who is the Authority. The priority of every church is to look to Jesus Christ for answers and direction.

His central presence in the church is pictured beautifully by the words "who walks in the midst of the seven golden lampstands" (cf. Revelation 1:20). When we come to the services of the church, it is our natural response to think of our own needs. We ask, "How is the church going to minister to me today?"

The real issue centers in the first and foremost objective of any church—the worship and praise of Jesus Christ our Lord! Is He the sovereign Authority and central Focus of your church (and your life)? How are you expressing that love and loyalty to Him?

A message about love. The key verse to the church in Ephesus reveals the real problem confronting this group of believers: "Nevertheless I have this against you, that you have left your first love."

The problem of neglected priorities centers in a person's departure from that "first love." The word *first* could refer to the love one feels when he first becomes a Christian. More likely, it refers to priorities. What love should be first? In the words of Jesus: "'You shall love the LORD your God with all your heart, with all your soul, and with all your mind.' This is the first and great commandment. And the second is like it: 'You shall love your neighbor as yourself.' On these two commandments hang all the Law and the Prophets" (Matthew 22:37-40).

The first love is the love we should have for God Himself and His Son, Jesus Christ. Most of our problems center in that central issue. When our love for God diminishes, many problems develop that have no solution except a return to that first love.

Our Efforts Cannot Be Substituted for Love (2:2-3)

Jesus Christ had some wonderful things to say about this church. He knew all about their work and their faithfulness. In each letter to these seven churches we find the phrase from the lips of Jesus, "I know your works." Nothing is hidden from His knowledge. He knows us better than we know ourselves (cf. Hebrews 4:13).

In 1 Corinthians 13 Paul emphasized an important point about love that John deals with in his letter to the Ephesians. You cannot substitute your own efforts for love. It is commendable to have an abundance of gifts and abilities and to perform exemplary deeds; but without love, there is no real spiritual profit nor lasting effect upon people.

Jesus Christ speaks of the Ephesian dedication and commends it. He used words such as *labor* and *patience*. The labor of this church represents an intense effort, perhaps to the point of exhaustion. They were tireless in their efforts to serve the Lord. That is commendable, but it is no substitute for an intense love for God Himself. *Patience* speaks of endurance, bearing up under a load. These believers were not quitters. In spite of the pressures of ministry and the heaviness of their responsibilities, they remained faithful. We need more people like that in today's churches.

Verse 3 emphasizes that these efforts were done for the Lord Himself—"labored for My name's sake." In contrast to many believers who suffer burnout in their service for the Lord, these Ephesian believers did "not become weary." What a wonderful testimony they had.

In addition to their faithful service and tireless efforts, these people were strong in their convictions and able to discern the difference between the false and the true. Two things characterized their doctrinal purity: (1) "You cannot bear those who are evil"; and (2) "You have tested those who say they are apostles and are not, and have found them liars."

The toleration of sin and wicked people in our churches adds greatly to our powerlessness and ineffectiveness in serving the Lord and honoring Him in what we do and say. The Ephesian believers simply did not tolerate "those who are evil" and investigated all claims of apostleship before granting their approval or support.

The term *apostles* in verse 2 probably is used in the wide sense of our term *emissaries*, rather than the restricted sense of the Twelve or those set apart to receive direct revelation from God that would become a part of the Bible (cf. Ephesians 2:20 and 3:5). It was not uncommon in early times for people to claim the authority of apostles or emissaries of the churches and to be looked upon, therefore, as worthy spokesmen. It was imperative that churches investigate such claims before granting approval and support. The Ephesian church was to be commended for their efforts in these matters.

Another issue which was a part of these doctrinal investigations is found in verse 6: "But this you have, that you hate the deeds of the Nicolaitans, which I also hate." They hated what the Lord hated.

It is difficult to determine exactly who the Nicolaitans were, though they seem to be identified here and in 2:14-15 as a heretical sect, perhaps with gnostic influences. The name Nicolaitans means to "conquer the people," and may have been the name they used for themselves or perhaps Christ's derogatory title for them.

In 2:6, the emphasis is on the "deeds" of the Nicolaitans; in verse 15, in the message to the church in Pergamos, it mentions "those who *hold the doctrine* of the Nicolaitans." In Ephesus, the believers "hated" what the Nicolaitans were doing; in Pergamos, the Nicolaitans were a part of the church. In both places, the Lord says that He hates the teaching and deeds of such people.

In summary, the Ephesian church was doctrinally strong and service-oriented. Their efforts remain as an example to all believers. We commend them as does the Lord. But, there is a problem.

The Lord's Evaluation Reveals
the Real Problem (2:4)

Nevertheless is a word of great contrast. Do not think for a moment that the problem of these believers is minor. Though they are commended highly for their efforts and loyalties, it is a sharp contrast which the Lord makes when He accuses them of neglected priorities and expresses how He feels about it ("I have this against you").

It is quite amazing how we can rationalize our lack of love by emphasizing our works. Churches can appear outwardly to be all God wants them to be and do, but inwardly be cold and indifferent toward the Lord Himself. Where are you in this matter? Have you left the first love?

There is disagreement among Bible teachers concerning the first love. We suggested earlier in this chapter that the primary thought is love for the Lord Himself. Other suggestions that flow out of that include: (1) Love for other believers, (2) love for the second coming of Christ, and (3) love for nonbelievers.

The central thought is critical when we consider the intensity of the Lord's reaction to this church. Is He concerned that the church cares more about its doctrinal integrity than reaching nonbelievers with the gospel? That is a point worthy of our careful evaluation. Is He saying that you can stand for what's right, but not care for people in the process? Good point, but is that the "first love"?

It is fascinating to read the last verse of the apostle Paul's letter to these same Ephesians, written some thirty years prior to this letter in Revelation: "Grace be with all those who love our Lord Jesus Christ in sincerity. Amen."

The "first love" is the love we should have for the Lord Himself. Everything else flows from that. Therefore, the most serious and often neglected priority of the church is a sincere and intense love for the Lord. All else is secondary.

His Exhortation Reveals How Important That Love Is (2:5)

Jesus' strong words here reveal the seriousness of leaving your first love in at least the following ways:

In realizing that we have fallen from the place where He wants us to be. The exhortation is to "remember." How easy it is to forget in the midst of our efforts to serve the Lord that love for Him is the most important attribute He desires. Maybe we should take a short break at this point and start that process of remembering. Do you remember when your love for the Lord was the most important thing in your life? Perhaps that has never really been a part of your experience as a Christian.

Maybe you have been taught to get busy for the Lord, and in the process you have missed Him.

In repenting. Repentance means a change of mind and conduct. We need to think differently about our priorities and then start manifesting that difference in the way we think, speak, and perform. Repentance suggests the need for radical change. Some of us may not sense that need because we have become so used to a performance orientation. We have been taught to "do" more than to "love."

In responding to His instruction. Jesus says to "do the first works." The "first love" causes us to do the "first works." Perhaps the issue of loving others and seeking to win lost people to Jesus Christ are part of what is meant by "first works." The text does not go into detail as to what the "first works" represent. We do know that it is an issue of love. In the book of Ephesians, Paul wrote about the greatness of love (3:17-19) and its importance in the unity, growth, and edification of believers (4:2, 15-16; 5:2).

In removing their testimony and influence. Jesus said, "Or else I will come to you quickly and remove your lampstand from its place." The churches are referred to as "lampstands." They are to be lights to this dark world, drawing people to the light of Jesus Christ. According to our Lord, the influence of a church will be diminished and even removed when the first love is neglected. Neglected priorities is a serious matter.

His Personal Encouragement to Us Reveals That He Expects Us to Respond (2:7)

This is truly a remarkable statement and promise. The message we have just studied was intended for all the churches. It comes from the Holy Spirit and requires a listening ear and heart. Have you heard this message with the ears of your heart, and do you find yourself responding to it?

The phrase "to him who overcomes" is repeated in each of the messages to the seven churches. It is not referring to a Christian who gets victory over some particular problem in his or her life. It is referring to those who are true believers. Those who overcome are believers, and those who do not overcome are not believers. John makes that clear in his first epistle (1 John 5:4-5). If you believe that Jesus is the Son of God and have put your faith in Him, you are an overcomer.

The promise of Revelation 2:7 deals with eternal issues. To all overcomers comes the privilege of eating from the tree of life, a symbol of eternal life originally found in the garden of Eden (Genesis 2:9). When Adam and Eve sinned, God sent them out of that paradise and guarded its entrance so that they would not partake of the tree of life.

In Revelation 22:2, we find that the tree of life is mentioned again, this time as a prominent feature in the heavenly city. It stands as a symbol of everlasting life. This promise of Revelation 2:7 involves assurance of eternal life—being with the Lord forever in the "Paradise of God." The garden of Eden was merely a symbol of what our future holds.

This promise of eternal life causes us to dwell a moment longer on the issue of neglected priorities. It is very possible that the Lord's message is revealing how easy it is for a church (or an individual believer) to look good and appear to be orthodox, yet be far from the Lord. Perhaps it is much like what Jesus said in Mark 7:6-7 when He quoted Isaiah 29: "This people honors Me with their lips, but their heart is far from Me. And in vain they worship Me, teaching as doctrines the commandments of men."

May God give us all wisdom to understand the seriousness of neglected priorities. Have you left the first love?

Chapter 5

Satanic Opposition

(2:8-11)

At the end of each church letter, there is this simple admonition: "He who has an ear, let him hear what the Spirit says to the churches." These letters are intended for all of us in each generation of church history. That these were messages to particular churches existing in John's day does not eliminate its intended goal of reaching all of us. That is made clear by the plural form "churches," undoubtedly implying that more people were to be affected by the letter than simply the members of a first-century church.

What Do We Know about Smyrna?

Smyrna is a beautiful city today on the western shore of Turkey. In ancient times it was known as the "Beauty of Asia" and the "City of Life and Strength." It is located some thirty- five miles north of Ephesus and was also a seaport city like Ephesus.

Its loyalty to Rome was well known. In 195 B.C. (before the days of the Empire), Smyrna had erected a temple to the goddess of Rome during the days of the Roman Republic. The city became the seat of emperor worship, and in A.D. 26, when several cities were competing for the privilege of erecting a temple in honor of Emperor Tiberius, Smyrna was granted the honor.

According to various ancient sources, it appears that a large colony of Jews lived there with considerable influence upon the civil and political authorities. Some years after John's death, the Jewish leadership, along with some Gentiles, formed a mob and called for the death of the local bishop, Polycarp, who was a disciple of the apostle John. Church leaders Tertullian and Irenaeus claim that Polycarp was the bishop at Smyrna at the time John wrote this letter and that John not only discipled him personally but also appointed him as bishop. If Polycarp died in A.D. 166 as most scholars have concluded, and if he was older than the eighty-six years which he claimed was his service for Christ, it means that he was a young pastor about twenty to thirty years old when this letter was delivered to his church.

The church at Smyrna endured intense persecution, but in a real sense this persecution yielded a fragrance that affected many lives for Jesus Christ. That can happen to us as well if we will but see the hand of God behind all that we are called upon to endure. Tertullian insisted that the "blood of the martyrs is the seed of the church."

What Jesus Christ Says to Smyrna
(2:8-11)

[8]"And to the angel of the church in Smyrna write,

'These things says the First and the Last, who was dead, and came to life: [9]"I know your works, tribulation, and poverty (but you are rich); and I know the blasphemy of those who say they are Jews and are not, but are a synagogue of Satan. [10]Do not fear any of those things which you are about to suffer. Indeed, the devil is about to throw some of you into prison, that you may be tested, and you will have tribulation ten days. Be faithful until death, and I will give you the crown of life. [11]He who has an ear, let him hear what the Spirit says to the churches. He who overcomes shall not be hurt by the second death." '"

Smyrna holds a special message for every believer, regardless of his circumstances. The world is no friend. Jesus said, "If the world hates you, you know that it hated Me before it hated you. If you were of the world, the world would love its own. Yet because you are not of the world, but I chose you out of the world, therefore the world hates you. . . . If they persecuted Me, they will also persecute you" (John 15:18-19, 20).

We should all be prepared. Hostility will come to all who live for the Lord and honor Him in their lives. The message to the church of Smyrna is good preparation for us all. It emphasizes who Jesus Christ is, what He knows, what He commands, and what He promises.

Who Jesus Christ Is (2:8)

These words were introduced in 1:17-18, but the statement that He is "the First and the Last" is used elsewhere (Isaiah 41:4; 44:6; 48:12) to identify Him as the eternal God, the Creator of all. It implies that nothing happens outside the realm of His character and control. He is there at our conception and at our death; all that takes place in between is known to Him and is a part of His divine plan for us.

When we are reminded that He died and then rose from the dead, we are assured that we will have the ultimate victory no matter what persecutions may come our way or what circumstances we may face in this life. The day of our own resurrection is guaranteed by the resurrection of Jesus Christ from the dead (cf. John 11:25-26)!

What Jesus Christ Knows (2:9)

To each church He says, "I know your works." Everything we say and do is known to Him. Nothing escapes His knowledge. We need to remember that when we try to do things that are sinful and wrong (Hebrews 4:13). We are not hiding it from Him.

It is also a comfort to believing hearts to know that He knows all we have said and done for Him. Sometimes we think that what we do is not important or is too insignificant to be noticed by the eternal God. The Bible teaches us otherwise (Hebrews 6:10).

There are three things about the experiences of believers in Smyrna that Jesus says He already knows:

Jesus Christ knows all about tribulation. This word *tribulation* primarily refers to pressure from without as opposed to pressure from within. It was not coming from other believers within the church but from the antagonism of people with whom they came in contact. It was not easy to be a Christian and live in Smyrna, the seat of emperor worship.

It is possible to allow the government itself, the laws of the land, or human judges to take precedence over the laws of God and devotion to Jesus Christ. This happens on a regular basis in many countries of the world. This was the situation in Smyrna. It leads to persecution of all who will not bow the knee to human authority.

The Christian faces the dilemma of having to submit to human authority (Romans 13:1-7; 1 Peter 2:13-17), but not at the expense of disobeying God (Acts 5:29). There is constant tension between those two relationships. Christians are asked to submit to authorities who are unbelievers, but not to obey that which violates the clearly revealed will of God. It should be obvious why Christians are often subjected to tribulation and persecution.

The good news is that Jesus Christ knows our struggle and what we suffer. When a businessman loses his job because he will not lie, cheat, or manipulate, Jesus knows about it and has promised great reward in the future. When a student refuses to take drugs, get involved in illicit sex, and suffers rejection and mockery because of it, Jesus knows and will one day reward that young person for the courage displayed (Matthew 5:10-12).

Jesus Christ knows about your poverty. The word *poverty* refers to a beggar who is destitute. It means one who has lost his property and possessions. Perhaps it was stolen or confiscated because the person was a believer.

Our Lord calculates differently than we do. He says "I know your . . . poverty (but you are rich)." Material wealth is no barometer of spiritual riches. You may not be materially wealthy but the Bible says of believers that we can have "treasure in heaven" (Matthew 6:20), and be "rich in faith and heirs of the kingdom which He promised to those who love Him" (James 2:5). Second Corinthians 8:9 lays before us the example of Christ: "For you know the grace of our Lord Jesus Christ, that though he was rich, yet for your sakes He became poor, that you through his poverty might become rich."

The "unsearchable riches of Christ" (Ephesians 3:8) are not to be compared with the corrupt riches, moth-eaten garments, and corroded gold and silver of unbelievers who face the judgment of God (James 5:1-3).

Jesus Christ knows all about the blasphemy we have received. This "blasphemy" refers to the slander of others. It was the kind of reaction Polycarp would receive some seventy years after this letter was written. It is the blasphemy to which Jesus was subjected and about which Peter wrote:

> For this is commendable, if because of conscience toward God one endures grief, suffering wrongfully. For what credit is it if, when you are beaten for your faults, you take it patiently? But when you do good and suffer for it, if you take it patiently, this is commendable before God. For to this you were called, because Christ also suffered for us, leaving us an example, that you should follow His steps: "Who committed no sin, nor was guile found in His mouth"; who, when He was reviled, did not revile in return; when

He suffered, He did not threaten, but committed Himself
to Him who judges righteously (1 Peter 2:19-23).

What a wonderful lesson to all of us who are rebuked, criticized,
mocked, slandered, or misrepresented. Leave it to the Lord, to Him
who judges righteously. No one gets away with anything. One day all
accounts will be settled before our eternal Judge.

The source of this blasphemy toward Christians is described as being
"a synagogue of Satan." It was composed of those "who say they are
Jews and are not." These antagonists claimed to be Jewish, but their
hearts were far from God and the Messiah. They demonstrated their
unbelief by the slander they gave to the believers in Smyrna, who
included both Jews and Gentiles. Because of their attitudes and actions
of blasphemy they were doing the work of Satan himself; Satan was
behind these attacks. In 1 Peter 5:8-11, the apostle makes it clear that
Satan is attacking believers. But God is in ultimate control. He allows
Satan to do this, not to defeat us but actually to make us stronger than
ever.

What Jesus Christ Commands (2:10)

Jesus Christ knows our works, tribulation, poverty, and blasphemy.
He understands and sympathizes. In the midst of it all, He gives us
two commands: (1) "Do not fear any of those things which you are
about to suffer"; (2) "Be faithful until death."

Be fearless and faithful—that's a message we all need to hear in the
midst of a pagan and hostile society that seeks to eliminate Christian
witness and remove God's standards from public life.

When our Lord tells us not to be fearful, He reminds us that times
will come that will test our courage. It is relatively easy to be courageous
when there is no crisis, no test. The problem of fear arises when it
hits us personally. Consider the following interesting facts about Revelation 2:10:

1. Jesus Christ predicts that we are going to suffer in some way. If you have
not suffered as yet, cheer up . . . you will! Second Timothy 3:12 says,
"Yes, and all who desire to live godly in Christ Jesus *will* suffer persecution." Perhaps this is the real reason many Christians remain silent
when they should speak and inactive when they should act. We are
aware that persecution, resentment, criticism, and worse will come to
all who live for the Lord. We often retreat into a comfortable zone in
which we do not let those around us know of our faith and continue

to agree with their views of life, morality, and values by either our silence or our active participation. Christians in the past called that problem "worldliness." Each of us needs to ask, How worldly am I?

2. *The devil is behind this persecution of believers* . Jesus said to this church "Indeed, the devil is about to throw some of you into prison." The devil, according to Revelation 12:10, is the "accuser" of believers, and He keeps it up "day and night."

The Bible teaches that the devil can disrupt and cause dissension. It teaches that he can inflict pain, disease, and bodily harm. He can influence and tempt us to do wrong, and is the father of lies. He deceives the whole world. He is behind many of our struggles and conflicts, and the Bible pictures our battle with Him as spiritual warfare necessitating the special armor and protection of God Himself. Although he is not omnipresent, he appears to be so because he has a vast army of demons—evil spirits—who do his bidding.

3. *The purpose behind this satanic opposition is to test us*. Verse 10 tells us the devil throws some of the believers into prison that they "may be tested." Whatever happens, the design of God is behind it. Job writes: "But He knows the way that I take; when He has tested me, I shall come forth as gold" (23:10). And Peter adds these encouraging words about our trials:

> In this you greatly rejoice, though now for a little while, if need be, you have been grieved by various trials, that the genuineness of your faith, being much more precious than gold that perishes, though it is tested by fire, may be found to praise, honor, and glory at the revelation of Jesus Christ (1 Peter 1:6-7).

We are being tested by our trials, not to defeat us, but to make us more beautiful and strong.

4. *The tribulation will not last long*. The text says, "and you will have tribulation ten days." A great deal of discussion has centered on this statement. Many Bible teachers speak of the "ten days" as though it refers to ten Roman persecutions. Some begin with the persecution by Nero. However, John wrote this letter some thirty years later than Nero's time, and the text places the ten days of tribulation in the future.

Some believe the "ten days" refer to ten years of persecution by the emperor Diocletian (A.D. 303-313), but that seems highly unlikely in that it would have no significance to the church in Smyrna to which this letter was originally sent.

The best view of the meaning of the "ten days" is that the persecution would not last long; it would be brief, though real and difficult to endure. Genesis 24:55 uses the term "ten days" to refer to a brief time, as does Daniel 1:12.

While not conclusive, it would appear that the "ten days" of Revelation 2:10 could easily mean a short time of persecution for the believers in Smyrna and, by broader application, that all believers in any age will suffer only for a short time. God's love will not allow us to endure more than we can bear (1 Corinthians 10:13).

Be faithful until death. The command to "be faithful until death" is not a reference to dying grace or the ability to endure bad health until it culminates in physical death. God's grace can indeed strengthen us in such moments and give us an inward peace and joy in the midst of our suffering and trial. But the point in this passage must be taken from the days of Smyrna and the persecution that was coming from the unbelievers of that day. To be faithful until death is to be faithful to one's commitment to Christ no matter what persecution, torture, suffering, or means of death one must face.

Revelation 6:9 refers to the "souls of those who had been slain for the word of God and for the testimony which they held." Many believers have died for their faith. We call them *martyrs*. This English word comes directly from the Greek word referring to a "witness." We are to be witnesses for the Lord even in death.

The great need among Christians in our generation is a deepened sense of commitment and loyalty to Jesus Christ our Lord. Weak Christianity leads to compromise and moral defeat. Jesus challenges us all to "be faithful until death." We have nothing to lose and everything to gain. Commitment at the point of death is built on a continual pattern of commitment throughout one's life.

What Jesus Christ Promises (2:10-11)

A Christian song says "It will be worth it all, when we see Jesus. Life's trials will seem so small, when we see Christ." All of our suffering and trials are known to the Lord and He has promised to reward us for them (cf. 2 Timothy 2:12; Romans 8:18). In our present passage, Jesus specifically promises two things: (1) "I will give you the crown of life"; and (2) He who overcomes shall not be hurt by the second death."

What is the "crown of life"? James 1:12 tells us "the crown of life" is something "the Lord has promised to those who love Him." The context deals with those who have endured trials. Some say this is a special crown given only to those who suffer martyrdom. However, the text does not indicate that every believer will experience this. It simply urges us to be faithful, even if it means death.

This crown symbolizes victory (perhaps an allusion to the wreath or garland of the Greek games, well known at Smyrna) and is used often in the Bible. It would be best to argue that the crown is eternal life which all believers will experience. It is the reason we should not fear death or persecution from unbelievers. Our future is to live forever with the Lord, and that reward makes it possible for us to endure trials in this life.

What about the "second death"? This is the other side of receiving the "crown of life." The "second death" is mentioned in Revelation 20:14-15 and refers to a final separation of the unbeliever from God forever in a place called "the lake of fire." It is eternal death, the final consequence of unbelief.

Overcomers—those who believe in Jesus Christ as Lord and Savior—will not be hurt by the second death but rather be rewarded with the crown of life. Have you made that commitment, and are you being faithful to it?

Are we listening? This message to the church in Smyrna is intended for all believers in every age and culture. Are we listening? The message comes from the Holy Spirit and is about commitment under pressure to conform and turn one's back on Christ. Have we been faithful under such pressure? What do we do when those around us begin to attack, criticize, or mock the followers of Christ? Are we faithful to our commitment to Him?

Chapter 6

Religious Compromise

(2:12-17)

We won't find many commendations in this chaper—primarily rebuke! Things in Pergamos have really deteriorated.

What Do We Know about Pergamos?

Pergamos is located seventy miles north of Smyrna and fifteen miles from the coast of the Aegean Sea. In 29 B.C. Pergamos was given permission to erect and dedicate a temple to Augustus, making it the official Asian center for the imperial cult. A great university was located in Pergamos with a library of over 200,000 volumes, which were sent to Alexandria by Mark Antony as a gift to Cleopatra.

The acropolis at Pergamos is beautiful to behold. After visiting the top of this thousand-foot elevation and seeing the ruins of an ancient amphitheater (perhaps holding ten thousand people) and the massive altar to Zeus, one cannot help being impressed with the glory of this ancient city.

A short distance from the altar to Zeus was an elegant temple to the goddess Athena. Dionysus and Demeter were also worshiped there, and Asklepios, the god of healing, was honored with a great medical school whose college of medical priests was associated with the worship of this god. The idol of Asklepios was shaped like a serpent, a symbol still used by the medical profession today, though many do not understand its ancient associations.

Worship of the emperor was very strong in Pergamos. In some cities Christians were in danger only on the day of the year in which incense was to be burned and Caesar declared to be "Lord." In Pergamos, Christians were in danger year-round.

What Jesus Christ Says to Pergamos
(2:12-17)

[12] "And to the angel of the church in Pergamos write,

'These things says He who has the sharp two-edged sword:
[13] "I know your works, and where you dwell, where Satan's throne is. And you hold fast to My name, and did not deny My faith even in the days in which Antipas was My faithful martyr, who was killed among you, where Satan dwells.
[14] But I have a few things against you, because you have there those who hold the doctrine of Balaam, who taught Balak to put a stumbling block before the children of Israel, to eat things sacrificed to idols, and to commit sexual immorality. [15] Thus you also have those who hold the doctrine of the Nicolaitans, which thing I hate. [16] Repent, or else I will come to you quickly and will fight against them with the sword of My mouth. [17] He who has an ear, let him hear what the Spirit says to the churches. To him who overcomes I will give some of the hidden manna to eat. And I will give him a white stone, and on the stone a new name written which no one knows except him who receives it."'"

The Sword of the Lord (2:12)

One simple but powerful description of Jesus Christ begins this letter: "He who has the sharp two-edged sword." Verse 16 reminds us that it is "the sword of My mouth" (cf. 1:16; 19:15). The sword of His mouth symbolizes the judgment which can come when He speaks the word. This is a church facing severe judgment if they do not repent. Christianity and paganism were opposites, but the Christians at Pergamos were trying to coexist. The result was religious compromise and sinful practices in the church.

A Dangerous Environment (2:13)

As in each of the letters, Jesus Christ says "I know your works." We cannot hide from Him. The emphasis in His words to this church centers on "where you dwell." The environment is dangerous; it is where "Satan's throne" exists, probably a reference to the giant altar to Zeus, elevated about eight hundred feet from the plain below and visible for miles. It could also refer to all that was dominating and controlling the life and culture of this city; it was truly a seat of satanic power. The serpent god, Asklepios, would also serve as a symbolic picture of Satan and his power.

The environment in which we live is often a test to our faith. Satan was not only present at Pergamos, he was ruling ("throne"). Some cities in our present day have become "thrones of Satan." It's a reminder to all Christians that the pressures we face often come from the enemy of our souls, the devil himself. It is our profession of faith that is the special target of satanic attack. That was true in Pergamos as well.

Jesus commends these believers with the following words: "And you hold fast to My name, and did not deny My faith even in the days in which Antipas was My faithful martyr, who was killed among you, where Satan dwells."

Two things are said of these believers in their struggle with satanic influence and pagan worship: (1) "You hold fast to My name," and (2) "You did not deny My faith."

The first implies that the key battleground was the deity of Jesus Christ. His "name" is above every name, but a city devoted to emperor worship could have none of that kind of commitment and loyalty among its citizens. It was war between Caesar and Christ. Who is Lord? That was the heart of the struggle, and it is of supreme importance to all believers. Are we confessing Jesus Christ as our Lord and Savior, and are we doing that "before men"? Or are we ashamed of Him? (See Philippians 2:9-11; Romans 10:9-10; Matthew 10:32-33.)

His "name" refers to His character and essential nature—He is God in human flesh, the Lord of all, King of kings. Have we come to believe in and confess His name?

A second issue closely related to the deity of Jesus Christ is the matter of a public acknowledgment of what we say we believe. The statement "did not deny My faith" implies that under pressure they did not fold. They were not hesitant to declare their beliefs. That takes courage in a pagan and hostile environment that is antagonistic toward one's faith.

The pressure upon these believers evidently was especially severe when a person named Antipas was martyred. His name means "against all," which might suggest that he had to stand alone for his faith. Although many conjecture as to the person involved here, we really have no evidence. The church is commended for standing firm even when one of its members was killed for his faith.

A Serious Evaluation (2:14-15)

Jesus Christ begins His evaluation with these words "But I have a few things against you." In the letter to Ephesus He said, "I have this against you," implying just one matter. In this letter to Pergamos, the list has grown.

Two issues were confronted by our Lord with the statement "you have there those who hold the doctrine." Among these believers were two doctrines—the doctrine of Balaam and the doctrine of the Nicolaitans—that were infiltrating their fellowship and destroying their testimony and effectiveness. These doctrines were being tolerated rather than confronted and removed. The modern church with its emphasis on self and individual rights needs to hear the message of Pergamos and to take heed. We tolerate much today in order not to offend anyone. This kind of superficial, weak love is undermining our commitment to biblical truth and standards just as it was doing in the ancient church at Pergamos.

What is the doctrine of Balaam? The teaching of Balaam refers to a story in the book of Numbers, chapters 22-25. Balaam was a prophet of God who was asked by Balak, king of Moab, to curse the people of Israel. But instead Balaam blessed the people of Israel as God told him to do. However, all was not right with the counsel of Balaam. According to Numbers 31:16, he advised the people of Israel to commit immorality with the women of Moab and to participate in their pagan rituals (cf. Numbers 25:1-3).

The doctrine of Balaam walks softly on immorality and encourages intermarriage with unbelievers and compromise with pagan worship. Second Peter 2:12-16 refers to false teachers who encourage immoral practices and pagan behavior. We read that they have "eyes full of adultery" and "cannot cease from sin." Verses 15-16 relate these practices to Balaam:

> They have forsaken the right way and gone astray, following the way of Balaam the son of Beor, who loved the wages of unrighteousness; but he was rebuked for his iniquity: a dumb donkey speaking with a man's voice restrained the madness of the prophet.

Jude 11 warns against such false teachers who promote an immoral lifestyle and who compromise with the world and its beliefs. It says that such teachers "have run greedily in the error of Balaam for profit."

The "way of Balaam" is religious compromise for a few coins. Balaam was covetous of what the king of Moab could give him, though he spoke piously about being free from the love of money.

Our Lord's sharp condemnation of the doctrine of Balaam shows the critical nature of separation from the world. The Christians of Pergamos had a good confession of faith and showed a degree of loyalty to the Person of Christ, but their association with unbelievers in that city and their desire for monetary success had led them to religious and spiritual compromise. The immorality and idolatry of that ancient pagan culture was being absorbed by the Christians and made a part of their lives.

What a message this is to the culture of our day! Religious leaders have fallen for a few coins or pleasure. Attitudes of holiness and godly living have become mere words as leaders have adopted immoral practices and succumbed to the secular attitudes and beliefs of society around them. But God's standards have not changed. The doctrine of Balaam is still condemned by the One to Whom we must all give account.

What is the doctrine of the Nicolaitans? In the letter to the church in Ephesus we read: "But this you have, that you hate the deeds of the Nicolaitans, which I also hate" (2:6). Now we find that the believers in Pergamos have people in their fellowship who hold this doctrine. God hates it, and some believers hold it! We should hate what God hates. In Ephesus, they hated the "deeds" of the Nicolaitans; in Pergamos some hold the "doctrine" they teach.

Later Christian tradition linked the Nicolaitans with Nicolas, the proselyte from Antioch (Acts 6:5) who was chosen by the Jerusalem church as one of the seven who would serve tables, distributing food and funds to needy widows. Supposedly, he became a heretic and led others to follow him. Though plausible, this view should be approached with caution.

The prevailing view is that the Nicolaitans were an antinomian sect (opposed to the law) with possible gnostic influences. The close association of verse 15 which mentions the doctrine of the Nicolaitans and verse 14 which mentions eating things sacrificed to idols and committing immorality suggests that the doctrine proclaimed by these people led to such excesses and sinful practices. This would explain the strong rebuke.

Whenever the leadership suggests wrongdoing or sinful practices as possible alternative lifestyles or tolerates that which God clearly condemns for the believer, the doctrines of Balaam and the Nicolaitans are present.

A Strong Exhortation (2:16)

When Christ our Lord deals with the problems in the churches, His favorite exhortation is "repent." Not much is heard about repentance in modern preaching, but it is still the only way to get right with God and to see our churches return to powerful witness and influence for the Lord. Five of the churches are given the exhortation to repent (only Smyrna and Philadelphia are exceptions).

This exhortation is based on two things: Jesus' warning that He would come to them quickly and that He would fight against them with the sword of His mouth.

Is this a reference to the second coming of Christ, which is the main theme of the book, or to a special coming of judgment upon the church in Pergamos? It is not an easy choice. Since the message is intended for all churches, it could mean that failure to deal with such religious compromise results in the removal of the church's influence and testimony, as suggested by the wording to the church in Ephesus (2:5).

However, the reference to the "sword of My mouth" and its obvious connection with the second coming in chapter 19, plus the relationship of our Lord's words "I will come quickly" in the rest of the book, seem to favor relating this exhortation to the second coming of Christ.

In either case, the message to the believers remains— *repent!* The imminence of the Lord's return and the prospect of facing His judgment upon the world of unbelievers is sufficient reason to get right with God, to make sure that we really know the Lord. The implication throughout these letters to the churches is that many are merely professing to be Christians but are not true overcomers—that is, ones who have placed their faith and trust in the Person and work of Jesus Christ alone.

It is fascinating to observe the change in pronouns in verse 16. Jesus says, "I will come to *you* quickly and will fight against *them* with the sword of My mouth." The believers apparently will suffer if they do not deal with the doctrines of Balaam and the Nicolaitans held by members in the church. Those who hold these doctrines are going to suffer the judgment of the second coming—the sword of Christ's mouth—which suggests these are unbelievers who are professing to be Christians and have been received into the fellowship of the church in Pergamos.

When we tolerate pagan views and sinful practices among believers, we face the possibility of losing our testimony and influence as a church. We no longer are a "lampstand" to shine for Jesus Christ drawing others to Him. When we adopt the lifestyle of the world around us and engage in immorality and idolatry, we are manifesting unbelief, no matter what we profess (cf. Matthew 7:21-23).

A Wonderful Encouragement (2:17)

Once again, all believers are encouraged to listen to the Spirit's message to all the churches, not just the church in Pergamos. Encouragement is given "to him who overcomes," a statement that refers to true believers, as we learned previously.

Two things are to be given to the overcomers by Jesus Christ as special rewards and encouragement: Hidden manna to eat, and a white stone with a new name on it.

What is the "hidden manna"? "Hidden" means that we do not know about it now, but the blessings of it will be revealed at a later time. "Manna" connects it with the food God supplied for the people of Israel in the wilderness, and which John 6 uses in symbolism to refer to the life of the Lord Jesus Himself. He is the true Bread from heaven; if we eat of it, we shall live forever.

No doubt there is a connection with the pot of manna that was kept in the ark in the tabernacle and later in the temple. It, of course, was hidden. Revelation 11:19 reveals that the ark is presently in heaven. It was believed in past history that Jeremiah hid the ark before the destruction of Jerusalem, where it would not be discovered until Israel is restored to its Messianic hope and glory.

Perhaps several thoughts need to be associated with the phrase "hidden manna." John 6 makes it clear that Jesus Christ is the real manna from heaven of which the manna in the wilderness was merely a type. We now experience a personal relationship and fellowship with Him by faith, but the full expression of that experience will not be known until He comes again. Therefore, the spiritual manna, the food which gives eternal life, is "hidden" at the present time, though real. But when Jesus Christ returns it will no longer be "hidden" but fully enjoyed by believers forever. The symbolism of the pot of manna "hidden" inside the ark of the covenant relates well to this possible interpretation.

What is the "white stone" with a "new name" on it? This is a most difficult symbolism and requires some careful research and investigation. Stones were used in ancient times to render a verdict, a white stone indicating acquittal and a black stone condemnation. However, there is no mention or comparison of a white stone with a black stone in this passage.

Some choose to relate this stone to the stones on the breastplate of the high priest in the Old Testament, representing the twelve tribes of Israel. However, not one of those stones was said to be a white stone or even a diamond, if that is what the white stone looks like.

Others choose to emphasize the ancient practice of using stones as counters in calculations. The idea here is that if you have been faithful to the Lord (overcomer), you will be counted among those who are saved. However, this does nothing to explain the whiteness of the stone or the new name written upon it.

One of the most interesting and plausible arguments about the use of stones in the ancient world comes from the practices of the Roman Empire. When the Roman Empire gave free doles of bread and free admission to entertainments, the tickets were often in the form of a white stone with a person's name on it. It was a well-established practice to reward the victors at the games with such a ticket to a special feast. Since the "hidden manna" probably implies eating at a feast in the future, namely, the marriage supper of the Lamb (Revelation 19), or enjoying the blessings of fellowship forever, it is quite possible that the white stone implies our entrance ticket to that heavenly feast.

The words "new name" do not imply new from the standpoint of time, but rather new in quality or essential nature. The name may not be referring to the name of Jesus Christ, but rather to a special name that reveals the eternal relationship of the overcomer to the promises of God.

Our Lord has so many wonderful promises to those who are the true believers, the overcomers. First Corinthians 2:9 reminds us all: "Eye has not seen, nor ear heard, nor have entered into the heart of man the things which God has prepared for those who love Him."

Chapter 7

Immoral Practices

(2:18-29)

What Do We Know about Thyatira?

It was my pleasure to visit the ruins of the ancient city of Thyatira, located about forty miles southeast of Pergamos. The surrounding countryside is most beautiful. Thyatira was a small city, easily conquered, but commercially profitable due to its location on a major route to more prominent cities. Because of its size, however, it was not really important to Rome or the worship of the emperor.

The pagan culture of Thyatira was not dominated by emperor worship, but each trade guild had its own god, and members of the guild were pressured into participation in the pagan feasts and immoral practices of guild members. Christians would face a problem of job security and acceptability if they refused to participate.

According to Acts 16, Lydia was from Thyatira. She was a seller of purple. History records that Thyatira was well known for its cloth industry and its special dyes. Though Lydia was converted in the city of Philippi in Macedonia, some believe it was through her testimony that the church was begun in the city of Thyatira. Unfortunately, the church may have ceased to exist by the end of the second century.

What Jesus Christ Says to Thyatira
(2:18-29)

[18] *"And to the angel of the church in Thyatira write,*

'These things says the Son of God, who has eyes like a flame of fire, and His feet like fine brass: [19] *"I know your works, love, service, faith, and your patience; and as for your works, the last are more than the first.* [20] *Nevertheless I have a few things against you, because you allow that*

67

woman Jezebel, who calls herself a prophetess, to teach and beguile My servants to commit sexual immorality and to eat things sacrificed to idols. [21]And I gave her time to repent of her sexual immorality, and she did not repent. [22]Indeed I will cast her into a sickbed, and those who commit adultery with her into great tribulation, unless they repent of their deeds. [23]And I will kill her children with death. And all the churches shall know that I am He who searches the minds and hearts. And I will give to each one of you according to your works. [24]But to you I say, and to the rest in Thyatira, as many as do not have this doctrine, and who have not known the depths of Satan, as they call them, I will put on you no other burden. [25]But hold fast what you have till I come. [26]And he who over-comes, and keeps My works until the end, to him I will give power over the nations—

> *[27]'He shall rule them with a rod of iron;*
> *As the potter's vessels shall be broken to pieces'—*

as I also have received from My Father; [28]and I will give him the morning star. [29]He who has an ear, let him hear what the Spirit says to the churches." '"

The Examination of the Church (2:18)

Several years ago our church underwent an examination by a fine Christian organization dedicated to helping the church evaluate itself and make improvements. Their materials were excellent and based upon biblical principles. Their attitudes were kind, humble, and ser-vice-oriented. They pointed out some ways in which we could improve our ministry to people. It was most beneficial and well worth the investment we made in it.

But in spite of that examination's benefits, it is far more important to know what the Head of the church thinks about our ministry, methods, and message. Each of these seven churches is confronted with a unique portrayal of Jesus Christ—a portrayal that reflects the specific need of each church.

Two things are brought to our attention in this letter to Thyatira: (1) Jesus is the Son of God, and (2) He has eyes like a flame of fire and feet like fine brass.

This is the only place in Revelation where we find the title "the Son of God," a title John used frequently in his gospel account. Some believe John is marking the contrast between the authority of Jesus Christ and that of the emperor. While that is possible, emperor worship was not prominent at Thyatira as it was at Pergamos.

A more likely connection is with the Messianic teaching of Psalm 2 since a verse from that psalm (v.9) is quoted in this letter to Thyatira (v. 27). In this psalm, the nations are declared to be Messiah's unique inheritance, and He will ultimately demonstrate His sovereignty over them: "You shall break them with a rod of iron; / You shall dash them in pieces like a potter's vessel" (2:9).

The deity, sovereignty, and authority of Jesus Christ must always be reestablished in the minds of believers if sinful practices are to be dealt with as God intends. It is not our authority that roots out evil, but our submission to His will. The issues are not merely temporary ones; they affect eternal destiny and reward.

The reference to His "eyes" and "feet" reminds us of the vision of chapter one (vv. 14-15) where we learned of His scrutiny, seeing all that we think, say, and do, and His severity, treading with His feet in the winepress of God's wrath against sin and unbelief.

Verse 23 verifies this interpretation of the eyes like a flame of fire when it says, "I am He who searches the minds and hearts." Verse 27 mentions ruling with a rod of iron, a clear connection to Revelation 19:15 where His feet tread "the winepress of the fierceness and wrath of Almighty God."

This church needed to know Who was about to examine their spiritual condition. They needed to remember His authority, deity, and sovereignty over all, and His knowledge of all that was going on in the church, and His role in judging them if they did not repent.

The Evidence of Spiritual Life (2:19)

Is it possible to have a growing and maturing church and yet be compromising with sin? Judging from the initial remarks of Jesus, that is a real possibility. Appearances may deceive us, but God looks on the heart.

Their deeds. Our Lord's examination of this church reveals four basic things worthy of commendation—love, service, faith, and patience.

1. They had a proper motivation ("love"). This is the only church that received commendation for love. Ephesus was rebuked for leaving its first love. It is a striking paradox when reading the terrible things going on in Thyatira to see that the Lord commends them for love.

A great lesson is revealed in mentioning the "love" of believers in Thyatira, a church that is strongly rebuked for compromising with sin.

Immoral Practices

God's love does not mean we tolerate sin. In the name of "love" many sinful practices are allowed in today's churches. No one wants to confront, rebuke, or discipline believers. We are told we have no right to tell people how to live their lives. Some say it is an invasion of privacy and legally wrong to be concerned about the lifestyles of people who attend our churches. We have lost sight of what Jesus thinks of the church, and have substituted our own insufficient and powerless viewpoints.

2. They demonstrated an effective ministry ("service"). The Greek word for service gives us our English word *deacon*, and indicates voluntary service focused on the needs of people. It was used of those who waited on tables, serving food to others. All believers are to be equipped for the work of "ministry" (Ephesians 4:12), which includes using the spiritual gifts God has given to them (1 Peter 4:10-11).

The church in Thyatira had a proper motivation (love) that resulted in effective ministry (service). Most of us would be delighted to be a part of such a fellowship and active church.

3. They were committed to a right message ("faith"). The works of these believers in Thyatira demonstrated their commitment to *"the* faith," the body of truth (found in the Bible) which is the ground for our salvation and growth in the Lord. But it is not only the content of our faith that may be indicated by this word, but also our faithfulness to that content. Thus many translate "faithfulness" here, or a commitment to the faith.

4. They endured with a tough mentality ("patience"). Patience is "bearing up under" a heavy load. Trials were expected; persecution was everywhere; problems would not go away. These believers were commended for endurance, not giving up. They had the patience James speaks about that develops maturity and contentment (James 1:2-4).

It is hard to believe the church was in such peril when these qualities were being manifested in their midst.

Their spiritual development. In addition to their deeds giving evidence of strong spiritual life and a growing ministry in Thyatira, their spiritual development was also obvious. Our Lord says of them "and as for your works, the last are more than the first."

Unlike many churches, they were not depending upon a rich past, nor boasting of what things were like "in the good old days." They did not rest on previous blessings, but in fact were seeking to serve the Lord more and more. We cannot help being impressed with this little congregation, located in the smallest of the seven cities.

But . . .

70

The Example of Moral Decay (2:20-21)

In spite of the good things Jesus had to say, He continues His examination of this church with these ominous words: "Nevertheless I have a few things against you."

Just because I am being blessed and am active in the ministry of my church, motivated properly and committed to the message of God's Word in my life, does not mean that everything is okay—that God is pleased with everything I say and do.

Who is Jezebel? Verses 20-21 inform us that Jezebel is a woman, that she calls herself a prophetess, that she teaches and deceives the believers about sexual immorality and food sacrificed to idols, that she is guilty of sexual immorality herself, and that she is unrepentant. Verse 24 adds that those who hold to the doctrine of Jezebel claim to know the "depths of Satan." So we can say further about her that she was involved with occultic practices associated with satanic influence.

The name recalls a familiar Old Testament character, Jezebel, the wife of Israel's king Ahab. What we learn about Jezebel in Revelation 2 is uniquely tied to the account of Jezebel and Ahab in 1 and 2 Kings. The similarities are there. The question is, Is the reference to Jezebel in Revelation 2 merely symbolic of the Old Testament woman by that name, or was there a woman named Jezebel in the church of Thyatira?

I believe this passage describes a real woman in the church, but the depiction of her as Jezebel is symbolic. This calling to mind of the Old Testament account underscores for us how serious and sinful the situation at Thyatira really was. The reference to Balaam in the message to Pergamos is a similar use of symbolism in the book of Revelation.

Some suggest that an evil spirit (demon) was involved in the woman in Thyatira, producing through her life the same evil qualities of the woman Jezebel who lived almost a thousand years previous. One writer even suggests that this Jezebel was the wife of the pastor-bishop of this church!

In any event, this prominent woman in the church, identified symbolically as Jezebel, claimed to be a prophetess and desired to mislead the people into immorality, idolatry, and occultic practices. Her teaching and deception is like that mentioned previously in the church at Pergamos—those who hold the teachings of Balaam and the Nicolaitans. However, it was no doubt in connection with the trade guilds in Thyatira that this teaching and deception found fertile soil. Christians were being persuaded that it was acceptable to be involved in these sinful practices because it was a part of their job. It was a relief to these believers to think that the Spirit of God might be approving of these things because a prophetess was proclaiming its acceptability.

Today we have many leaders who claim to be prophets or prophetesses of God. They say God talks to them and gives them special messages in addition to what is already found in the Bible. The danger of this should be obvious no matter how sincere the individual may be. A given teaching is right or wrong based upon the authority of the Bible, not the personality or claims of a given leader.

What about Christian liberty? Some argue that the grace of God frees believers to do whatever they want or deem necessary to achieve their goals in life. This is turning the grace of God and our liberty in Christ into license to sin. We are never free to sin; we are still under the moral laws of God. And if we are true believers, we desire to do His will and to obey His commandments (Romans 5-6).

The Explanation of God's Judgment (2:22-23)

The Lord Himself is very patient. Verse 21 states, "and I gave her time to repent." How wonderful is God's long-suffering toward us. He gives us time to get right with Him, but we should never assume that He will not judge us. If we do not judge ourselves, we will be judged by God (1 Corinthians 11:31-32).

God's judgment will come upon Jezebel and her followers. Notice the words "I will," which appear three times. God will execute His judgment upon all who refuse to repent.

1. Physical disease for Jezebel ("I will cast her into a sickbed"). A play on words exists in this statement: the bed of immorality to which she often resorted will become a bed of sickness. Perhaps the sexual diseases so prevalent in our society today are a valid understanding of this sickbed that Jezebel would experience.

It is also possible because of the connection with the words "great tribulation" that the "bed" is the tribulation itself with all its horrible sufferings.

2. Great distress for her followers ("and those who commit adultery with her into great tribulation"). While this could refer to actual adultery, it would either make the group involved exceedingly small or would indicate her enormous capacity for sexual sin. A more likely explanation is that the emphasis is on spiritual adultery—going along with her viewpoints (which included sexual sin).

The "great tribulation" would refer to the judgment of God upon all unbelievers which will soon unfold before our eyes in the book of Revelation.

3. Coming death for her children ("and I will kill her children with death"). Her "children" are distinguished from "those who commit adultery with her." The latter group refers to professing believers in the church who were influenced by her teaching and deception to go along with the sinful practices of the trade guilds of Thyatira.

The "children" refers to the next generation or all those who are committed to her viewpoint and continue to propagate it, whether they were living in the generation immediately after the one mentioned in Thyatira or people living today. The coming result for all who advocate such teaching is death—final, eternal, and fully justified.

God's judgment should affect the attitudes of all the churches. Verse 23 says, "And all the churches shall know that I am He who searches the minds and hearts." The simple point here is that we cannot escape the judgment of God. We cannot tolerate what went on in Thyatira and expect to avoid the coming judgment of God. God knows what we are doing—nothing is hid from His knowledge and presence (Hebrews 4:13)—and we are accountable to Him.

God's judgment will come to every one of us. Verse 23 adds a final note: "And I will give to each one of you according to your works." This truth is presented in the Bible over and over again (Romans 14:10, 12; 1 Corinthians 4:5; 2 Corinthians 5:10). There is no escape.

To the believer in Jesus Christ, the judgment of Christ is for reward, not to determine eternal life and personal salvation. To the unbeliever, the judgment of Christ results in eternal punishment. All of us will give account.

This is a strong admonition to every church and every believer to resist teachings and insinuations by professing Christians that tolerate sexual sin and approve of carnal involvements with unbelievers. God's Word emphasizes separation from sinful practices as the standard for Christian conduct and ministry.

The Exhortation to the Faithful (2:24-25)

It was not easy to be a Christian in the environment of ancient Thyatira. Many were compromising their Christian convictions in order to keep their jobs.

The appeal here is to a godly remnant within the church, a noticeable change from the first three letters. Things are obviously worse in Thyatira.

The Lord understands the struggles of the faithful, and He places no other burden upon them than remaining faithful to the admonition of this letter, which simply stated is to stay away from sexual sin (cf. 1 Thessalonians 4:1-8) and pagan practices that lead to the toleration and acceptance of sinful lifestyles.

The Encouragement to the Overcomer (2:26-28)

The overcomer is the true believer. He demonstrates his faith by obedience ("keeps My works until the end") through all his days. It does not mean that he never makes a mistake or has his moments of defeat. It means he is characterized by obedience to God's will.

The word *keeps* is used by John thirty-six times in his writings. It is followed by "My word," "My commandments," and in this case "My works." It is a phrase emphasizing obedience to God's will; that is the major evidence of true belief in the Lord.

Two promises are given to the overcomer in Thyatira and to all overcomers throughout church history: (1) "I will give power over the nations," and (2) "I will give him the morning star."

Power over the nations implies great authority in the coming kingdom of the Messiah. It is similar to Christ's promises to believers that we will rule and reign with Him. If we have been faithful in a few things, He will make us ruler over many things.

The quotation from Psalm 2 emphasizes the final victory of the Messiah over the nations of the world, which Revelation 19 predicts as well. Believers will share that victory and provide leadership in the coming kingdom on earth.

The authority, dominion, and conquering of the nations of the world by the Messiah is that which He received from the Father Himself ("as I also have received from My Father").

What is the "morning star"? Jesus Christ is certainly the morning star (Revelation 22:16), but is that what it means in the letter to overcomers in Thyatira? Jesus Christ says, "I will give him the morning star." Does He mean that He will give Himself? Possibly, but not likely.

The star of the morning may be considered the brightest, and the symbolism here indicates the glory the righteous will experience in the Messianic kingdom (2 Peter 1:19); we will shine "like the stars forever and ever" (Daniel 12:3). Of course, Jesus Christ as *the* Morning Star makes that all possible. What a glorious future awaits us!

Repetition Aids Learning (2:29)

Once again we read the phrase: "He who has an ear, let him hear what the Spirit says to the churches." Are we listening and responding? The Holy Spirit has dealt with four essential issues in the four letters we have studied so far:

Ephesus: *neglected priorities*
Smyrna: *satanic opposition*
Pergamos: *religious compromise*
Thyatira: *immoral practices*

And in each letter our Lord gives us His exhortation:

Ephesus: *repent*
Smyrna: *do not fear and be faithful unto death*
Pergamos: *repent*
Thyatira: *hold fast what you have*

Finally, in each letter there are promises to overcomers:

Ephesus: *eat from the tree of life*
Smyrna: *the crown of life and no second death*
Pergamos: *hidden manna and a white stone with a
            new name*
Thyatira: *power over the nations and the morning star*

Four down . . . three to go. What are we personally going to do in response to these challenges from our Lord and Savior Jesus Christ?

Chapter 8

Spiritual Apathy

(3:1-6)

Several things about this letter are similar to the others we have studied. Jesus Christ gives a description of Himself, taking it from previous statements in the book. He repeats the words of each letter, "I know your works," and He tells them to "hold fast and repent." He gives some wonderful promises to the one "who overcomes" and ends the letter with a familiar challenge: "He who has an ear, let him hear what the Spirit says to the churches."

But there are also some unique statements which are not found in the other letters, and give us some insight into the situation and need of the church in Sardis.

What Do We Know about Sardis?

Sardis, located about fifty miles due east of Smyrna and about thirty miles south of Thyatira, was the capital of the province of Lydia. The city was built on the acropolis and was thus able to defend itself quite well from possible invaders. Later in its history, a second city was built on the slopes of this fifteen hundred foot plateau for convenience and easier access.

The Lydian kingdom began around 1200 B.C. and was the center of opposition to European forces. Sardis in particular was the one great enemy of Ionian cities. In the great conflicts between Asia and Europe, Sardis stood as an impregnable fortress of defense for the cities of Asia. It was known as the "First Metropolis of Asia, and of Lydia, and of Hellenism." It was powerful in its influence, bolstered by an exceedingly wealthy and prosperous economy.

Spiritual Apathy

The conquest of Sardis by King Cyrus of Persia in the sixth century B.C. was a shock to the Greeks who had tried so often to conquer it. King Croesus of Sardis and Lydia had attacked Cyrus on the promise of victory by a Delphic oracle, but was soundly defeated. After Croesus returned to Sardis, Cyrus brought a surprise attack and caught the city unprepared. Three hundred years later, Antiochus the Great also captured the city and later it was taken by the Romans.

In A.D. 17 the city was devastated by an earthquake, but through the kindness of Emperor Tiberius, the city was able to recover. In appreciation, the city minted a special coin in honor of Tiberius and erected a temple as well.

The economy of the city was affected by a fertile territory that was carefully cultivated, and by an active trade with other parts of the world. Its main industries dealt with the production of woolen goods and jewelry. Like Thyatira, Sardis was known for its dyes and its ability to produce beautifully colored garments.

Its religious background is more difficult to ascertain. The evidence of emperor worship, pagan temples and idols, and occultic practices are present, but no particular influence stands out. Its coins have religious symbols, including the Greek god Zeus, and a specific temple was built by the city to the goddess Cybele who seems to be connected with nature in Greek mythology. From the fourth century B.C. there was a temple to Artemis, the multibreasted goddess of sex and fertility so fervently worshiped by the Ephesians.

As in several cities of Asia province (western Turkey), healing powers were associated with pagan gods. The interesting point about Sardis is that such healing power was expanded to include restoring the dead. Perhaps this was connected with the hot springs which were located close to the city. One cannot help but connect this fact with the words of this letter "you have a name that you are alive, but you are dead," words that would have reminded the residents of this city of their glorious past and their meaningless present situation.

When John wrote the book of Revelation, Sardis had already lost its former glory. The acropolis was no longer inhabited and the city was faced with a glorious past and no future.

The Church in Sardis

Not much is known about the church prior to the writing of this letter. Neither its founding or development is referred to in the New

Testament. One of its early bishops, Melito, wrote one of the first known commentaries on the book of Revelation near the end of the second century A.D.

In spite of the past wealth of the city, there is no boasting in this letter like that of Laodicea (3:17). There does not seem to be a problem of persecution like other cities faced. There is no emphasis upon the impact of pagan religions or religious opposition. The church has a reputation and appears to be a normal congregation in the eyes of others. Herodotus, the Greek historian, said that the citizens of Sardis had a reputation for lax moral standards and open licentiousness which might explain the emphasis of verse 4 concerning a few people who had not "defiled their garments."

The general impression one gets when reading this letter is that the church is dying through apathy and indifference. The struggle against pagan influence and worldly viewpoints has been lost. The Christians have given up the fight and are not reaching their world for Jesus Christ. It's the problem so many fine churches of our day have experienced. They talk of the past and still have all the ingredients and message of former days, but they have lost their zeal, compromised with the world around them, and have a terminal illness. If the present trend continues, the church will soon be a relic of the past, a reminder of how easily God's work can die when spiritual apathy sets in.

What Jesus Christ Says to Sardis
(3:1-6)

[1] *"And to the angel of the church in Sardis write,*

'These things says He who has the seven spirits of God and the seven stars: "I know your works, that you have a name that you are alive, but you are dead. [2] *Be watchful, and strengthen the things which remain, that are ready to die, for I have not found your works perfect before God.* [3] *Remember therefore how you have received and heard; hold fast and repent. Therefore if you will not watch, I will come upon you as a thief, and you will not know what hour I will come upon you.* [4] *You have a few names even in Sardis who have not defiled their garments; and they shall walk with Me in white, for they are worthy.* [5] *He who overcomes shall be clothed in white garments, and I will not blot out his name from the Book of Life; but I will*

confess his name before My Father and before His angels.
⁶He who has an ear, let him hear what the Spirit says to
the churches." '"

His Assessment of This Church (3:1)

Consider the following observations from this one simple verse:

The message comes from Jesus Christ. The "seven Spirits" are the seven angels which are God's messengers in the book of Revelation. One is assigned to each church. Their ministry is under the Lord's control; He holds them in His right hand (1:20; 2:1). They are simply communicating what the Lord wants us to hear. None of us can run away from that fact; this comes from Jesus Christ, the Head of the church.

The truth about each church is known by Jesus Christ . A person can hide the truth from his family, friends, and fellow employees, but not from God. A church may have a good reputation, but Jesus Christ knows the real truth about its spiritual condition and effectiveness. When He says, "I know your works," it is a solemn reminder that nothing escapes His notice and analysis (Hebrews 4:13). According to verse 2, their "works" were not what the Lord desired. They fell short of His standards even though they produced a good reputation for the church in Sardis in the eyes of others.

The spiritual condition of a church is not easily known. We think we know what a church is like if we have been a member for a number of years. That may or may not be true. What we think and what the Lord thinks are not always the same.

This church had a good reputation ("you have a name that you are alive"). Spiritual life is the point, of course. In the eyes of other people, the church in Sardis was spiritually alive. But Jesus sees the real condition and says "but you are dead." It is rather startling to realize that there can be such a contrast between what people say about a church and what Jesus might say about the same church.

What is true about a whole congregation is also possible for individual believers. Friends may think we are spiritually alive by what they see us do, but it is possible for us to be spiritually dead in the eyes of the Lord no matter what others say.

Here is a good lesson: Don't be too quick to judge outward appearance or performance. The important questions deal with the inward man, the realm of the unseen, the heart of the individual. Are we really in right relationship to God in the innermost recesses of our hearts?

Our reputation is no guarantee of inward character. Many of us major in a good reputation. We want people to think well of us and to say nice things about us. However, our reputation is only what people think we are; our character is what God knows us to be. This church had a "name," a profession, a reputation, but it was not the truth about their spiritual condition.

The Bible warns us often concerning outward appearance versus inward reality. We enjoy hearing the praises and commendations of others, but the one who walks with the Lord desires to hear these words from the lips of his Lord and Savior: "Well done, good and faithful servant. . . . Enter into the joy of your Lord" (Matthew 25:21,23). It is His approval that we need, not the plaudits of men.

His Appeal to This Church (3:2-3a)

The appeal Jesus Christ makes to this church is based on the true condition of these believers as well as the commitment they must make if things are to change.

Their real condition in the eyes of the Lord. His words reveal at least three things:

1. They were unconcerned about their spiritual condition. When He says "be watchful," it literally means "to wake up." They are asleep spiritually—unconcerned, apathetic, indifferent. It reminds us of Paul's words to the Ephesian believers, "Awake, you who sleep, / Arise from the dead, / And Christ will give you light" (Ephesians 5:14). These words would have special meaning to the citizens of Sardis. Their city had fallen on two previous occasions to surprise attacks (from Cyrus and Antiochus the Great) when they were militarily asleep.

There is also a ray of hope here. While the church suffers from apathy, it is not hopeless. The fact that the Lord challenges them to wake up shows that things can be different. Our Lord has not given up on this church.

2. They were unaware of how serious their condition was. When Jesus Christ tells this church to "strengthen the things which remain," He added what must have been a shock to these believers in Sardis—things "that are ready to die." By the statement that follows, this appears to be a reference to their "works," which were not what the Lord wanted them to be. The efforts of this church were becoming so routine and mechanical, lacking in real spiritual vitality, their ministry and influence were about to be removed.

3. They were unresponsive to what the Lord wanted. In His appeal, our Lord tells them the truth about their performance: "I have not found your works perfect before God." Too much concern about our reputation before men can take our minds and hearts away from what God thinks.

The word "perfect" carries the idea of completion or fulfillment. The works of these believers were not fulfilling the purpose of God. As to what is meant, we can only conjecture. No doubt their works were not coming from hearts filled with "first love" as described in the letter to the Ephesian believers. Perhaps they were not done to praise and glorify the Lord and to attract others to Him (Matthew 5:16), but only to build a good reputation.

Another sense in which their works might not have been complete or fulfilling the purposes of God is that they were not centered in reaching others for the Lord but only in convincing themselves that they were spiritually alive.

The commitment required to change things. Jesus told this church to do three things—remember, hold fast, and repent.

1. We must remember what the Bible teaches. To remember what you have "received and heard" is a reminder to all of us of the importance of God's Word. Not much change occurs permanently that does not rest solidly upon biblical counsel. When real commitment takes place, it is motivated by biblical truth. We begin to see again what God thinks and says we are to do, and we act on it because we fear the Lord and desire to do His will in our lives.

2. We must re-establish our loyalty and obedience to what God teaches in His Word. The simple words "hold fast" are mentioned in four of the seven letters, but the word in Greek used here is not the same as Revelation 2:13, 25, or 3:11. It is often translated "keep" and is used by John frequently in his epistles. He concluded that true believers were those who "keep His commandments." Revelation 3:8 and 10 use the word when they speak of those who "kept My word" and who "kept My command."

The level of commitment and loyalty here demands continual obedience. That's where many of us grow weak and become ineffective; we stop being obedient to God's Word. If we want to change, we need to remember the importance of God's Word and re-establish our loyalty and obedience to what God says.

3. We must repent of our wrong attitudes and practices. This one word "repent" is used frequently in the Bible, and yet is seldom heeded by believers. It demands change. It is a change of mind primarily, but results in a change of conduct or lifestyle. We must bring our attitudes and habits into conformity with what the Bible teaches. Radical change is necessary or little will happen to stop the spiritual decline.

The Action Jesus Threatens to Take (3:3b)

Things began to change when we wake up ("watch"). If we do not, we will suffer the consequences. Our Lord is patient with our spiritual apathy and indifference, but if it continues and we fail to respond, He must bring His judgment upon us.

These words reminded the believers in Sardis of their past history. It was said of king Cyrus that he invaded Sardis like a "thief in the night," before anyone had time to put his shoes on.

These same words to Sardis could be said to us today regarding the second coming of Jesus Christ. We don't know the hour when He will come, but we are exhorted to be ready and watching. However, the primary meaning here is not the second coming but the judgment of Jesus Christ upon a dying church that refuses to respond to His challenge. He will come in the sense that He mentioned in the letter to Ephesus (2:5) and remove its lampstand or influence—the church will die. History has verified that this is precisely what happened to Sardis. The church eventually ceased to exist and exercise any influence for the Lord. The area surrounding Sardis became a center of Moslem influence in later history and continues to this day.

The Assurance Jesus Gives (3:4-6)

It is both sad and encouraging to read His words "You have a *few* names even in Sardis." A small group of believers who loved the Lord and were spiritually alive existed in that church. Jesus reaches out to them with wonderful words of encouragement and promise. His assurance to them is based upon two things and gives us insight into why the other believers were apathetic and spiritually dying.

He gives assurance because of their moral purity. The phrase "have not defiled their garments" is a symbolic expression for moral purity. The tolerance of immorality and acceptance of pagan sexual practices in John's day is well known. Sardis was no exception. Many believers were asleep spiritually because some of this moral impurity was entering their lives and causing them to be apathetic and indifferent to spiritual truth. Sexual sin can deeply affect our ability to respond to God's

Word. We hear God's Word and may even say we believe it, but no repentance occurs. We remain indifferent and unresponsive.

He gives assurance because of their personal practices. When verse 4 says "for they are worthy," it uses a word meaning "having the weight of" something. It was used in the marketplace of a balance which determined the value of an item. When Paul exhorted us in Ephesians 4:1 to "walk worthy," he meant the same thing we mean when we say "practice what you preach." If our life is balanced with what the Bible teaches, then our walk matches our talk, our performance proves what we say we believe.

Moral purity refers to what we *do not* do, and personal practices refer to what we *do*. These few believers were receiving these words of encouragement from Jesus Christ because they were staying away from sinful practices and were demonstrating daily their obedience to the Lord.

He gives three wonderful promises. Jesus directs these words to the one "who overcomes," the true believer (cf. 1 John 5:4-5). The three eternal realities are perfection, security, and acceptance.

1. Perfection. Verse 4 says, "they shall walk with Me in white," and verse 5 agrees—"clothed in white garments." The "white" pictures the purity of Christ's righteousness, the past not only forgiven but wiped away forever. What good news!

According to Revelation 4:4, the twenty-four elders in heaven are "clothed in white robes." In 6:11 we learn that a "white robe" is given to each of the souls who have been martyred. In 7:9 the great multitude which comes out of the tribulation is "clothed with white robes." We are told in that same chapter (v. 14) that the robes are white because they were made white "in the blood of the Lamb." We cannot help but see the forgiveness, cleansing, and righteousness of our Lord being pictured by these white garments (cf. Revelation 19:8, 14).

2. Security. No matter is more important, no security as powerful as this promise of Jesus Christ: "I will not blot out his name from the Book of Life." This "Book of Life" is mentioned in Revelation 13:8, 17:8, 20:12, 15, 21:27, and 22:19. From these passages we learn the following:

1. It is a book that uniquely belongs to the Lamb of God and is related to His death (13:8; 21:27).

2. Your name must be written in this book in order for you to enter the heavenly city (21:27).

3. If your name is not found written in this book, you are cast into the lake of fire (20:15).

4. Those who dwell on the earth during the tribulation and marvel at the beast do not have their names written in this book, nor have their names been there since the foundation of the world (17:8).

These passages do not allow for names to be written in this book and then later be removed. Although some writers argue for this, it is impossible to prove and appears to be wrong on the simple evidence of these verses.

The promise that names will not be blotted out of the book does not necessitate a belief that some names will be blotted out, though many argue that possibility. This promise is a simple yet powerful statement of assurance to all who place their faith and trust in Jesus Christ as Lord and Savior—you cannot have your name removed from the Book of Life! No true believer can ever lose his salvation.

3. Acceptance. "I will confess His name before My Father and before His angels." We are admonished in the Bible to confess with our mouths that Jesus is Lord (Romans 10:9) and urged to confess before men (Matthew 10:32) that we have come to believe in Him as our only Savior from sin. The opposite of confession is denial.

When we one day stand before God, Jesus Christ will confess us as His own before all the angelic hosts and the Father Himself. What wonderful acceptance! We belong to Him, and He will proclaim it before all who dwell in heaven.

Unbelievers who have denied Him will also stand before God at the Great White Throne judgment (Revelation 20). Jesus Christ will publicly deny them because they have refused to confess Him as their Savior and Lord.

What about you? Have you made a personal and public confession of Jesus Christ as your Lord and Savior? "He who has an ear, let him hear what the Spirit says to the churches."

Chapter 9

Eternal Security

(3:7-13)

What Do We Know about Philadelphia?

Philadelphia was located in a beautiful valley some twenty- five miles southeast of Sardis. It sat on a great trade route that in Byzantine times became the greatest trade route in the whole country. Philadelphia was connected vitally to the main communications line of Rome itself by which it maintained control and influence over much of the ancient world.

The name of the city (which means "brotherly love") comes from the loyalty which King Attalus of Pergamum, who sponsored the founding of the city, demonstrated to his brother King Eumenes. The original purpose behind this key city was to make it a center for spreading Greek language, culture, and manners throughout the Asian provinces, such as Lydia and Phrygia. Its success is seen in that the Lydian language ceased to be used by 20 A.D. and was replaced by Greek.

While the evidence is sparse, it appears that the influence of Greek culture affected religious life in Philadelphia. Its coins reveal pagan gods such as Artemis and Asklepios, as well as pagan temples. Since grapes were one of its main crops, it's not surprising to learn that the pagan god, Dionysus, the god of wine and revelry, was worshiped here. In Byzantine and Medieval times, this church seemed to grow in influence as did the city itself.

When you visit the site of this ancient city, you are reminded of its vulnerability to natural disaster. It is located in a region where volcanoes have erupted producing large quantities of black lava. The earthquake of A.D. 17 that devastated Sardis also struck Philadelphia, and the continual aftershocks caused a state of panic for several years.

Philadelphia is known for its resistance to Moslem influence in the Middle Ages. While most of the surrounding cities fell early to the forces of Mohammedanism, Philadelphia remained Christian until the fourteenth century. The city remains to this day with a population around twenty thousand and even has a bishop with five churches, claiming about a thousand Christians.

The message to this church deals with the promises of God to those who are faithful to Him. It is important to see those promises clearly when faced with unbelief and persecution. Some believe no problems exist in this church. However, in spite of the absence of specific words of condemnation, there is the subtle implication that some have begun to question God's promises, wondering if they are true and if commitment to Christ is worth the pressure and hostility that inevitably comes.

What Jesus Christ Says to Philadelphia
(3:7-13)

[7] *"And to the angel of the church in Philadelphia write,*

'These things says He who is holy, He who is true, "He who has the key of David, He who opens and no one shuts, and shuts and no one opens": [8] *"I know your works. See, I have set before you an open door, and no one can shut it; for you have a little strength, have kept My word, and have not denied My name.* [9] *Indeed I will make those of the synagogue of Satan, who say they are Jews and are not, but lie—indeed I will make them come and worship before your feet, and to know that I have loved you.* [10] *Because you have kept My command to persevere, I also will keep you from the hour of trial which shall come upon the whole world, to test those who dwell on the earth.* [11] *Behold, I come quickly! Hold fast what you have, that no one may take your crown.* [12] *He who overcomes, I will make him a pillar in the temple of My God, and he shall go out no more. And I will write on him the name of My God and the name of the city of My God, the New Jerusalem, which comes down out of heaven from My God. And I will write on him My new name.* [13] *He who has an ear, let him hear what the Spirit says to the churches." '"*

The Power of Jesus Christ Is Behind It All (3:7-8)

You cannot read these words without realizing that the Lord is controlling everything. He is in charge. It is His authority that is behind the open door. Notice three things about our Lord in these two verses:

His character ("These things says He who is holy, He who is true"). These two attributes are used of the Lord in Revelation 6:10 and are appealed to by the martyrs concerned with God's revenge upon those who have killed them and seemingly escaped God's wrath. God's holiness demands that justice be done, and the fact that He is true (genuine/faithful) demonstrates that His character can be relied upon. Justice will come in God's timing.

All of God's promises to the faithful are based upon His unchanging character (Hebrews 6:17-19). Because God is holy (will not lie) and because He is true (totally reliable), we can trust Him to reward us wonderfully when we respond to Him.

His control ("He who has the key of David, He who opens and no one shuts, and shuts and no one opens"). The "key of David" is referred to in Isaiah 22:20-25. In that passage, it is given to a man called Eliakim, a steward over King Hezekiah's household (descendant of King David). He was able to open and shut the doors that led into the treasures of the king. In that sense, he points to Jesus Christ who also possesses the key of David, and opens and shuts the door into His Messianic kingdom. If the "door" is the symbol of opportunity and entrance as most argue, then the "key" is the symbol of authority and control.

Jesus has the control—He opens and shuts. That control is also obvious in the phrase repeated in each letter: "I know your works." It is placed within this context to let us know that Jesus knows all about our efforts for Him, and He wants to encourage us by reminding us of His promises to those who are faithful to Him.

His challenge ("See, I have set before you an open door, and no one can shut it; for you have a little strength, have kept My word, and have not denied My name"). Is this a challenge to spread the gospel? Is this speaking of expanded missionary opportunities? The Philadelphian believers were located in a strategic city, a gateway to many areas of the ancient world, a city dedicated to the spread of Greek language and culture. Is the point behind these words of Jesus Christ that these believers must now dedicate themselves to the spread of the gospel?

A more probable interpretation is that this open door speaks of certain entrance into the Messianic kingdom of our Lord. The connection with the prophecy in Isaiah 22 supports this view. It also better fits the other letters—appeals to the faithful and promises to the overcomers, the true believers, of our eternal hope. This view also relates better to what is said in verses 9-12. The challenge to "hold fast" in verse 11 is hard to connect with the view that this is a missionary challenge.

Why the Philadelphians? What made this group of believers so special that they would receive such encouragement from the Lord? Three reasons are given:

1. Dependence upon the Lord's strength ("for you have a little strength"). This statement, and the two that follow it, are simply facts which the Lord knows about the believers in Philadelphia and the reasons why they are given such promises in the midst of what appears to be a difficult environment.

The truth about these believers is that they were not the strongest Christians in the empire nor the most influential. They did not have great numbers of people when John wrote to them, nor any outstanding leaders or unusual talents. But their "little strength" brought encouragement from the lips of our Lord. What wonderful assurance that brings to our own struggles!

2. Dedication to God's Word ("have kept My word"). They guarded the Word of God in such a way as to warrant the commendation of the Lord. Their loyalty proves the validity of their faith and provides one of the reasons for the wonderful encouragement given in this letter. Obedience to God's Word is still the proof of our love for Christ (John 14:21; James 1:22-25). We need to ask ourselves, Am I a "doer of the Word"?

3. Devotion to the Lord Himself ("and have not denied My name"). These Philadelphian believers were loyal to the name and character of Jesus Christ, as were some of those who lived in Pergamos (Revelation 2:13). They believed that He is God in human flesh and that to deny His true nature means you are not a believer and that you have the spirit of antichrist (1 John 2:22-23; 4:2-3), issues with which the apostle John was deeply concerned.

The Protection of Jesus Christ Is All We Need (3:9-10)

This protection of Jesus Christ deals with two great issues: the hostility of unbelievers and the hour of trial which shall come upon the whole world.

Jesus Christ will honor us in the eyes of unbelievers who have been hostile to us. These are such wonderful words to a believing heart, especially for the one who has endured a great deal of pressure and hostility from unbelievers. No matter how extensive the verbal and even physical abuse some believers have experienced, the Lord will one day show to them how much He loves them.

The "synagogue of Satan" was discussed previously in the letter to the church in Smyrna. The same language is used here as there. It was a synagogue composed of those who "say they are Jews and are not." Revelation 3:9 says they "lie," and Revelation 2:9 speaks of their "blasphemy" of the Christians in Smyrna.

These words are not intended to reflect on all Jewish people. It is quite clear in this text that these people are lying when they say they are Jews; they are not true Jews at all. A true Jew is one who has expressed his faith and confidence in the promise of God to Abraham, Isaac, and Jacob, and has come to believe in God's Messiah, who alone can offer redemption and salvation as the prophets of old clearly taught. Such Jews know that the salvation of Gentiles is a part of that promise (Galatians 3:6-9).

Those who do not have faith in the promises of God may claim to be part of God's chosen and beloved people (Israel), but because of their unbelief they become tools in the hands of the devil himself to persecute both Jewish and Gentile Christians. That's why their religious meetings are described as a "synagogue of Satan." He is using them to further his attacks on true believers, whether they be Jew or Gentile.

According to this text, Jesus Christ "will make them come and worship" at the feet of true believers, and these unbelievers will then know how much the true believers are loved by Jesus Christ.

It's fascinating to look at some of the Old Testament parallels to our text. In Isaiah 45:14 the Lord promises that "the labor of Egypt and the merchandise of Cush and of the Sabeans" will "bow down" to the people of Israel and they will "make supplication" saying, "Surely God is in you, and there is no other; there is no other God." In Isaiah 49:23 we read similar words about kings and queens who shall "bow down" to the people of Israel and know that the Lord is their God. Isaiah 60:14 says "the sons of those who afflicted you / Shall come bowing to you / And all those who despised you shall fall prostrate at the soles of your feet; And they shall call you The City of the LORD, / Zion of the Holy One of Israel."

The believers in Philadelphia are likened to the believers in Israel who will one day see that all those who have opposed and resisted them and their message will in the end acknowledge that they are deeply loved by the Lord.

Jesus Christ will keep us from the hour of trial which shall come upon the whole world. The reason for this promise is the perseverance of the believers under persecution and pressure from the society in which they lived. God has a wonderful reward for all who stand firm in their faith and remain dedicated to the Word of God no matter what trials they face.

Christians disagree whether or not Revelation 3:10 promises a *removal* of believers from the hour of trial, or an *immunity* from the trials that will characterize that period of time. It is a debate between pre-tribulationists and posttribulationists.

Posttribulationists rightly argue that there are believers who live during the tribulation period. Pretribulationists agree but insist these are not church-age believers but a multitude who become Christians during the tribulation period on earth (cf. Revelation 7).

Posttribulationists believe Jesus' words in John 17:15—"I do not pray that You should take them out of the world, but that You should keep them from the evil one"—support their interpretation of Revelation 3:10 as a promise of immunity or protection without removal.

Pretribulationists argue that the most natural reading of this verse in the light of its grammar, construction, and context (both here and throughout Revelation), is that church-age believers will not be found on earth during the tribulation period. It is a promise of complete deliverance.

Obviously, it is a tremendous promise and encouragement to all, whether you believe the rapture of the church will occur before or after the tribulation period.

The Purpose behind This Message
All Believers Should Heed (3:11)

It is interesting to observe that Jesus did not say "I will come to you quickly," as He said to the Ephesians (2:5) and to the believers in Pergamos (2:16). To the believers in Sardis He said: "I will come upon you as a thief" (3:3). Here it is not referring to a special coming to judge a particular church and remove their testimony and influence, but it is a reference to the overall theme of the book—the *second coming of Jesus Christ* to this earth! Jesus said those exact words three times in the last chapter of Revelation (22:7, 12, 20).

The imminence of His return (can occur at any moment) is evident. When He does come, it will happen "quickly." Surprise and suddenness are present in this declaration from Jesus Christ.

The challenge. The challenge is to "hold fast what you have." This was stated before in these letters (2:13, 25; 3:3). Dedication and loyalty are being urged. Today we might emphasize this message with the word *commitment*. How committed are you to the message of God's Word? What do you do when pressured to deny Him or to remain silent when you should speak? John wrote elsewhere: "And now, little children, abide in Him, that when He appears, we may have confidence and not be ashamed before Him at His coming" (1 John 2:28).

The consequence. Jesus Christ urged us to be faithful and loyal "that no one may take your crown." He did not say "crowns," but used the singular form. It is the "crown of life" (2:10) to which He is referring. It is the symbol of final victory—living forever with the Lord. Those who deny the Lord and do not hold fast to their commitment will be lost forever. There will be no crown for them.

The Promises to Overcomers Encourage Us to Be Faithful (3:12)

Jesus promises to do two things: He will make the overcomer a pillar, and He will write on him some wonderful names. These are issues of permanence, security, and identity.

It is the promise of a permanent place. The Lord will make this happen; we can't. "A pillar in the temple of My God" is, of course, not to be taken literally but figuratively. According to Revelation 21:22, there is no literal temple in the eternal city. The "temple of My God" refers to the dwelling place of God, and the fact that we are described as "a pillar" indicates that we have a permanent place with the Lord forever and ever.

While inscriptions were frequent on the pillars of ancient temples, there is a custom in Roman times to which this promise may be related. It was customary for a religious leader of the imperial cult (worship of the emperor) to erect a statue in the temple on which was inscribed his name, his father's name, his place of birth, and the year of his office as official priest of the Roman Empire.

These words call to mind a wonderful promise from Isaiah 56:5:

> "Even to them I will give in My house
>   And within My walls a place and a name
>   Better than that of sons and daughters;
>   I will give them an everlasting name
>   That shall not be cut off."

Surely the apostle John was reminded of this passage when he penned these beautiful words of assurance.

When Jesus says, "and he shall go out no more," He means we shall never be separated from Him. We will "dwell in the house of the LORD forever" (Psalm 23:6). As Paul wrote so beautifully: "For I am persuaded that neither death nor life, nor angels nor principalities nor powers, nor things present nor things to come, nor height nor depth, nor any other created thing, shall be able to separate us from the love of God which is in Christ Jesus our Lord" (Romans 8:38-39). Nothing can ever separate us!

It is the promise of a special identity. In three ways we are assured of a special identity and relationship to the Lord forever. The Lord will write three things on us: (1) "The name of My God," (2) "the name of the city of My God, the New Jerusalem," and (3) "My new name."

It is said of the 144,000 Jewish evangelists of the tribulation period that they have "His Father's name written on their foreheads" (14:1). Revelation 19:12 says of Jesus that "He had a name written that no one knew except Himself." Verse 13 adds, "His name is called The Word of God." Verse 16 says, "And He has on His robe and on His thigh a name written: KING OF KINGS AND LORD OF LORDS." Revelation 22:4 says of believers in the eternal city, "His name shall be on their foreheads."

Our relationship to God the Father and God the Son and the eternal city, the New Jerusalem, are all made secure by this wonderful promise. It's like one giant summary statement— *we belong to the Lord*—nothing can ever change that fact! This wonderful letter of encouragement to the faithful and the overcomers is a reminder that one day it will be worth it all when we see Jesus.

The letter concludes as always with this penetrating thought: "He who has an ear, let him hear what the Spirit says to the churches."

Chapter 10

Material Prosperity

(3:14-22)

What Do We Know about Laodicea?

Laodicea was the ancient capital of the province of Phrygia. It was a part of a tri-city metropolitan area which included the cities of Hierapolis and Colossae. Located in the Lycus Valley on a major highway, the city was surrounded by mountains, and its location made it an excellent fortress to guard the main road and the greater metropolitan area. It was located about forty miles southeast of Philadelphia.

In addition to being the judicial seat of the province, it was a center for the banking industry, and included a prosperous economy with manufacturing of cloth as one of its primary assets. Beautiful garments and carpets were designed from the wool of the black sheep of this region. The wool was known to be extremely soft in texture and glossy black in color, making it highly desirable around the empire.

The medical school was quite famous, and its physicians claimed success in mixing medicines for certain diseases. They produced an ointment for the ears as well as a powder for the eyes. Aristotle called it "Phrygian powder." The physicians demonstrated allegiance to the serpent god Asklepios, which dominated the medical school of Pergamos.

Laodicea was a center of emperor worship as one might expect after seeing its strategic location. Although destroyed by an earthquake in A.D. 60, the city was rebuilt without any financial help from Rome. It proudly refused imperial financial assistance in rebuilding.

In his letter to the Colossians, the apostle Paul refers to a letter he wrote to the Laodiceans (4:16). His words in Colossians suggest the possibility that Epaphras was the founder or present pastor of the church in Laodicea (cf. 1:7; 4:12-13). If Epaphras was the pastor or church-planter in this region, then the Laodiceans were blessed with godly leadership in the beginning days of their ministry. Epaphras had a servant's heart and was fervent and faithful in his prayers for these people. He earnestly desired their maturity in the Lord.

What Jesus Christ Says to Laodicea
(3:14-22)

[14] *"And to the angel of the church of the Laodiceans write,*

'These things says the Amen, the Faithful and True Witness, the Beginning of the creation of God: [15] *"I know your works, that you are neither cold nor hot. I could wish you were cold or hot.* [16] *So then, because you are lukewarm, and neither cold nor hot, I will spew you out of My mouth.* [17] *Because you say, 'I am rich, have become wealthy, and have need of nothing'—and do not know that you are wretched, miserable, poor, blind, and naked—* [18] *I counsel you to buy from Me gold refined in the fire, that you may be rich; and white garments, that you may be clothed, that the shame of your nakedness may not be revealed; and anoint your eyes with eye salve, that you may see.* [19] *As many as I love, I rebuke and chasten. Therefore be zealous and repent.* [20] *Behold, I stand at the door and knock. If anyone hears My voice and opens the door, I will come in to him and dine with him, and he with Me.* [21] *To him who overcomes I will grant to sit with Me on My throne, as I also overcame and sat down with My Father on His throne.* [22] *He who has an ear, let him hear what the Spirit says to the churches." '"*

His Character Is behind This Message (3:14)

He is "the Amen." When "Amen" is said it indicates assent or agreement; it is confirmation of something said or done. The main point of this unique title of Jesus Christ (used only here) is that what He says to this church is totally reliable.

He is "the Faithful and True Witness." In Revelation 1:5 Jesus Christ was called "the faithful witness," one Who proclaims accurately the revelation of God. His witness should be received because it is not only reliable, but accurate (John 3:11-12, 32- 34). Since Laodicea was not characterized by faithfulness to God, this characterization of Jesus Christ carried a powerful message to this church.

He is "the Beginning of the creation of God." Revelation 1:8 calls Him "the Beginning," which is the same as saying that He is the Originator of all things—the Creator Himself (Colossians 1:15-18; John 1:3). It is a clear statement of His pre-existence (before His birth in Bethlehem) and power.

The Condition of This Church Made Him Sick (3:15-17)

Though the familiar words "I know your works" appear here, no words of commendation follow. This church has nothing in its ministry that honored the Lord or brought His favor and blessing. Like so many churches of today, its indifference makes the Lord sick. Two things specifically characterized this church:

They were indifferent to the work of the Lord. When visiting the site of this church some years ago, I was deeply impressed with the hot mineral waters that flowed over the cliffs of Hierapolis. The water tasted terrible—it was lukewarm. It was a vivid and personal illustration of this passage. Just as I wanted to spit that bad tasting water out of my mouth, so the Lord says the same about these lukewarm believers in Laodicea.

Some have suggested that "hot" refers to true believers, "cold" to unbelievers, and "lukewarm" to carnal believers. In spite of efforts to describe the "lukewarm" condition of the Laodiceans as that of true believers who are not presently walking with the Lord (carnal Christians), the language and force of our Lord's words seem to indicate otherwise. A more probable view is that "lukewarm" refers to those who profess to be Christians but clearly are not, and face the consequences of an eternity without God and without hope. This would also explain why Christ said that He wished they were "cold" or "hot" rather than "lukewarm." It also matches the impact of verse 20 where Christ is outside the church knocking on the door and extending an invitation to individuals within to receive Him.

Are we lukewarm? Being spit out of the mouth of the Lord suggests rejection by Him. Solemn and thought-provoking to say the least! It is easy to profess, but more difficult to live like our Lord wants us to live. We can say the right words and make people think that we are Christians, but do we obey the Lord's Word as a habit of life?

Material Prosperity

They were insensitive to their spiritual need. Their pride and self-confidence is evident in their claims: "I am rich, have become wealthy, and have need of nothing." They were confident of the amount of wealth they had as well as their acquiring of that wealth. There was no dependence upon the Lord; they didn't need Him. They came to the tragic conclusion that they had "need of nothing." Our Lord said they "do not know" their true condition. That's how self-confidence and material prosperity can blind our eyes. We don't see our true condition before God. Material prosperity seems like a blessing, but it often becomes a curse and blinds our minds to our real spiritual needs.

It is possible that their profession of wealth is referring to spiritual riches and not primarily to material gain. Even so, they are making claims that cannot be proven. Jesus uses five highly descriptive words to speak of their real condition—wretched, miserable, poor, blind, and naked—all of which reveals that they were not true Christians at all. They claimed it, but their attitudes demonstrated the exact opposite.

It is sad indeed to see so many so-called Christians who never demonstrate the lifestyle of an "overcomer." Their attitudes, habits, and convictions all speak of unbelieving hearts. It is not enough to profess that we are Christians. John Bunyan remarked "A heart without words is ten thousand times better than words without a heart." How true! Are we really committed to Jesus Christ as our Lord and Savior? Have we placed our lives and futures into His hands? Are we depending completely upon His death on the cross for our sins and His resurrection from the dead to guarantee that we will live forever?

His Counsel Must Be Heeded (3:18-19)

Jesus Christ urges these Laodiceans to do three things: (1) They must *recognize* their spiritual need, (2) they must *realize* why He rebukes and chastens them, and (3) they must *respond* with repentance.

Do we recognize our spiritual need? These Laodiceans were "poor, blind, and naked." Now Christ urges them to acknowledge their need and to do something about it.

To solve their spiritual poverty, they need to "buy" from the Lord "gold refined in the fire, that you may be rich." The Lord is urging a group of people known for their material prosperity to buy that which cannot be bought with money. Gold that is "refined in the fire" is pure; the dross has been removed. Peter speaks of "the genuineness of your faith, being much more precious than gold that perishes, though it is tested by fire" (1 Peter 1:7). The reference here is to a purified faith, not a mere profession that was not genuine.

When the Lord urges them to buy "white garments, that you may be clothed" there can be little doubt that He is referring to His own righteousness. The "white garments" were promised to the overcomers in the church of Sardis (3:5) and were also used of the tribulation believers mentioned in chapter 7. It is a picture of God's righteousness, holiness, and purity—a symbol of true salvation. One cannot help but contrast the "white garments" the Laodiceans needed with their own "black wool," a major source of their fame and wealth.

The instruction to "anoint your eyes with eye salve, that you may see" would have special meaning to the Laodiceans, whose school of medicine was known for its special ointments for the eyes and ears. The connection with the anointing of the Holy Spirit seems inescapable. John wrote elsewhere:

> But you have an anointing from the Holy One, and you know all things. . . . Therefore let that abide in you which you heard from the beginning. If what you heard from the beginning abides in you, you also will abide in the Son and in the Father. And this is the promise that He has promised us—eternal life. These things I have written to you concerning those who try to deceive you. But the anointing which you have received from Him abides in you, and you do not need that anyone teach you; but as the same anointing teaches you concerning all things, and is true, and is not a lie, and just as it has taught you, you will abide in Him (1 John 2:20, 24-27).

The issue is salvation (eternal life) made possible by the anointing of the Holy Spirit. Their eyes needed the eye salve of the Holy Spirit in order that they might see God's viewpoint. Spiritually, they needed to have their eyes opened. Do we?

Do we realize why the Lord rebukes and chastens? "As many as I love, I rebuke and chasten." These words remind us of Proverbs 3:12 and Hebrews 12:6 where we learn that a son is chastened by a father because the father loves him. It is love that causes our Lord to be so strong in His rebuke of these Laodiceans.

Some believe Jesus' words here are in sharp contrast to what preceded them, making this statement an appeal to a faithful remnant in Laodicea who are not the objects of our Lord's earlier rebuke. As attractive as that may appear, there is no warrant for such a view. The words are simply reminding these professing believers in Laodicea that it is the Lord's love that causes Him to attack their profession of faith.

When a preacher of today attacks false profession and rebukes a group of people for "easy-believism," he may be doing them a great favor and may be speaking out of love for them. It is God's love that seeks to correct false views and challenge people to true faith and repentance.

Will we respond with repentance? The words "be zealous" imply that the problem in this church is indifference to the true gospel message of Jesus Christ. There is a lack of enthusiasm and desire to do anything more. They are satisfied with what they are and profess. They are "lukewarm" and about to be rejected by the Lord unless some serious action takes place that would change their minds and conduct. Repentance requires radical change, not gradual development.

Repentance is not an out-of-date word—it is essential to becoming a true believer in Jesus Christ. Are we bringing our minds into conformity to the Bible's teaching about Jesus Christ? Have we changed our conduct, or do we still act and behave like we did as unbelievers?

His Challenge to Open the Door (3:20)

Flowing out of the motive of love (v. 19) comes this beautiful picture of our Lord urging individuals to respond to His invitation. It reminds us of the Song of Solomon passage (5:2) where the Bridegroom knocks on the door of the Bride's chamber, urging her to open the door to Him.

What is the "door"? Good Bible teachers disagree. It's not easy to be dogmatic on this matter. The "door" could represent: (1) The door of the church in Laodicea, (2) the door of an unbeliever's heart, (3) the door of a believer's heart, or (4) the door through which Jesus Christ will come again.

That the door represents an individual's heart seems quite strong on the basis of our Lord's promise "I will come in to him." The picture of dining with him may suggest fellowship for the believer, underscoring the "lukewarm" Laodiceans' need of fellowship with the Lord or strengthening their personal relationship with Him.

However, the overall context of this letter indicates that these Laodiceans are guilty of false profession. They are not true believers. To view this "door" as the door of a church that has Jesus Christ on the outside, then, seems to fit the Laodicean situation. Nevertheless, the personal nature of our Lord's invitation is hard to reconcile with such a view. When He comes in through the open door, it is to an individual that He comes, not a whole church.

It is possible that the door does refer to the second coming of Jesus Christ. The letter to the church in Philadelphia mentions "an open door." We concluded that this is the door into the Messianic kingdom. Jesus Christ is the door through Whom we must enter His eternal kingdom. When Jesus said "I have set before you an open door" (3:8), it is possible that the meaning here is the same. He stands at the door into the Messianic kingdom and invites the unbeliever to open the door and come in and dine with Him. These statements remind us of other biblical references that connect the symbolism of the door to the coming kingdom of our Lord (Matthew 24:33; Luke 12:36; James 5:9).

In any case, the invitation of Jesus Christ is clear—He is offering eternal salvation to any person who will respond to Him. Sitting down at His table in the Messianic kingdom is promised to all who respond. Revelation 3:20 clearly invites nonbelievers to open the door to Jesus Christ and experience the marriage supper of the Lamb (cf. 19:7-9).

The Consequence for All Overcomers (3:21)

The wonderful promise is to all true believers. We shall one day rule and reign with Jesus Christ in His kingdom on earth. It will be on that Messianic throne that true believers will also sit, ruling and reigning with Him (Isaiah 9:7; Matthew 19:28; Luke 1:32-33; 22:29-30). This identification with Jesus Christ by believers is like the position and relationship which Jesus has to His Father's throne. We do not sit on that throne, the position of the sovereign God ruling the universe, but Jesus was granted that privilege to sit down with His Father on His throne when He had finished His work on the cross in dying for our sins.

Hebrews 1:3 tells us that when He had purged or cleansed our sins, He sat down at the right hand of the Majesty on High. Just as Jesus was given that privilege by the Father, so we also will be given that privilege by Jesus Christ to rule and reign with Him on the Messianic throne, called "the throne of his father David."

A Thought-Provoking Conclusion (3:22)

The conclusion to this letter sent to the Laodiceans is the same one given in each letter: "He who has an ear, let him hear what the Spirit says to the churches."

Material Prosperity

The phrase "to the churches" means that all churches are to listen carefully to what has been said to these seven churches in Asia Minor during John's day. These messages deal with "what the Spirit says." We will heed them carefully if we are sensitive to the leading of the Holy Spirit. They are appeals to true believers, reminding them of God's wonderful promises. The "overcomers" will be mightily blessed of the Lord when Jesus Christ comes again.

There is also a message to mere professing Christians, who do not really walk with the Lord—"repent," before it is too late. God's patience and love are being demonstrated by the appeals of these letters. But one day there will no longer be "an open door" for us. Now is the day of salvation; now is the time to get right with the Lord! Are we ready for the second coming of Jesus Christ? Have we settled our personal commitment to Jesus Christ as our Lord and Savior? If not, why not stop reading at this point and make that decision to commit your life and future to Him?

Once we've settled the matter of our personal relationship to Jesus Christ, we are now ready to take a look at what goes on in heaven!

Chapter 11

The Throne of God

(4:1-11)

No chapters of the Bible are so inviting, thrilling, and worshipful as chapters 4 and 5 of the Revelation. The Lord welcomes us to heaven itself, giving us a brief look at what takes place there and what we can anticipate for ourselves in the future.

In chapter 4, the primary focus is on God the Father, sitting upon His throne, enjoying the worship of His creatures. In chapter 5, the focus is on God the Son, the Messiah, our Lord Jesus Christ, Who is also the One Whom all heaven adores and worships. What tremendous insights are to be found in these two chapters about the unique relationship of the Father and the Son.

The central feature of chapter 4 is the throne of God. Forty-five times the Revelation refers to thrones, and only fifteen times in the rest of the New Testament. Here is the throne book of the Bible!

The Throne of God
(4:1-11)

¹*After these things I looked, and behold, a door standing open in heaven. And the first voice which I heard was like a trumpet speaking with me, saying, "Come up here, and I will show you things which must take place after this."* ²*Immediately I was in the Spirit; and behold, a throne set in heaven, and One sat on the throne.* ³*And He who sat there was like a jasper and a sardius stone in appearance; and there was a rainbow around the throne, in appearance like an emerald.* ⁴*Around the throne were twenty-four thrones, and on the thrones I saw twenty-four elders sit-*

ting, clothed in white robes; and they had crowns of gold on their heads. ⁵And from the throne proceeded lightnings, thunderings, and voices. And there were seven lamps of fire burning before the throne, which are the seven Spirits of God. ⁶Before the throne there was a sea of glass, like crystal. And in the midst of the throne, and around the throne, were four living creatures full of eyes in front and in back. ⁷The first living creature was like a lion, the second living creature like a calf, the third living creature had a face like a man, and the fourth living creature was like a flying eagle. ⁸And the four living creatures, each having six wings, were full of eyes around and within. And they do not rest day or night, saying:

> *"Holy, holy, holy,*
> *Lord God Almighty,*
> *Who was and is and is to come!"*

⁹Whenever the living creatures give glory and honor and thanks to Him who sits on the throne, who lives forever and ever, ¹⁰the twenty-four elders fall down before Him who sits on the throne and worship Him who lives forever and ever, and cast their crowns before the throne, saying:

> *¹¹"You are worthy, O Lord,*
> *To receive glory and honor and power;*
> *For You created all things,*
> *And by Your will they exist and were created."*

The Second Vision of John (4:1-2a)

The first vision John received began with his words, "And having turned I *saw* . . ." (1:12), and continued until the end of chapter 3. It included a glorious revelation of the Person of Jesus Christ, and a message from the lips of Jesus to be sent to seven churches in Asia Minor.

According to Revelation 1:19, John was to write what he saw about the risen Christ and about "the things which are," a phrase dealing with the seven churches. After the messages to the seven churches, John was to write about "the things which will take place after this." The words "after this" or "after these things" refer to everything John saw from Revelation 4:1 until the end of the book.

Revelation 4:1 begins with the same prepositional phrase as the end of Revelation 1:19—"After these things." The verse also ends with that phrase. John is making sure that we understand where this fits in his outline. All that follows comes after the message to "the churches." The word *church* is not even mentioned again. The book refers to "saints" and "brethren," and to the children of Israel and a great multitude of believers in the tribulation period; but, there will be no further reference to a church or group of churches.

The phrase "after these things" is used eleven times in the book in connection with the words "I saw." It implies an order or sequence of events, but not necessarily a chronological order. Rather, it suggests the order in which visions of the future were given to John—first vision, second vision, third vision, and so on. It does not necessarily imply that what was said in each vision takes place chronologically.

The door in heaven. When people speak of a door through which one enters heaven, they are speaking accurately. You may have heard people speak of Peter being at the gates of heaven and checking people before they enter. While that is stretching things a bit, it is interesting that it was to Peter that Jesus Christ gave the "keys" to the kingdom of heaven. This does not refer to him standing at the gate of heaven to make sure that everyone entering really belongs; it refers to his introducing the gospel to the Gentiles (Acts 10) at the house of Cornelius and, in general, to all who will believe in Jesus Christ as Lord and Savior.

According to Revelation 4:1, this door was "standing open in heaven." This is the only place where such a picture is given except when John saw the second coming of Jesus Christ on a white horse and said, "Then I saw heaven opened" (19:11). During the tribulation period on earth, there is no reference to the door of heaven being opened, and the words of Revelation 19:11 might indicate that the door has, in fact, been closed during that period of time.

The voice in heaven. The voice John heard inviting him to heaven "was like a trumpet speaking with me." The voice also said, "I will show you things which must take place after this." This voice is the same as the one he heard earlier (1:10) when he said, "I heard behind me a loud voice, as of a trumpet." That voice is clearly stated to be Jesus Christ our Lord. It is Jesus Christ Who is showing him the visions of this book.

He was "in the spirit." As discussed previously (1:10), this is not referring to being Spirit-filled, but rather to a spiritual transference. It is the realm of the Spirit in contrast to the realm of the flesh into which John was placed. This was necessary so he could visualize and see the events of the future (cf. 17:3).

The Throne of God

The Wonder of the Throne of God (4:2-7)

What a spectacular sight this must have been! As we read it today, we are still amazed at the description of this throne of God in heaven. Human words are inadequate, but they will have to do. They are our only means of understanding what God wants to convey to us about heaven. The word "behold" suggests the need to pay special heed to what is being said and described. It deserves our alertness and attention.

These verses are organized around four prepositional phrases concerning the throne of God: "on the throne" (v. 2); "around the throne" (vv. 3, 4, 6); "from the throne" (v. 5); and "before the throne" (vv. 5 and 6).

Who is on the throne? The One on the throne is the "Lord God Almighty" (v. 8), the Lord Who "created all things" (v. 11). John is immediately affected by His appearance, which was "like a jasper and a sardius stone." The word "like" signals a simile— likeness in appearance, but not the same as. God is not a stone, obviously; His appearance to John was *like* a jasper stone, clear as crystal. The "sardius" stone is named after the city of Sardis, where beautiful red stones have been found. Most liken this stone to a blood-red ruby. Together, and in conjunction with the rainbow around the throne, they create a dazzling impression of transcendent glory.

What was around the throne? Three things are depicted "around the throne": a rainbow, twenty-four elders, and four living creatures.

1. Why a rainbow? In Genesis 9:13 God said, "I set My rainbow in the cloud, and it shall be for the sign of the covenant between Me and the earth." This covenant made with Noah and his family is the promise that God will never again destroy all humanity with a flood. The rainbow is a sign of that covenant, a visible evidence that God will be faithful to the terms of that promise. He is totally reliable in what He says. Second Peter 3 reminds us, however, that God *will* destroy the world once again—not with a flood but with fire!

2. Who are the twenty-four elders? The identification of this group in heaven is a major factor in one's view of the rapture of the church. If the twenty-four elders represent church-age believers in heaven, and if the number of them represents the completed body of Christ in heaven, then church- age believers will not go through the tribulation on earth but will be in heaven during that time.

In Revelation 4, we learn the following about this unique group: (1) They are called "elders"; (2) they are sitting on twenty-four thrones;

(3) they are clothed in white robes; and (4) they have crowns of gold on their heads.

In both Jewish and Christian history, "elders" refer to the key leadership of the congregation. They are the decision makers and the authorities for the people of God; they are to represent the people before the Lord and to carry out the Lord's will among His people. In the history of Israel, the priests played an important role in the worship of the people and in representing the people before God. In the New Testament church, all believers are "priests" and the leadership rests in the hands of the "elders."

It is more likely that a reference to "elders" in Revelation refers to church leadership than to the leadership of the nation of Israel. This seems especially appropriate in that we have just completed a look at the seven letters to seven churches. Israel was not a part of that vision though she will be a factor later in the book.

An important footnote to the identity of the elders is a remark made in Revelation 7. One of the elders inquires as to the identity of the great multitude who come out of the tribulation. Obviously, the great multitude of believers in the tribulation period are not to be identified with the twenty-four elders. In addition, "all the angels" of God are distinguished from the elders in Revelation 7:11, so the elders cannot refer to either the great multitude who come out of the tribulation or to angels.

It is also difficult to see how the twenty-four elders could represent the completed nation of Israel, since Revelation 7 speaks of 144,000 Jews on earth during the tribulation, and Revelation 12 speaks of the nation's persecution by Satan during the tribulation period (as do many of the prophets in the Old Testament).

The only completed group of God's creatures left (excluding Israel, angels, and the great multitude who come out of the tribulation) is the church. They are not mentioned as being on earth during the tribulation. It was to the church in Philadelphia that the Lord promised (3:10): "Because you have kept my command to persevere, I also will keep you from the hour of trial which shall come upon the whole world, to test those who dwell on the earth."

But does the number twenty-four indicate *a completed body*? The Bible is the best source for understanding isolated words, verses, and passages found within its pages. Does the number twenty-four appear elsewhere?

In 1 Chronicles 24 we have a listing of the divisions of priests who come from the line of Aaron. His son, Eleazar, had sixteen "heads" of priestly families and his son, Ithamar, had eight. Verses 7-18 name each of the twenty-four divisions and indicate that they were to serve in the temple according to this order or listing. In 1 Chronicles 25, musicians are organized in a similar fashion. Those who were highly skilled in music numbered 288. Their time for service in the temple was based on the order listed in verses 9-31, which included twenty-four divisions of singers to match the twenty-four divisions of priests.

The number twenty-four when used of the priests and singers represents the whole nation of Israel. It is not speculation, therefore, to suggest that the twenty-four elders represent a completed body of people in heaven while the tribulation is happening on earth.

Daniel 12:1-3 is quite clear in teaching the resurrection of Old Testament believers at the end of the tribulation period. In addition to Old Testament believers, those who become believers during the tribulation period and are killed during that time will be resurrected at the end of the tribulation. All of which presents us with the problem of the twenty-four elders in heaven during the tribulation on earth, for these elders are clothed in white robes indicating that their resurrection has already taken place.

Perhaps the most important key for identifying these elders, however, is found in the description of them in Revelation 4:4. As we noted earlier, these twenty-four elders sit on thrones, are clothed in white robes, and have crowns of gold on their heads. How fascinating to read in the letters to the seven churches that these are the promises given to the overcomers:

1. Sitting on thrones (Revelation 3:21);
2. Clothed in white robes (Revelation 3:5);
3. Wearing crowns of gold (Revelation 2:10).

Therefore, we draw the conclusion that the twenty-four elders represent the completed body of Christ, the church, including all believers, both Jewish and Gentile, from the Day of Pentecost (Acts 2) until the rapture of the church—symbolized by Revelation 4:1, clearly preceding the great tribulation on earth.

3. What about the four living creatures? These creatures are mentioned several times in Revelation and are associated with the worship of God (4:9; 5:8, 11, 14). They are also the ones who speak to John about the first four seal judgments in which four horsemen and horses are pictured (Revelation 6:2-8).

These four living creatures are mentioned in the book of Ezekiel twelve times in the first ten chapters. Ezekiel 10:20 clearly identifies the living creatures as cherubim.

The appearance of these four living creatures is likened to a lion, a calf (ox), a man, and an eagle. The word "like" expresses a similarity in appearance and should not be regarded literally. These four characterizations are the same as those in Ezekiel 1:10, and it is difficult to decipher their meaning. Some of the viewpoints expressed by various scholars include:

1. The angels have the characteristics of these four creatures;
2. It pictures Jesus Christ as seen in the four gospels (very difficult to prove);
3. It illustrates the attributes of God (majesty, strength, intelligence, sovereignty);
4. It reminds us of Israel's encampment around the tabernacle. Their tents were pitched in the order which placed Judah (lion), the first of three tribes on one side; Ephraim (ox) on one side; Reuben (man) on one side; and Dan (eagle) on one side (interesting, but again difficult to prove).

The first view seems the most likely. There is a sense in which these angels represent all the angels of God. They hold a unique position in relation to the throne of God. While all the angels are "around the throne" (5:11), the four living creatures are said to be "in the midst of the throne, and around the throne" (4:6). Because of what they say (4:8) in praising God's holiness, we are reminded of the angels of Isaiah 6 called "seraphim." It is fascinating to read in the Isaiah account that these angels were standing above the throne of God, constantly praising God for his holiness, power, and preeminence. In one sense, we can describe these four living creatures as the worship leaders of heaven, inspiring by their words and actions all of heaven's residents to pour out their worship toward the One Who sits on the throne!

The statement that these creatures are "full of eyes around and within" is suggestive of the omniscience of the One Who sits on the throne. They do His bidding with a deep awareness of His desire and plan. They also "do not rest day or night" which is a reminder that God never sleeps or slumbers; He is constantly working out His plan, making decisions in heaven and earth that will bring all things to a grand climax and fulfillment, demonstrating that He is to be worshiped and praised forever and ever.

What comes from the throne? The simplest understanding of the lightning, thunder, and voices that proceed from the throne is that this display announces a coming storm of judgment that will be poured out upon the earth. "Lightnings, thunderings, and voices" seem to suggest or introduce a mighty display of God's presence, power, and wrath (cf. Psalm 18:13-15; Job 37:2-5; Revelation 8:5; 11:19; 16:18).

What is before the throne? Verses 5 and 6 tell us that there were "seven lamps of fire burning before the throne, which are the seven Spirits of God," and that "before the throne there was a sea of glass, like crystal."

1. Seven lamps of fire. These seven lamps of fire before the throne "are the seven Spirits of God," mentioned previously in Revelation 1:4 and 3:1 (and noted again in 5:6). As we noted in an earlier chapter, the seven spirits are the seven angels who stand before God, ready to do His bidding. We see them again in Revelation 8:2 where John says, "I saw the seven angels who stand before God."

2. A sea of glass. In Revelation 15:2, John saw this "sea of glass" again and this time it was "mingled with fire." He saw tribulation believers "standing on the sea of glass, having harps of God" and they were singing praise to God for His judgment and power.

In Exodus 24:10, Moses, Aaron, Nadab, Abihu, and seventy elders of Israel received a similar manifestation of the presence of the Lord: "And they saw the God of Israel. And there was under His feet as it were a paved work of sapphire stone, and it was like the very heavens in its clarity."

It is well known that ancient monarchs created something similar in front of their thrones—an area paved in a way to indicate the separation between the king and his subjects. It emphasized their majesty and greatness over all. Perhaps the primary point of the sea of glass before the throne of God is to picture the holiness, majesty, and purity of God Himself, and that He is separate from His creation. The transparency or clearness of that sea of glass might emphasize God's penetrating gaze into all things that take place on earth.

The Worship of All Those in Heaven (4:8-11)

Fourteen times in this one chapter the word *throne* appears. Not only is Revelation the "throne book of the Bible," but Revelation 4 is the "throne chapter of the Bible." It centers in the exaltation of God the Father and climaxes with the worship of all heavenly creatures. It clearly reveals the primary objective of all believers and all creation—the glory, praise, and worship of Almighty God!

The continual response of the four living creatures. Verse 8 says that "they do not rest day or night" in their praise and worship of the Lord. It is a *continual* response.

1. What these creatures say. "Holy, holy, holy, Lord God Almighty, Who was and is and is to come!" These creatures worship and praise the Lord for three basic things: His holiness, His power, and His eternal nature and plan. Like the seraphim (angels) of Isaiah 6:3, they proclaim the holiness (separateness) of God. The repetition of the word "holy" might be for added emphasis or it may suggest the triunity of God—He is one God, but exists as three Persons. God is holy in two ways: He is separate from all that He created and is not to be identified with the physical and material universe; He is also separate from sin. The holiness of God emphasizes both His transcendence as well as His moral purity.

In referring to God as "Lord God Almighty," these creatures speak of His mighty power which shall be uniquely displayed on earth during the tribulation period (cf. Revelation 11:17; 15:3-4). The worship of those in heaven seems to focus on the holiness and power of God, exalting His attributes and His actions.

These four living creatures praise God for His eternal nature and plan by calling Him "Who was and is and is to come!" He is the eternal God, living, governing, in past, present, and future history. These same words are applied to Jesus Christ in Revelation 1:8, establishing His identity as God the Son.

2. Why these creatures say what they do. One motive is certainly to recognize the greatness and worthiness of the One they are praising. Why should we praise the Lord? Because He alone is worthy of such worship and praise. These creatures give "glory and honor and thanks" to God the Father as a habit of life. What an example these heavenly beings are to all of us.

That suggests a second motive—to reveal to us what we should do. The twenty-four elders represent the completed church in heaven, and their actions help all of us to know how we should respond as believers. We are to worship the Lord and to give Him honor, glory, and thanks as a habit of life. *Whenever* the four living creatures give worship to God, the twenty-four elders respond.

The immediate reaction of the elders. Taking their cue from the four living creatures who serve as the worship leaders of heaven, the twenty-four elders react immediately with worship and praise to God the Father on His throne.

1. The way they react. When they "fall down before Him" they give recognition to His authority and position. It is a lesson to all believers; we need to submit to His authority as a daily principle in our lives. That's why it is a good thing to kneel when we pray to indicate our submission to the Lord.

When they "worship Him" they display a reverence and love for Him and His attributes. In the New Testament, and particularly in the Revelation of John, the word *worship* denotes a prayer of adoration for God and His works. It is a royal acclamation of His worth. Do we love and adore Him for Who He is?

When they "cast their crowns before the throne," they show a deep realization of His worthiness when compared with their accomplishments (for which we shall all be rewarded by the Lord). While we are motivated in the New Testament to be faithful to the Lord on the basis of future reward, it is good for us to pause and realize that the worthiness of the Lord Himself causes our rewards to seem quite insignificant by comparison.

2. The words they repeat. Their words speak of *what* He deserves—"glory and honor and power"—as well as *why* He deserves it—"for You created all things, and by Your will they exist and were created."

God the Father is worthy of praise and worship because of two basic things we should always remember: It was *His power* that created all things, and it is *His purpose* (will) that brought everything into existence and gives meaning to it all. If we refuse to acknowledge the power and purpose of God in creation, then, as Paul so graphically portrays, we deserve His judgment (Romans 1:18-23).

A Closing Thought

Why are we here on planet earth? What is the real meaning of our lives? Do we feel frustrated at times trying to put the pieces together, wondering why things happen as they do? What are our goals and objectives? What are we really trying to accomplish?

Revelation 4 is a clear testimony of what heaven is going to be like and gives us fresh and concise information on Who and what is behind all the events and circumstances of our lives.

God the Father, the Creator of everything, deserves and desires our worship and praise. We should honor, glorify, and give Him thanks every day of our lives because He created all things and has a Divine purpose for it all. To Him belongs all the glory!

Chapter 12

Worthy Is the Lamb!

(5:1-14)

The worship of Revelation 4 centers on the One Who sits on the throne—God the Father; the worship of Revelation 5 focuses on the One Who sits at the right hand of the Father, the Lamb of God, Jesus Christ (cf. Romans 8:34; Hebrews 1:3; Revelation 22:3).

John is still in heaven (4:1) and begins this section with the familiar words "I saw." In verses 2, 6, and 11 he repeats those words. The passage also says that he "heard" the voices of heavenly creatures (vv. 11 and 13). One of the twenty-four elders spoke to him directly (v. 5). What a thrilling opportunity for this first century believer and apostle! He was there, in heaven, seeing and hearing these wonderful things as an eyewitness. The apostles, who were responsible for giving us the New Testament, received direct and marvelous revelations from God that are now written for us to read and understand.

The Scroll with Seven Seals
(5:1-7)

¹And I saw in the right hand of Him who sat on the throne a scroll written inside and on the back, sealed with seven seals. ²Then I saw a strong angel proclaiming with a loud voice, "Who is worthy to open the scroll and to loose its seals?" ³And no one in heaven or on the earth or under the earth was able to open the scroll, or to look at it. ⁴So I wept much, because no one was found worthy to open and read the scroll, or to look at it. ⁵But one of the elders said to me, "Do not weep. Behold, the Lion of the tribe of Judah, the Root of David, has prevailed to open the scroll and to loose its seven seals." [6] *And I looked, and behold, in the midst of the throne and of the four living creatures, and in the midst of the elders, stood a Lamb as though it had been slain, having seven horns and seven eyes, which are the seven Spirits of God sent out into all the earth.* [7] *Then He came and took the scroll out of the right hand of Him who sat on the throne.*

A certain degree of drama is connected with this scroll. There is an apparent emphasis here on the importance of this scroll as it relates to the total message of the book. The scroll unravels the events of the tribulation period, and appears to be a summary of what God intends to do in bringing world history to a grand finale.

The Identity of the Scroll (5:1)

Its location. All of the authority and sovereignty of the heavenly Father is behind the simple statement "in the right hand of Him who sat on the throne." He controls the destiny of our lives; the future is in His hands. It reminds us that the events of human history are proceeding from the throne of God. He is truly directing the affairs of this world. Being "in the right hand" of the Father suggests not only that He is the source and controller of all events, but that He has a plan that has already been determined.

Its design. This scroll (called a "book" in some English translations) was rolled up from both ends. It was written on both sides, and it was necessary to break the seals in order to unroll it. That it was written on both sides probably indicates the extensiveness of its message and terms, a symbolic statement indicating that the scroll contains great deal about the future.

A Roman law required that a will was to be sealed seven times. The wills of Caesar Augustus and Emperor Vespasian were sealed in this way. Some see this scroll as the "last testament" of the One Who died for us, containing the terms of His wrath upon those who reject His love and sacrificial death.

It is of great interest to prophecy students that the book of Daniel predicts much of what is recorded in Revelation. In Daniel 12:4 we read that Daniel was instructed to "shut up the words, and *seal the book* until the time of the end." Verse 9 repeats, "the words are closed up and *sealed* till the time of the end." Here in Revelation, the scroll with seven seals is unrolled, each of the seven seals being broken and revealing a special message of what God will do to planet earth in "the time of the end."

The Importance of the Scroll (5:2-4)

The scroll contains much more than what is said in chapter 6. The seventh seal that is broken reveals seven trumpet judgments of which the last one announces seven last plagues to be poured out upon the earth. It is implied that the seven-sealed scroll contains everything that is depicted in chapters 6 through 22.

The proclamation by a strong angel. The word "strong" could emphasize the importance of the angel and his message, but it could also be a clue as to which angel is involved. Some Bible teachers hold that it refers to the angel Gabriel whose name means "strength of God." It was the angel Gabriel who communicated to Daniel about future events (Daniel 8:16).

The text uses a Greek word for "proclaiming" that speaks of a herald, one who simply proclaimed a message without added commentary or explanation. A herald spoke with urgency and was under orders to proclaim it in behalf of a higher authority.

When the Bible says the angel spoke with a "loud voice" we are reminded that this message is one of great concern and urgency. Loud voices are mentioned frequently in Revelation to denote the importance of what is being said. A person who is "worthy" is sought in order to break the seals and open the scroll.

The problem John faced. Combining the importance of the scroll with the fact that no one in God's universe was "worthy" to open the scroll caused John many tears. If we read this outburst correctly, it is possible that John is heartbroken because no redeemer can be found.

The Introduction of the Worthy One (5:5-7)

One of the elders urges John not to cry because there is a worthy one who can loose the seven seals. The elders—these representatives of the completed body of believers in heaven, the church—know of Him. It is the church in heaven (Hebrews 12:23-24) who know full well that Jesus is the only "Mediator of the new covenant."

He is the Lion. My office is filled with lions—pictures, plaques, signs, emblems—you name it, I've got it. Our family crest has a lion as its symbol, and my study of them has convinced me that I bear some of this animal's characteristics! The word occurs 155 times in the Old

Testament in various forms but only 9 times in the New Testament, of which 6 are found in the book of Revelation.

While in some cases the lions are described as those which devour people (Daniel 6; 2 Timothy 4:17) and prey (Numbers 23:24), they are also seen as symbols of strength (Judges 14:18) and boldness (Proverbs 28:1). The Lord describes Himself as a lion who devours his prey (Hosea 5:14).

In describing Jesus Christ as "the Lion of the tribe of Judah, the Root of David," the elder who speaks with John is referring to the Messianic promise given to Judah, the son of Jacob. The prophecy of Genesis 49:8-10 reads:

> "Judah, you are he whom your brothers shall
>   praise;
> Your hand shall be on the neck of your enemies;
> Your father's children shall bow down before you.
> Judah is a lion's whelp;
> From the prey, my son, you have gone up.
> He bows down, he lies down as a lion;
> And as a lion, who shall rouse him?
> The scepter shall not depart from Judah,
> Nor a lawgiver from between his feet,
> Until Shiloh comes;
> And to Him shall be the obedience of the people."

The One to Whom the "scepter" belongs will come out of the line of Judah (the name means "praise"). The Messiah comes from Judah, and is described as a lion, the animal we call "the king of the jungle." Jesus Christ is the Messianic Lion who will rule and reign over all the earth.

The phrase "Root of David" reminds us that it is a special son of Judah from which the Messiah will come. Revelation 22:16 quotes Jesus as saying: "I am the Root and the Offspring of David." The "Root of David" is a reference to Isaiah 11:1-2:

> There shall come forth a Rod from the stem of Jesse,
> And a Branch shall grow out of his roots.
> The Spirit of the LORD shall rest upon Him,
> The Spirit of wisdom and understanding,
> The Spirit of counsel and might,
> The Spirit of knowledge and of the fear of the LORD.

The mother of Jesus came from the line of David through his son Nathan. Jesus fulfilled the promise that the Messiah would be "the fruit" of the body of David (Psalm 132:11). Joseph was a direct descendant of David's son Solomon. When Joseph married Mary, Jesus was adopted as his son, and thus became the legal heir to the throne of His father David. Jesus was both the "child" (by virgin birth—Isaiah 7:14) and the "son" (by adoption) Who would sit on the throne of His father David (2 Samuel 7:12-13; Isaiah 9:6-7).

Luke 1:31-33 contains this wonderful message to Mary by the angel Gabriel: "And behold, you will conceive in your womb and bring forth a Son, and shall call His name JESUS. He will be great, and will be called the Son of the Highest; and the Lord God will give Him the throne of His father David. And He will reign over the house of Jacob forever, and of His kingdom there will be no end."

He is the Lamb. What a paradox—lion and lamb! The symbol of a lamb is powerful when applied to our Savior Jesus Christ. Obviously, the picture here is symbolic—in the midst of this throne room setting stood "a Lamb as though it had been slain, having seven horns and seven eyes." This is an unusual looking lamb, to say the least.

1. His centrality ("in the midst of"). In Revelation 1:13 we saw a picture of the risen Christ "in the midst of the seven lampstands." In the message to the church in Ephesus, Jesus Christ referred to Himself as the One "who walks in the midst of the seven golden lampstands." Now we see Him "in the midst of" the throne, the four living creatures who serve as the worship leaders in heaven, and the elders, who represent the church, the completed body of believers in heaven.

Because He is in the middle of the throne, He is to be worshiped, and because He is in the middle of the four living creatures, He is the One directing the worship of all heavenly creatures, and because He is in the middle of the elders, He is the object of the worship and praise of the church over which He is the Head. To Him belongs all the glory and praise forever and ever!

The text also says He is standing, which means He is no longer seated at the right hand of the Father (Hebrews 1:3). His new position causes all of heaven to break forth in praise and worship and reminds us that He is now ready to take action against the inhabitants of the earth and to set up His kingdom over all.

2. His condition ("as though it had been slain"). The Greek verb is in the perfect tense, indicating a past event with results that continue into the present. He died over nineteen hundred years ago, but the effects of what He did at the cross continue until this present hour.

The symbolism of a slain lamb reminds us all of the sacrificial system of the Jews. A sacrifice for sin must be provided in order for redemption to take place. When John the Baptist introduced Jesus, he said: "Behold! The Lamb of God who takes away the sin of the world!" (John 1:29). Peter says of our salvation: "knowing that you were not redeemed with corruptible things, like silver or gold, from your aimless conduct received by tradition from your fathers, but with the precious blood of Christ, as of a lamb without blemish and without spot" (1 Peter 1:18-19).

Jesus Christ is the Lamb of God Who takes away our sin. He was a "lamb without blemish and without spot." Because He had no sin in Himself nor did He ever commit an act of sin, He did not have to die for His own sin but could substitute His life for us (Hebrews 4:15; 7:26; 2 Corinthians 5:21). As God in human flesh, His infinite life could substitute for the sum total of all human life which He Himself created. As 2 Corinthians 5:19 tells us, "God was in Christ reconciling the world to Himself."

The picture of this slain Lamb of God is not of an animal lying on the altar of sacrifice; the Lamb "stood" in the midst of heaven's audience reminding us all that He arose from the dead.

Though the picture of a Lion represents the power, strength, and majesty of the Messiah as our conquering King, ready to roar from the heavens and devour His enemies, it only appears this one time in chapter 5. The picture of the Lamb, however, is used twenty-eight times in the book of Revelation. God does not want us to forget what His Son did on the cross when He died for our sins. The motto of the Moravian church is "Our Lamb has conquered!"

3. *His characteristics* ("having seven horns and seven eyes"). "Horns" are symbols of authority and power, sometimes representing individual rulers and at other times representing nations (Daniel 7). It is possible that the seven horns represent the fullness of the slain Lamb's power and authority to rule and reign.

The "seven eyes" of the Lamb of God are said to be "the seven Spirits of God sent out into all the earth." These "seven Spirits" were mentioned in Revelation 3:1 and were compared with "seven stars," which represent angels (1:20). It seems that these "seven Spirits" are the seven angels who appear often in the book and carry out the wishes of Jesus Christ.

According to Zechariah 4:10, the "seven eyes" represent the Lord's knowledge of what transpires on earth:

> "For who has despised the day of small things?
> For *these seven* rejoice to see
> The plumb line in the hand of Zerubbabel.
> *They are the eyes of the LORD,*
> Which scan to and fro throughout the whole earth."

Nothing happens on earth that is not known by the Lord. He sees it all and is controlling all events and circumstances. His sovereign will is being executed through the seven angels who stand before Him, ready to do what He wants. They are the instruments through whom His message to the seven churches was given, and they are the ones who blow the trumpets and pour out the plagues, announcing His judgments upon planet earth.

John simply declares: "Then He came and took the scroll out of the right hand of Him who sat on the throne" (v. 7). In great symbolism, we are reminded that the kingdom of the Messiah is given to Him by the heavenly Father. The Son is to be honored and worshiped as the Father, and that comes with the Father's approval and blessing.

The Song to the Lamb
(5:8-14)

⁸*Now when He had taken the scroll, the four living creatures and the twenty-four elders fell down before the Lamb, each having a harp, and golden bowls full of incense, which are the prayers of the saints. ⁹And they sang a new song, saying:*

"You are worthy to take the scroll,
And to open its seals;
For You were slain,
And have redeemed us to God by Your blood
Out of every tribe and tongue and people
and nation,
¹⁰*And have made us kings and priests to our*
God;
And we shall reign on the earth."

¹¹*Then I looked, and I heard the voice of many angels around the throne, the living creatures, and the elders; and the number of them was ten thousand times ten thousand, and thousands of thousands,* ¹²*saying with a loud voice:*

"Worthy is the Lamb who was slain
To receive power and riches and wisdom,
And strength and honor and glory and
blessing!"

> **¹³ And every creature which is in heaven and on the earth and under the earth and such as are in the sea, and all that are in them, I heard saying:**
>
> > **"Blessing and honor and glory and power**
> > **Be to Him who sits on the throne,**
> > **And to the Lamb, forever and ever!"**
>
> **¹⁴ Then the four living creatures said, "Amen!" And the twenty-four elders fell down and worshiped Him who lives forever and ever.**

John speaks of Jesus Christ in this book with many wonderful titles given to him by Jesus Himself. But the key title is the one John uses twenty-eight times: "Lamb." Jesus is *the Lamb of God!*

The Reaction to the Taking of the Scroll (5:8-10)

Two things happened immediately—the four living creatures and the twenty-four elders "fell down before the Lamb," and "they sang a new song." The first was an act of humility and submission; the second an act of praise and worship.

They reacted with submission, recognizing His sovereignty. What a picture—bowing down in front of a lamb! This all happened when He took the scroll out of the right hand of the One Who sat on the throne, the heavenly Father. At that moment, the worship leaders of heaven knew what to do, and as we learned earlier, whenever the four living creatures respond in worship, the twenty-four elders do the same.

The harps these elders played were a part of that worship response, reflecting the traditional instrument of worship from the Old Testament (Psalm 33:2-3; 98:5; 147:7). It is with some amusement that people speak of harps being played by heavenly beings. However, the Bible speaks of it as reality, not fantasy. Since the twenty-four elders represent the completed body of believers we call "the church," perhaps we shall all be harpists in heaven!

We are told the elders also have "golden bowls full of incense, which are the prayers of the saints" (cf. 8:3-4). The altar of incense in front of the second veil of the tabernacle and temple was the place where the priest symbolized his role in representing the people to God (Luke 1:8-10). The incense spoke of the people's prayers rising up to the nostrils and attention of God (Psalm 141:2).

It is possible that the prayers of the elders reveal that the church in heaven will be interceding for those who become believers in the tribulation period as well as for the nation of Israel. It is also possible that these prayers represent the long-standing prayer of God's people which our Lord instructed us in Matthew 6:10 to pray—"Your kingdom come."

They reacted with singing, recognizing His salvation. The twenty-four elders have the harps and the golden bowls of incense; they also are the ones who sing the new song. This new song speaks of redemption, something the angels desire to understand but, in fact, do not experience (1 Peter 1:10-12).

What is the "new song"? The Greek word used here for "new" does not mean new from the standpoint of time, but new in quality, fresh, unique. The Psalms speak often of singing a "new song" to the Lord (33:3; 96:1; 98:1; 144:9; 149:1). Isaiah 42:10 also says, "Sing to the LORD a *new song*, / And His praise from the ends of the earth." The 144,000 Jewish believers from the tribulation period sing a "new song" which no one else could learn (Revelation 14:3).

The words of this "new song" are recorded for us, and we learn some wonderful things from this song to the Lamb:

1. It tells us why the Lamb is worthy to take the scroll and open its seals. He is worthy because He was slain, because He has redeemed us, and because He has made us kings and priests.

2. His worthiness is based on His death. What more moving words could we read about His suffering and death for us than those recorded in Isaiah 53.

3. His blood was the price of our redemption. Our redemption is not based on our performance or personal worthiness—we were bought at a price and therefore belong to God (1 Corinthians 6:19-20; 1 Peter 1:18-19).

4. The twenty-four elders represent every tribe and tongue and people and nation. It was the instruction of Jesus Christ to make disciples of all nations (Matthew 28:19). Revelation 14:6 speaks of the everlasting gospel being preached to "every nation, tribe, tongue, and people."

5. Our relationship to God as kings and priests has been made possible by His redemption, and guarantees that we shall reign on the earth. Notice carefully that our role as kings and priests is to be directed toward God Himself (cf. 1:6). We serve Him.

The Big Problem

In these verses we have a very important textual problem. Some translations have rendered these words from the lips of the 24 elders as referring to someone other than themselves or at best just praising the Lord for whoever is redeemed.

Consider the rendering in the New American Standard Bible:

> ". . . And didst purchase for God with thy blood men from every tribe and tongue and people and nation. And thou has made *them* to be a kingdom and priests to our God; and *they* will reign upon the earth."

Notice that the word "us" does not appear after the word "purchase" (redeemed). Also, notice the pronouns "them" and "they" in the text instead of "us" and "we." The New International Version does the same.

George Eldon Ladd in his book, *A Commentary on the Revelation of John,* says the following on page 92, illustrating the importance of this problem:

> This is very important for determining the identity of the elders. If the King James Version is right, the elders are identified with the redeemed, but if the Revised Standard Version is right, the elders are sharply and clearly distinguished from the redeemed. In terms of our knowledge of the history of the text, there is hardly any question as to which reading is correct, for this is one of several places where the King James Version is clearly incorrect because it was based upon a late inferior Greek text. It is surprising to find any modern commentary still following the incorrect King James Version. The elders sing praise to the Lamb not for their own redemption but for the redemption of the church.

Is it really that "incorrect," and is there "hardly any question as to which reading is correct"? As you might guess, George Eldon Ladd does not believe that the 24 elders represent the completed church in heaven. If we take what he says in the above quote, the King James rendering of the "new song" settles the issue of whether or not the 24 elders represent the church or not. If they do represent the completed church in heaven during the tribulation period, it would be a powerful argument in favor of those who believe that the rapture of the church will take place *before* the tribulation period ever begins!

John Walvoord in his book *The Revelation of Jesus Christ* says on page 117:

> If the text of the Authorized Version is correct, the twenty-four elders in their new song declare that God has redeemed

them by His blood out of every kindred, tongue, people, and nation and has made them kings and priests. If the twenty-four elders are actually redeemed by the blood of Christ, it is clear that they could not be angels but must be redeemed men.

Exactly what are the facts behind this textual variation? Let's consider the following:

1. In verse 9, the removal of the word "us" after the word "redeemed," is only found in Codex Alexandrinus. The majority of the manuscript readings, whether early or late, contain the word "us."
2. In verse 10, the word "them" and the third person plural rendering "they shall reign," are all variant readings. There is also a variant reading between the future and present tenses of the word "reign."
3. The Latin Vulgate translation of Jerome reads "us" in both verses as does the King James Version of A.D. 1634.
4. It is possible on the basis of all manuscript evidence to read "us" in verse 9 and "them" in verse 10, making verse 10 an editorial comment of the redeemed ones mentioned in verse 9.
5. The obvious connection with Revelation 1:4-6 where the remarks are given "to the seven churches" and the pronouns are first person plural ("us") seems to settle the issue in favor of the King James Version.

When we read about the "new song" sung to the Lamb of God by the twenty-four elders, we are reading about our response as the redeemed church in heaven—constantly glorifying and worshiping the Lord, singing songs of praise for His marvelous redemption. No wonder so many Christian songs speak of the Lamb of God and His worthiness to be praised!

The Response of All Creation (5:11-14)

When reading these verses, one feels the need to turn on the music of Handel's *Messiah*—which is what I'm listening to right now! What a blessing it is to hear.

This is a heavenly praise gathering, a worship service par excellence. May we never forget the marvelous scene depicted for us in these verses. How we need to understand the ultimate objective of God for all of His creation.

The great multitude involved. Imagine the joy that must have filled the apostle John when he saw and heard this marvelous display of worship and praise to God the Father and the Lamb of God! The number of angels indicated here is not to be taken as an exact mathematical calculation. Rather, this multitude of angels is innumerable—too many to count.

The statement in verse 13 that "every creature" was involved in this praise is remarkable indeed. Does it include the animal world? Romans 8:18-23 speaks about the present bondage of God's creation, and that all creation "eagerly waits for the revealing of the sons of God" (v. 19) and presently "groans and labors with birth pangs" (v. 22). What glory it will be when the curse is removed and all creation breaks forth in praise to God!

The creatures "under the earth" possibly refer to demonic spirits. They also shall praise the Lord and acknowledge His greatness.

The message which all creation proclaims. The ascription of praise to the Lamb Who was slain contains seven characteristics—power, riches, wisdom, strength, honor, glory, and blessing—indicating the fullness of worship that He deserves. Everything you can think of in terms of adoration should be given to Him. Four of these seven characteristics are repeated in verse 13 and ascribed to the One Who sits on the throne as well as to the Lamb.

Such praise, adoration, and worship will continue throughout eternity ("forever and ever"). There is no higher task for the believer than the praise and worship of Almighty God. To give such adoration to the Lamb clearly demonstrates His divine nature. Along with the Father, He is worthy of such praise.

The manner in which the living creatures and the twenty-four elders respond. The four living creatures who serve as worship leaders in heaven are also the "Amen corner" of heaven. They keep saying the word that speaks of agreement and affirmation of all that is being sung and said. The twenty-four elders (the church in heaven) respond as they did previously (4:10)—they "fell down and worshiped Him who lives forever and ever."

Can there be any doubt as to the grand and ultimate objective for the believer? Is not the worship and praise of Almighty God our primary goal? We will one day participate in that heavenly scene, but even now we can enjoy the privilege of exalting Him. As Paul exhorts us, whatever we do, let us do it to the glory of God (1 Corinthians 10:31).

Chapter 13

The Four Horsemen of the Apocalypse

(6:1-8)

In the opening chapters of Revelation, Jesus Christ is presented as Lord of the churches. He appeals to the churches through the letters sent to the seven churches of Asia. To those who merely profess faith but do not demonstrate that they are true overcomers, His message and challenge is to *repent*. To the true overcomers, He gives continual encouragement by His promises of eternal blessing and reward.

In chapter 5, the scroll with seven seals in the hand of the One Who sits on the throne, the heavenly Father, is given to the only One worthy to open the scroll and to loose its seals—the Lion of Judah, the Root of David, the Lamb Who was slain. All heaven breaks forth in praise, adoration, and worship of God.

Pronouncements of Judgment

The scene now shifts from the wonderful praise of heaven to the tragic judgments upon planet earth. Many Bible teachers believe chapters 6-19 are describing the great tribulation to which Daniel the prophet (Daniel 9:24-27; 12:1-2) and Jesus Christ referred (Matthew 24-25; Mark 13; Luke 21).

How Should We Understand These Events?

Throughout history there have been attempts to prove that the catastrophic events of Revelation have already been fulfilled. Often these attempts have centered on the tragedies and troubles of the Roman Empire, believing that its history more nearly represents what

The Four Horsemen of the Apocalypse

Revelation is trying to portray and occurred closer to the lifetime of the one who wrote about these things.

We not only have the problem of *when* these events occur, but also *how* and *why* they happen as they do. Is it possible that one-half of the world's population will be eliminated by these terrible judgments as Revelation seems to be teaching? And, if so, is that still future? Why would a loving God Who supposedly has a deep, personal interest in each individual want to destroy the world like Revelation describes? Revelation answers that question.

Three sets of seven judgments—seals, trumpets, and bowls—are recorded in chapters 6-16. Some Bible teachers believe the judgments mentioned in the seven seals are the same as those in the seven trumpets and in the seven bowls of wrath. Attempts to draw this conclusion are often based on comparing the sixth seal judgment of a great earthquake with the seventh bowl of wrath, also said to be a great earthquake. Since the second and third trumpet judgments (chapter 8) affect the seas, rivers, and springs of water, these events are judged to be similar to the second and third bowls of wrath (chapter 16).

However, this interpretation is highly unlikely. In spite of some similarities, the differences are most pronounced. In addition to the obvious differences, the text indicates that these three sets of judgments will happen in order, one following the other:

Scroll with the Seven Seals Is Opened

> *First seal*: rider on white horse
> *Second seal*: rider on red horse
> *Third seal*: rider on black horse
> *Fourth seal*: rider on pale horse
> *Fifth seal*: martyrs
> *Sixth seal*: a great earthquake

The Great Day of His Wrath Has Come

> *Seventh seal*: Seven Angels Sound Seven Trumpets

> *First trumpet*: trees and grass burned up
> *Second trumpet*: bloody seas
> *Third trumpet*: bitter waters and springs
> *Fourth trumpet*: partial eclipse

Fifth trumpet: locust plague
Sixth trumpet: demonic horsemen
Seventh trumpet: Seven Bowls of Wrath Poured Out

In Them the Wrath of God Is Complete

First bowl: terrible sores
Second bowl: sea life destroyed
Third bowl: bloody rivers and springs
Fourth bowl: sun scorching with great heat
Fifth bowl: total eclipse
Sixth bowl: battle of Armageddon
Seventh bowl: mighty earthquake

It Is Done!

The Four Horsemen
(6:1-8)

¹*Now I saw when the Lamb opened one of the seals; and I heard one of the four living creatures saying with a voice like thunder, "Come and see."* ²*And I looked, and behold, a white horse. And he who sat on it had a bow; and a crown was given to him, and he went out conquering and to conquer.*

³*When He opened the second seal, I heard the second living creature saying, "Come and see."* ⁴*And another horse, fiery red, went out. And it was granted to the one who sat on it to take peace from the earth, and that people should kill one another; and there was given to him a great sword.*

⁵*When He opened the third seal, I heard the third living creature say, "Come and see." And I looked, and behold, a black horse, and he who sat on it had a pair of scales in his hand.* ⁶*And I heard a voice in the midst of the four living creatures saying, "A quart of wheat for a denarius, and three quarts of barley for a denarius; and do not harm the oil and the wine."*

⁷*When He opened the fourth seal, I heard the voice of the fourth living creature saying, "Come and see."* ⁸*And*

The Four Horsemen of the Apocalypse

> *I looked, and behold, a pale horse. And the name of him who sat on it was Death, and Hades followed with him. And power was given to them over a fourth of the earth, to kill with sword, with hunger, with death, and by the beasts of the earth.*

The moment the Lamb opens one of the seals, one of the four living creatures speaks with "a voice like thunder." Throughout Revelation we read of "loud voices in heaven" that sound like thunder. When the seventh angel sounds his trumpet (11:15) "there were loud voices in heaven." When the seven bowls of wrath are introduced (16:1) John says, "Then I heard a loud voice from the temple." These judgments are announced loudly; there is an atmosphere of great drama and intensity.

John is invited to "Come and see." Earlier he was told, "Come up here, and I will show you things which must take place after this" (4:1). Now he is invited to see the terrible judgments God's wrath will inflict upon a rebellious and unrepentant world. What a spectacle for his human understanding to absorb and accept.

First Seal Judgment:
A Rider on a White Horse (6:2)

Some have tried to see this white horse as a picture of good rather than evil. One view says it represents the gospel and its conquest of human hearts. Another says the white horse represents the second coming of Jesus Christ and pictures Christ Himself. A strong connection is made with Revelation 19:11: "Then I saw heaven opened, and behold, a white horse. And He who sat on him was called Faithful and True, and in righteousness He judges and makes war."

The rider is Jesus Christ in chapter 19, so why not believe that the rider on the white horse in chapter 6 is the same? Consider the following reasons why this rider on a white horse does *not* represent Jesus:

1. Jesus Christ is the One Who opens the seals. While not overpowering in its argument, it does seem strange that the first seal would represent the One Who opened the scroll with the seven seals in the first place. His worthiness to open the seals seems to place Him outside and above the messages written on the scroll.

2. The remaining seals deal with judgment and tragedy. Again not a strong argument, but it causes us to question why the first seal would depart from the overall scheme of things contained in these seals.

3. *The "crown" is not the same as that in Revelation 19.* In 6:2, the rider wears "a crown"; in 19:12, Jesus Christ wears "many crowns." Also, the Greek word used in 6:2 is not the one used in 19:12. On the head of Jesus Christ are many "diadems," the crowns of royalty, whereas the crown on the rider of a white horse in Revelation 6 is the crown of victory won by any conqueror, including those who participated in athletic contests.

Who is the rider on a white horse? That the rider rides "a white horse" probably suggests a counterfeit Christ. Jesus said in Matthew 24:4-5, "Take heed that no one deceives you. For many will come in My name, saying, 'I am the Christ,' and will deceive many." According to Jesus, there will be many attempts to deceive. There will be those who argue that the Christ has come and even invite us to go see him (Matthew 24:23-27). However, when the second coming of Christ takes place, the whole world will know it. No need for any private interview or instructions as to where He can be found.

In addition to being a counterfeit Christ, his authority and position was not earned but given—"a crown was given to him." That he had a bow depicts military conquest. The text says "he went out conquering and to conquer," indicating that his motivation is to achieve a military victory through his continual victories.

The Great Tribulation begins with a new ruler rising to power on the scene of world history. This is nothing new to those who have studied the Hebrew prophets. Daniel predicted that such a person would rise to power in the end times (Daniel 7, 9, 11). In 2 Thessalonians 2, the apostle Paul called this coming world ruler "the man of sin," "the son of perdition," and "the lawless one." In verse 4 Paul predicted what the prophet Daniel said over five hundred years before him: this son of perdition "opposes and exalts himself above all that is called God or that is worshiped, so that he sits as God in the temple of God, showing himself that he is God." The apostle John declared that "the Antichrist is coming" (1 John 2:18).

Putting all of this together, the first seal introduces us to a coming world leader who will deceive and convince people that he is a messiah. He will gradually rise to power and eventually become the dominant ruler in the world. That our present world desires such a leader is quite obvious. The "messiah syndrome" grips much of the world's populations, and it is not difficult to see how allegiance to a counterfeit Christ could be easily conceived and developed. The Bible teaches that this coming world ruler will be energized by the power of Satan himself (2 Thessalonians 2:9; Revelation 13:2).

The Four Horsemen of the Apocalypse

Second Seal Judgment:
A Rider on a Red Horse (6:3-4)

The symbolism of a "fiery red" horse has been traditionally a portrait of war and bloodshed. It is possible the rider is the same as the first seal judgment. The coming world ruler will arise in an atmosphere proclaiming peace, but he will soon take it from the earth.

Wars will increase before the end of human history as we now know it (Matthew 24:6-7). It appears that just prior to the return of Jesus Christ, wars among the peoples of the world will intensify, along with the cries for peace. Apart from the return of Jesus Christ to this earth, there appears to be no way to stop the constant fighting among the nations of the world. Senseless, bloody conflicts take place every day in some part of the world. We have become so used to news of war, we grow weary of the reports. The tragic fact is that thousands of people are being killed by these wars every day.

The horse is "fiery red," and we cannot help relating this to the description of Satan as "a great, fiery red dragon" (12:3). Satan is behind the wars and struggles of planet earth, but he himself is a conquered enemy. God's plan for human history is being worked out according to Divine schedule *not* satanic calendars.

What happens when the red horse appears? Three things are described: (1) world *peace* is ended, (2) many *people* are killed, and (3) military *power* is placed in the hands of one man.

The statement of Revelation 6:4, "it was granted to the one who sat on [the horse] to take peace from the earth," is awesome in its implications. Efforts to bring peace are constantly being advocated by world leaders. Here we have one man, a rider on a red horse, who is able to remove peace from the earth. What a contrast to the angels' proclamation at the birth of Christ (Luke 2:14):

> "Glory to God in the highest,
> And on earth peace, good will toward men!"

At the coming of Christ we are given hope of "peace on earth," but at the coming of the false christ peace is taken from the earth. The Messiah is called the "Prince of Peace" in Isaiah 9:6, but the false christ takes peace away.

Jesus Christ offers us real peace, not the world's kind, merely suggesting a cessation of hostilities, a signing of a paper to lay down arms for a time. The peace Jesus offers is the peace of the heart, no matter what tribulation goes on all around us (John 14:27; 16:33). His peace is settling the greatest hostility of all—the hostility between ourselves

130

and God! Have you made peace with your Maker? The Bible speaks of the "peace of God, which surpasses all understanding," a peace that will "guard your hearts and minds through Christ Jesus" (Philippians 4:7).

Many people will be killed. We cannot accurately determine how many people will be killed during the great tribulation on earth. In Revelation 6:8, one fourth of the world's population is killed. During the sixth trumpet judgment (9:15, 18), one third of the remaining population is eliminated. Those totals would equal one half of the world's population. At present world census figures, that means *over two billion people* will be killed during the tribulation period! These figures do not include other judgments depicted in Revelation that indicate death and destruction for the peoples of the world.

It is possible that this "fiery red horse" judgment is simply a panoramic picture of the killings that will take place throughout the tribulation, or it may speak of additional killings that will take place at the beginning of this time period. Revelation 6:4 tells us that people will kill (literally, "slaughter") one another. Some believe this refers to the rise of violent crime. People are killing each other with no apparent military or political reason.

What is the "great sword"? The text says "there was given to him a great sword." Remarkable military and/or governmental power is given to this rider on the fiery red horse.

When a ruler is given a sword, it usually expresses his right to exercise capital punishment (Romans 13:4). In this text, the rider is given a "great sword," emphasizing unusual powers, declaring his authority and influence over the affairs of planet earth. Revelation 13:7 says of the coming world ruler that "authority was given him over every tribe, tongue, and nation."

Third Seal Judgment:
A Rider on a Black Horse (6:5-6)

The color of the horse. Black pictures death resulting from famine and starvation. Lamentations 4:8-9 speaks of the appearance of famine-stricken people as being "blacker than soot." Famine usually follows war and bloodshed. Anyone who has witnessed scenes of the famine on the continent of Africa is aware of the terrible tragedy that literally devastates whole populations and destroys the will and strength of any people.

The Four Horsemen of the Apocalypse

The tragic condition this horseman brings.

1. Prices are going to change. The "pair of scales" suggests that the economic balance of things is going to be altered. Economic inflation will occur affecting the balance between necessities and luxury items.

2. Food prices will rise dramatically. A Roman "denarius" was equal to a normal day's wage. In the coming tribulation, inflation will cause food prices to rise so high that a whole day's earnings will be required to purchase enough wheat for one meal for an average family.

3. The quality of food will change because of the inflation. Barley is the food of animals. Families will turn to this kind of food in order to survive. Three meals a day could be provided from barley whereas only one meal could be produced from wheat.

4. Luxury items will not be affected by the inflation . "Oil and wine" are items used in the homes of the rich, and are consumed in meals as well as in moments of pleasure and leisure. With the prevalence of current famine conditions around the globe and the abundant consumption of alcoholic beverages, one could easily see how this predicted world condition could become reality within months. How easy it is for us in Western affluent culture to ignore the harsh realities around the world. We are but a step away from the black horse of Revelation 6!

Fourth Seal Judgment:
A Rider on a Pale Horse (6:7-8)

It is good to remember that the Lamb, our Lord Jesus Christ, is the One Who continues to open the seals, the only One Who is worthy to do so (cf. 5:9).

The identity of this pale horse. This horse is the color of a corpse and goes well with the name of its rider—"Death," the only horseman named. Some see it as a summary of the four horsemen and the consequences of their activity. This rider is followed by Hades, the abode of all wicked dead, suggesting that this horse and its rider describe the tragedies that shall befall the unbelievers of the tribulation period.

The impact of this horse and rider upon world conditions.

1. The scope of this impact affects one fourth of the world's population. Today's population figures are rapidly changing. By the year A.D. 2000, the world will contain over six billion people. If we understand this prediction, approximately one and a half billion people will die during the great tribulation because of this one judgment, the fourth seal opened by Jesus Christ.

2. The sources by which this mass extermination will occur. People will be killed, not merely die from old age or bad health, by four methods: sword, hunger, death, and beasts. The *sword* refers to murder or governmental action against its citizens. Perhaps military conflicts are pictured here as well. *Hunger* was pictured by the third seal judgment. A black horse and its rider revealed terrible conditions of famine and runaway inflation. People will die of starvation by the thousands. *Death* indicates death by plague or pestilence (cf. Ezekiel 14:21). Current studies regarding the dreaded and fatal AIDS problem, by which thousands have been affected with no cure in sight, have brought this passage into clearer understanding. Society has been affected already by plagues and diseases that have caused multiple deaths. Perhaps the most difficult source of mass killing to comprehend is that caused by *the beasts of the earth.* Apparently, wild beasts will kill many by their ferocious attacks.

Is There Any Hope for Planet Earth?

These four horsemen of the Apocalypse are enough to reveal the horror and catastrophe of the coming tribulation. Perhaps they describe the entire period of seven years. It is also possible, if not probable, that these judgments are merely the beginning of the tragedies that will afflict this planet.

Hope is found in personal faith and commitment to Jesus Christ as Lord and Savior. Have you made that most important decision to commit your life and future into the hands of the One Who died on the cross for your sins, and Who rose again from the dead to guarantee eternal life and future bodily resurrection for all who will trust in Him? Acts 4:12 tells us salvation will be found no where else but in Jesus, "for there is no other name under heaven given among men by which we must be saved."

Chapter 14

The Day of God's Wrath Has Come!

(6:9-17)

From the opening of the first four seals it is obvious the world is being plunged into a terrible and frightening time. This is the predicted period of seven years known as "the great tribulation," of which Jesus Christ said: "For then there will be great tribulation, such as has not been since the beginning of the world until this time, no, nor ever shall be. And unless those days were shortened, no flesh would be saved; but for the elect's sake those days will be shortened" (Matthew 24:21-22).

And Zephaniah the prophet said of this coming time of trouble (1:14-16):

> The great day of the LORD is near;
> It is near and hastens quickly.
> The noise of the day of the LORD is bitter;
> There the mighty men shall cry out.
> That day is a day of wrath,
> A day of trouble and distress,
> A day of devastation and desolation,
> A day of darkness and gloominess,
> A day of clouds and thick darkness,
> A day of trumpet and alarm
> Against the fortified cities
> And against the high towers.

The phrase, "the day of the Lord," is an eschatological term that not only applies to historical judgments that came upon the people of Israel in the past, but also refers to a future, terrible day when the judgments and catastrophes of planet earth will far exceed anything that preceded it. The seven seals that are opened, revealing the message and contents of the scroll, are the official proclamation by the Lord of the universe that *judgment day* has come!

The Great Day of God's Wrath Has Come
(6:9-17)

[9]When He opened the fifth seal, I saw under the altar the souls of those who had been slain for the word of God and for the testimony which they held. [10]And they cried with a loud voice, saying, "How long, O Lord, holy and true, until You judge and avenge our blood on those who dwell on the earth?" [11]And a white robe was given to each of them; and it was said to them that they should rest a little while longer, until both the number of their fellow servants and their brethren, who would be killed as they were, was completed.

[12]I looked when He opened the sixth seal, and behold, there was a great earthquake; and the sun became black as sackcloth of hair, and the moon became like blood. [13]And the stars of heaven fell to the earth, as a fig tree drops its late figs when it is shaken by a mighty wind. [14]Then the sky receded as a scroll when it is rolled up, and every mountain and island was moved out of its place. [15]And the kings of the earth, the great men, the rich men, the commanders, the mighty men, every slave and every free man, hid themselves in the caves and in the rocks of the mountains, [16]and said to the mountains and rocks, "Fall on us and hide us from the face of Him who sits on the throne and from the wrath of the Lamb! [17]For the great day of His wrath has come, and who is able to stand?"

Fifth Seal Judgment:
The Cry of the Martyrs (6:9-11)

One of the fascinating facts about the seven seals is that one of them speaks of those who have lost their lives because of their faith in the Word of God and their witness for the Lord. These are obviously the martyrs of history. They have a special place in the heart of God and here they are honored in a unique way.

The identity of these souls. We are told they were found "under the altar." This does not refer to the altar of incense, but rather the altar of sacrifice. Their lives had been sacrificed much like the sacrificial animals killed daily in the tabernacle and the temple.

Since the text says they "had been slain," it implies that their deaths occurred prior to this period of time. There will be many believers killed during the tribulation (as will be noted in verse 11). These martyrs are from past history.

Two reasons are given as to why they were killed: "for the word of God and for the testimony which they held." Both in conviction and in confession they were tested as to the reality of what they believed. They never saw the fulfillment of the promises they believed. Perhaps they are the ones honored in Hebrews 11:35-39.

The injustice they express. In the light of what they suffered and the long delay in the fulfillment of God's promises, it is no wonder they cry as they do "with a loud voice." They appeal to God's character and sense of justice as they cry, "How long, O Lord, holy and true, until You judge and avenge our blood on those who dwell on the earth?" God's holiness demands justice be done. Since He is true and faithful to His promises, He must carry out revenge against a world that has rejected Him and His servants. They also appeal to His sovereign authority over all the earth when they address him as "Lord."

Life is filled with many injustices. Victims are ignored while criminals go free. It is only natural to want revenge. However, the Bible is clear concerning the right of revenge. Vengeance and judgment belong to God (Leviticus 19:18; Deuteronomy 32:34-43; Romans 12:19).

This does not mean that people who commit crimes are to be tolerated and that no punishment is to be given. God instituted government and the principle of law to deal with the injustices and crimes of society. The exacting of punishment does not belong to the individual but to the civil authorities (Romans 13:1-7).

The martyrs of the past simply cry *when?* When will God do what He has promised and "avenge the blood of His servants"? It is clear that revenge belongs to the Lord, and it is clear that He has promised to avenge the blood of all His servants who have suffered because of their faith in His promises. These martyrs ask what many of us ask about the injustices and evils of society—"How long, O Lord?"

The instruction they receive. Verse 11 is filled with some fascinating and enlightening information:

1. The dead are conscious and aware of the promises of God. These martyrs were able to cry to God and express their concern over the fulfillment of God's past promises for avenging their blood and bringing justice to the world.

2. It is possible that those who have died have an intermediate body until they receive their final resurrection body. The text says, "and a white robe was given to each of them." Does the robe suggest a body? It is possible, though we don't have a great deal of evidence in the Bible for it. Some have suggested that if these martyrs represent those who have suffered during the church age only, and if the rapture of the church occurs before the tribulation period begins, then these believers would have already been resurrected with new bodies. However, it is difficult to prove that the martyrs who lived *before* the church age (and who will be resurrected at the end of the tribulation period [Daniel 12:1-3]) are not a part of these martyrs, especially in light of those named in Hebrews 11.

Some who question the possibility of an intermediate body (between death and the resurrection) base their doubts upon their reading of this text, which says "a white robe was given to each of them." If it was given to them at this point, then they did not have it previously. However, we cannot conclude that with certainty; this statement may refer only to the fact that the robes were given, not the timing of the giving.

The "white robe" or "white garments" description is used symbolically in Revelation 7:14 and 19:8, where it indicates the wearers' salvation and righteousness before God, a reminder of what grants them access to the heavenly kingdom.

3. Dead believers are resting. The text says "and it was said to them that they should rest a little while longer," meaning that their lives will soon be characterized by activity rather than rest. In the coming kingdom of Jesus Christ on earth, believers will rule and reign with Him. We will not be sleeping!

Revelation 14:13 adds that the dead are "blessed" because they "rest from their labors." The struggles, trials, and heartaches of this life are over for those who have died in the Lord.

4. God's plan is right on schedule. It might not seem like things are under God's control, but the Bible teaches that they are. God is working out His plan according to His timetable, not ours. These martyrs should rest a little while longer "until" others join them who will also be killed for their faith. Then this sad occurrence will be "completed"; the killing of believers will come to an end!

5. Many believers will be killed during the tribulation period. We will learn more about this tragedy when we come to Revelation 7. Here it describes additional martyrs with such terms as "fellow servants" and "brethren." This is a possible reference to both Gentiles and Jews who will suffer martyrdom during the tribulation.

In contrast to those who argue that believers will be spared and protected during the tribulation, this verse argues that many will be killed. One of the arguments that the church will go through the tribulation is that the promise of Revelation 3:10 ("keep you from the hour of trial") implies immunity rather than removal. But it is difficult to argue that viewpoint in the light of Revelation 6:11. If believers are protected, why are they killed?

Sixth Seal Judgment:
Cosmic Disturbances (6:12-17)

When the sixth seal is opened by Jesus Christ, John sees some amazing events that were predicted by the prophets long ago.

The worldwide catastrophe that will take place. Earthquakes have occurred often in the past and with increasing frequency in the latter half of the twentieth century. They have caused enormous devastation, with thousands killed and multitudes left homeless. Earthquakes reveal our helplessness and produce great anxiety and fear.

This particular earthquake is described as "a *great* earthquake." It coincides with changes in the heavens as well as remarkable alterations on the surfaces of the earth.

The extent of the catastrophe. In the heavens, the sun, moon, stars, and sky are affected by this catastrophe. The event depicted here was predicted by the prophets Isaiah, Joel, and Amos over twenty-five hundred years ago. The similarity of their imagery is remarkable (Isaiah 13:6-16; 34:1-4; Joel 2:30-31; Amos 8:9-10).

The explanation of this catastrophe. Some believe these events should be interpreted symbolically, depicting social and political upheaval. However, this view takes liberties with the plain sense of God's Word and tries to reinterpret events of the future in the context of present understanding and situations.

Many commentators believe these events are literal and will take place as described, but they disagree as to when they will occur. Among pre-millennialists there are three major viewpoints about the catastrophic events of the sixth seal judgment:

1. It refers to the earthquake that occurs at Christ's return at the end of the tribulation. Those who hold this view usually point out that a great earthquake does happen at the pouring out of the seventh bowl of wrath, described as the final plague on the earth (16:17-21). Yet, though they see the similarities between chapters 6 and 16, they fail to expound on the differences. This is not the same event. In chapter 6, the great day of God's wrath "has come"; in chapter 16, "it is done!" (v. 17). The one begins the judgment of God; the other ends it.

2. It refers to the earthquake that was predicted in Ezekiel 38:19. In speaking about a future earthquake, the prophet Ezekiel spoke of an invasion into Israel by a northern power in the end time, and that the following would happen: "Surely in that day there shall be a great earthquake in the land of Israel." Is this the earthquake of Revelation 6? Probably not—the one in Ezekiel 38 happens only in the "land of Israel," whereas the one in Revelation 6 causes "every mountain and island" to be moved out of its place.

3. It refers to a particular earthquake that will happen at the beginning of the tribulation. The words of Revelation 6:17 point to this view as the correct one: "For the great day of his wrath has come, and who is able to stand?"

The tremendous concern of the people of earth. The entire population is in a panic! World leaders and rulers have no answers but are filled with fear along with the rest of the population. The panic causes them to run and hide. This attempt to hide and to appeal to the mountains and rocks to fall on them demonstrates how severe and intense this state of panic really is. They are aware that this judgment is unusual. It is not a normal earthquake nor a normal period of time in history. They realize this is from God and that this catastrophe is a demonstration of the wrath of Jesus Christ Himself, the Lamb of God.

The cry of verse 17 is "who is able to stand?"—an echo of Malachi's words about the coming of the Lord: "But who can endure the day of his coming? And who can stand when he appears?" (3:2). During His earthly ministry, Jesus likewise spoke of this coming day of judgment:

> "And there will be signs in the sun, in the moon, and in the stars; and on the earth distress of nations, with perplexity, the sea and the waves roaring; men's hearts failing them from fear and the expectation of those things which are coming on the earth, for the powers of heaven will be shaken" (Luke 21:25-26).

There is no greater issue to face than eternal life and escaping the coming wrath of God. God's wrath will be poured out upon this planet during the coming tribulation period, but as awful as that will be, it is nothing compared to the wrath of God that executes the judgment of Hell upon those who refuse to put their faith and trust in Him.

Our present generation has no desire to hear of these things or to believe them. We want to be stroked and reminded of our self-worth and potential for success. The real issue has not changed—heaven and hell, life and death. Where will you spend eternity?

Chapter 15

Tribulation Believers

(7:1-17)

Although church-age believers (represented by the twenty-four elders) are in heaven during the tribulation period on earth, there are two groups of believers who will be living on earth during this tragic time. One group consists of 144,000 people who are supernaturally protected by God from the judgments and tragedies. The other group is an innumerable multitude who come from every nation and language and become believers during the tribulation.

When the fifth seal was opened, we saw the martyrs of history concerned with the justice and vengeance of God. In 6:11 a statement appears about those whose death is yet future. In this chapter we learn about those who become believers during the tribulation period and suffer martyrdom. We also learn about a group of Jewish believers who do not suffer martyrdom but are rather used by God to spread His message of salvation to the world.

The Sealed Servants of Our God
(7:1-8)

> [1] *After these things I saw four angels standing at the four corners of the earth, holding the four winds of the earth, that the wind should not blow on the earth, on the sea, or on any tree. [2] Then I saw another angel ascending from the east, having the seal of the living God. And he cried with a loud voice to the four angels to whom it was*

> *granted to harm the earth and the sea, [3]saying, "Do not harm the earth, the sea, or the trees till we have sealed the servants of our God on their foreheads." [4]And I heard the number of those who were sealed. One hundred and forty-four thousand of all the tribes of the children of Israel were sealed:*
>
> *[5]of the tribe of Judah twelve thousand were sealed;*
> *of the tribe of Reuben twelve thousand were sealed;*
> *of the tribe of Gad twelve thousand were sealed;*
> *[6]of the tribe of Asher twelve thousand were sealed;*
> *of the tribe of Naphtali twelve thousand were sealed;*
> *of the tribe of Manasseh twelve thousand were sealed;*
> *[7]of the tribe of Simeon twelve thousand were sealed;*
> *of the tribe of Levi twelve thousand were sealed;*
> *of the tribe of Issachar twelve thousand were sealed;*
> *[8]of the tribe of Zebulun twelve thousand were sealed;*
> *of the tribe of Joseph twelve thousand were sealed;*
> *of the tribe of Benjamin twelve thousand were sealed.*

The first eight verses of this chapter speak of the 144,000 servants of our God who are sealed by God on their foreheads. There have been many religious views concerning the identity of these servants of God. These views fall into two basic categories: symbolic and literal. Unless there are some obvious reasons in the text to make this passage symbolic, it is better to take the words literally.

Before we look at the identity of these servants of our God, we must first notice the vision of four angels and the instruction given to them.

The Purpose of the Four Angels (7:1-3)

The basic command these four angels received is to withhold judgment upon the earth, sea, and trees until the 144,000 servants of God are sealed or protected. When we look ahead to chapter 8, we observe that harm was done on a wide scale to the earth, trees, and sea (8:7-12).

These angels have as their purpose the will of God Himself as His wrath and judgment are being poured out upon earth. God grants them the authority and power to carry out this "harm" (v. 7), but does not allow them to do so until the 144,000 persons are sealed. These 144,000 sealed servants are not to be touched or harmed, and they appear to be the only ones during the tribulation that are so protected by God.

The People Who Are Sealed (7:3-8)

In order to interpret accurately, we must be careful with the details presented in this passage. We are told the following concerning the 144,000:

1. They are called the servants of God (v. 3);
2. They are sealed on their foreheads (v. 3);
3. They come from "all the tribes of the children of Israel" (v. 4);
4. Twelve thousand are sealed from each tribe listed;
5. Two tribes from past Jewish history are not listed: Ephraim and Dan;
6. Manasseh, Ephraim's brother, is listed and so is their father, Joseph, perhaps as a replacement for Ephraim;
7. Levi is listed, even though this tribe, the priestly tribe, had no land inheritance in Israel's past history.

The Scriptures contain twenty-nine lists of the tribes of Israel. This particular one is not the final list in the chronology of the nation. After the tribulation comes the kingdom of the Messiah on earth. The prophet Ezekiel speaks of a new temple of worship during the reign of the Messiah and a new division of the land of Israel among the twelve tribes. In the list of Ezekiel 48, Dan (absent from Revelation 7) is listed first, and Ephraim appears again in the place of Joseph, his father. Levi is not listed in the land divisions, but is honored with a special place and area immediately around the temple.

According to Ezekiel 48:30-34, the gates of the Messianic city, the new Jerusalem, will have the names of the twelve tribes of Israel. In this list, we find Reuben, Judah, Levi, Joseph, Benjamin, Dan, Simeon, Issachar, Zebulun, Gad, Asher, and Naphtali. Once again, like the list in Revelation 7, Ephraim is dropped out and his father Joseph appears in the list. Ephraim's brother Manasseh, is also missing, and is replaced by the priestly tribe of Levi. The interesting thing about this final listing is that it represents the original listing in Genesis 35:22-26 where only the sons of Jacob are listed, not the two sons of Joseph (Ephraim and Manasseh).

Because of God's promises of land to these twelve tribes, He keeps His Word and mentions those to whom He originally promised such an inheritance. However, in the role the 144,000 play during the tribulation and in the honor God bestows upon His people in the new Jerusalem, changes are made. The question is, Why?

In the case of the 144,000, the absence of the tribe of Dan might be the result of Dan's involvement in idolatry in Israel's past. Judges 18:30 states that it was the children of Dan who set up the carved image and that it was the descendants of Manasseh who performed the role of priests for this pagan system. The tribe of Dan continued this idolatry until the time of the captivity. Dan did not represent religious loyalty and commitment, and the predictions of Deuteronomy 29:14-29 may be the reason for Dan's removal.

This could also be the reason why Ephraim is not mentioned. According to 1 Kings 12:28-29, king Jeroboam set up two golden calves for worship—one in Dan and the other in Bethel, which is in the land of Ephraim. Hosea 4:17 says, "Ephraim is joined to idols."

Literal or symbolic? The number of each tribe, the listing of the tribe, and the specific statement that they are "tribes of the children of Israel" point to a literal interpretation. The absence of symbolic language is also a strong reason for avoiding any unusual speculation or interpretations of this group of 144,000. The listing of these twelve tribes helps refute the contention by some that certain tribes of Israel are "lost." They are obviously not lost in the mind and plan of God.

It is best to interpret this passage as it is written. It is speaking of 144,000 Jews who will be divinely protected from the judgments of the tribulation to carry on God's purposes and plan. Attention is given to these Jews again in Revelation 14:1-5.

The Saved Saints Who Come Out of the Great Tribulation
(7:9-17)

⁹*After these things I looked, and behold, a great multitude which no one could number, of all nations, tribes, peoples, and tongues, standing before the throne and before the Lamb, clothed with white robes, with palm branches in their hands,* ¹⁰*and crying out with a loud voice, saying, "Salvation belongs to our God who sits on the throne, and to the Lamb!"* ¹¹*And all the angels stood around the throne and the elders and the four living creatures, and fell on their faces before the throne and worshiped God,* ¹²*saying:*

"Amen! Blessing and glory and wisdom,
Thanksgiving and honor and power and might,
Be to our God forever and ever.
Amen."

¹³*Then one of the elders answered, saying to me, "Who are these arrayed in white robes, and where did they come*

from?" [14]*And I said to him, "Sir, you know." So he said to me, "These are the ones who come out of the great tribulation, and washed their robes and made them white in the blood of the Lamb.* [15]*Therefore they are before the throne of God, and serve Him day and night in His temple. And He who sits on the throne will dwell among them.* [16]*They shall neither hunger anymore nor thirst anymore; the sun shall not strike them, nor any heat;* [17]*for the Lamb who is in the midst of the throne will shepherd them and lead them to living fountains of waters. And God will wipe away every tear from their eyes."*

People will be saved during the tribulation on earth. That is the good news. The bad news is that they will suffer greatly and apparently be killed for their failure to submit to the edicts and laws of the Antichrist. They will not take his mark on their foreheads or on their hands. Because of this, he will eliminate them.

The People Who Are Described (7:9-10)

The phrase "after these things," which appears several times in Revelation, may suggest a connection between the two groups mentioned in this chapter. It is possible that the 144,000 Jews are the ones used by God to bring this great innumerable multitude to believe in Jesus Christ as their Messiah.

The size of this group. Many more people will be in heaven than we realize; the number of them cannot be counted They come from *all* nations, tribes, peoples, and tongues. Though there are language groups today that have yet to receive one verse of Scripture in their own tongue, this problem will be solved during the tribulation period. We are not sure how it will be done, but one possibility is that the 144,000 Jews will be empowered by God like the early disciples were on the day of Pentecost (Acts 2). They will speak with tongues—that is, they will have the ability to communicate the gospel in languages they themselves do not know.

The salvation of this multitude. It is quite fascinating to read the prophecy of Joel 2:28-32, which was quoted by Peter on the day of Pentecost. This prophecy states that God will pour out His Spirit on all flesh. That refers to the salvation of the Gentiles as well as the Jews. The prophecy says the sons and daughters of Israel will prophesy. Peter implies that these words are the explanation for what happened to the disciples when they all spoke in the very dialects of those attending the feast of Pentecost.

Since Joel's prophecy contains predictions about tribulation events (Joel 2:30-31), it is possible that the complete fulfillment of these words will happen when the 144,000 Jews preach the gospel in all the languages of the world during the tribulation period. Jesus did say in Matthew 24:14 that "this gospel of the kingdom will be preached in *all* the world as a witness to *all* the nations, and then the end will come." The "end" to which He is referring is the end of the tribulation period which culminates with the return of the Messiah in power and great glory (Matthew 24:29-30).

The situation in which this multitude is found. This great multitude of believers in the tribulation period is described as "standing before the throne and before the Lamb." This suggests they may have died as martyrs and may be the ones referred to in 6:11—"until both the number of their fellow servants and their brethren, who would be killed as they were, was completed."

They are "clothed with white robes," which clearly points to their righteousness (19:8) and salvation (7:14). The "palm branches in their hands" picture victory and rejoicing. The same thing was done at the time of the triumphal entry of our Lord into Jerusalem (John 12:13).

The Statement that Comes Out of Their Mouths (7:10)

The one thing that seems to capture the praise and worship of those in heaven is the issue of salvation. How easy it is to take our salvation for granted! We do not see what those in heaven see. With the eyes of faith, we have believed what the Bible has promised, but until we get to heaven we shall not be able to comprehend the glory, blessing, and joy which our salvation will bring.

The Praise of Those in Heaven (7:11-12)

This praise appears to be a response to the multitude who come out of every nation, tribe, people, and tongue. As seen often in this book the worship begins with an act of submission as "all the angels" and the "elders" and the "four living creatures" fall on their faces before the throne and worship God. There is so little of that in the lives of believers today. We are so concerned with ourselves that little praise comes forth, much less submission.

The statement that "*all* the angels" give this praise along with the "elders" clearly determines that the twenty-four elders are not angels. Their words of praise remind us of what was said in chapter 5 concerning the Father and the Lamb. Blessing, glory, honor, power, might, wisdom, and thanksgiving—all of it belongs to Him!

The Problem with Their Identity (7:13-14)

The phrase "who come out of the great tribulation" clearly separates these believers from any other group of saved people throughout history. They are unique to the tribulation period. Yet salvation is the same in the tribulation as it is today—they are in heaven because their robes have been washed and made white in the blood of the Lamb. Without the shedding of blood (Hebrews 9:22) there is no forgiveness or remission of sins. We are saved by the blood of Jesus Christ which paid for our sins. The message that will be preached during the tribulation will be the same message we preach today. There is only one gospel—Jesus Christ and Him crucified (1 Corinthians 1:18; 2:1-5).

Do those who fail to respond to the gospel now have a "second chance" to be saved during the tribulation? A good question. If it were up to us to decide, we would certainly hope that this would be the case. However, 2 Thessalonians 2:9-12 causes us to question such an assumption:

> The coming of the lawless one is according to the working of Satan, with all power, signs, and lying wonders, and with all unrighteous deception among those who perish, because they did not receive the love of the truth, that they might be saved. And for this reason God will send them strong delusion, that they should believe the lie, that they all may be condemned who did not believe the truth but had pleasure in unrighteousness.

The passage is speaking about the deception of the Antichrist, the lawless one, who will work miracles through the efforts of Satan. The ones who will be deceived are "those who perish," and the reason for this is "they did not receive the love of the truth, that they might be saved." It appears that those who hear the gospel now but do not respond to it are not going to receive it during the tribulation period either. God will see to it. He will send them "strong delusion, that they should believe the lie."

This no doubt implies that the multitude of believers who come out of every nation are those who have never heard the gospel of Jesus Christ or been given a chance to respond to it.

The Promises of God to This Multitude (7:15-17)

God promises them a special place. They will be "before the throne of God"—what a wonderful position to have! This is assurance of God's very presence, as the last phrase indicates: "He who sits on the throne will dwell among them." This is not only a place of God's presence, but it is a place of service—"serve Him day and night in His temple." The new city, the holy Jerusalem, has no temple (Revelation 21:22). This temple could be a symbolic term for the worship of heaven or a literal temple in heaven or the one that will be set up on earth during the millennial reign of Jesus Christ (Ezekiel 40-48).

We also learn in Revelation 21:25 that there is no night in the new Jerusalem. The statement that they serve God "day and night" could be written for our benefit (meaning "unending service"), or it could refer to their service for the Messiah during the millennium on earth, which follows the tribulation period out of which they come.

God promises them complete protection. These words are quoted from God's promises in the Old Testament (Isaiah 49:10; Psalm 121:6-7). What wonderful promises God has given to His people Israel. These are now applied to the tribulation believers.

The promise of God's protection is related to what they have faced in the tribulation period. To say that they will never hunger or thirst again implies that this was a part of their suffering during the tribulation. We do know that those who do not take the mark of the beast cannot buy or sell (13:17).

God promises them eternal peace. It is the Lamb of God, our Lord Jesus Christ, Who "will shepherd them and lead them to living fountains of waters." These words are reminiscent of Psalm 23 and its picture of wonderful peace. In the world they will have tribulation, but in Jesus Christ's presence, they will have eternal peace.

The last statement of verse 17 is repeated in 21:4—"And God will wipe away every tear from their eyes." This was promised long ago by God to His people (Isaiah 25:8). The Lord promised it, and He will remain faithful to all His promises. No more tears—gone forever!

The presence of "tears" does not mean they were shed in heaven and were then wiped away. It reflects back on our lives here on earth where we inevitably experience many tears and sorrows. The promise is that those tears will never again be present—God will wipe all of that away forever, including death itself!

Yes, there will be believers in the tribulation period. They will come to know the Lord during that period of time and will represent all nations and language groups of the world. They will suffer a great deal for their faith in the Lord and will be killed (cf. Revelation 6:11; 13:7, 15). But the Lord will fulfill His promises to them and to all of us who come to believe in Jesus Christ as our only Lord and Savior.

Chapter 16

Four Terrible Trumpets

(8:1-13)

The judgments of the tribulation period are found written in the scroll with seven seals which the Lamb of God took from the right hand of God the Father. The Lamb is the only one who is "worthy" to open the scroll and loose its seals. There are seven seals, six of which have already been opened. The seventh seal contains a rather extended message and reveals seven angels with seven trumpets. These trumpet judgments are found in the scroll after the seventh seal is broken.

The Prelude to Judgment
(8:1-5)

¹When He opened the seventh seal, there was silence in heaven for about half an hour. ²And I saw the seven angels who stand before God, and to them were given seven trumpets. ³Then another angel, having a golden censer, came and stood at the altar. And he was given much incense, that he should offer it with the prayers of all the saints upon the golden altar which was before the throne. ⁴And the smoke of the incense, with the prayers of the saints, ascended before God from the angel's hand. ⁵Then the angel took the censer, filled it with fire form the altar, and threw it to the earth. And there were noises, thunderings, lightnings, and an earthquake.

The silence is like the calm before the storm. After seeing and hearing all the praise and worship of heaven, this period of silence was a dramatic pause to the events that would soon follow. This silence is in direct contrast to the loud voices of the great multitudes of heaven.

Something unusual is about to take place—something of enormous importance.

John said he saw "*the* seven angels"—the ones previously referred to (1:4, 20; 2:1; 3:1; 5:6). They are the "seven Spirits who are before His throne" (cf. 1:4 and 8:2). They stand ready to do God's bidding, to carry out His orders. The seven trumpets were given to them by God, and these angels are entrusted with the responsibility to blow these instruments, announcing the judgments of Almighty God upon planet earth.

Trumpets have been used often in the life of Israel. A loud trumpet was blown at Mount Sinai at the giving of the law (Exodus 19:19). One of the feasts Israel celebrated was called the Feast of Trumpets (Leviticus 23:23-25). A trumpet was sounded on the Day of Atonement during the year of Jubilee (Leviticus 25:9). Two silver trumpets were used to assemble the children of Israel and direct them in moving from place to place during their wilderness journeys (Numbers 10:1-8). The trumpets were also used to sound the alarm for going to war and when sacrifices were offered at the various feasts and celebrations (Numbers 10:9-10). The prophet Joel speaks of a trumpet being blown to sound an alarm concerning the coming of the day of the LORD (Joel 2:1) and also speaks of a trumpet being blown to call the people of Israel to a fast and sacred assembly (2:15).

The Prayers of All the Saints (8:3-5)

The identity of the angel with the golden censer. Some Bible teachers believe this angel refers to Jesus Christ and His intercessory work as our High Priest. While interesting, it seems difficult to connect any angel in this book with Jesus Christ for the following reasons:

1. He is the One Who opens the scroll, and is continually described as the Lamb of God Who alone is worthy;

2. John is rebuked (Revelation 22:8-9) for trying to worship an angel, yet Hebrews 1:6 says of Jesus Christ: "Let all the angels of God worship Him";

3. The mention of the seven angels in verse 2 seems to govern the mention of "another angel" in verse 3;

4. The word *another* means "another of the same kind" and is a strong grammatical factor for concluding that this is an angel just like the seven mentioned in verse 2;

5. While the phrase "the angel of the LORD" seems to be a description of the Messiah in the Old Testament, there is no evidence in the New

Testament that the word *angel* refers to Jesus Christ. In fact, the exact opposite is implied.

This angel is one of many who reside in heaven and do God's work and will. They are truly "ministering spirits" (Hebrews 1:14).

The incense that is offered. Here is a beautiful picture of an Old Testament practice. Every morning and evening, the priests would use a golden censer to put incense on the altar of incense in front of the second veil of the tabernacle or temple. Behind this veil was the Holy of Holies into which only the High Priest could go once a year on the Day of Atonement. The Lord told Moses that this is "where I will meet with you" (Exodus 30:6).

The role of the priest is to offer the prayers of the people to God. The smoke of the incense burning on the altar was a picture of prayer rising to God. According to Revelation 8:3, this incense represents "the prayers of *all* the saints." No doubt this refers to the martyrs' cry to God: "How long, O Lord, holy and true, until You judge and avenge our blood on those who dwell on the earth?" (6:10). Chapter 8 brings the answer from God—*now*—as the trumpet judgments are announced and God begins to avenge the blood of His servants.

The altar here is described as being "the golden altar which was before the throne." It seems unlikely that this special altar and its special place would be an altar of sacrifice. More likely, it is a beautiful fulfillment of the altar of incense which God commanded the Jews to build for worship in the tabernacle and temple. An altar in heaven is mentioned seven times in Revelation (6:9; 8:3-twice; 8:5; 9:13; 14:18; 16:7).

The impact of these prayers. For one thing, these prayers are being answered. Verse 4 says they "ascended before God." Also, the angel fills the censer with fire from the altar which is then thrown down to the earth. That dramatic act demonstrates that the trumpet judgments are answers to the prayers of God's people throughout history.

To demonstrate how important these prayers are in bringing these judgments, a familiar response takes place—"noises, thunderings, lightnings." Such response, we learned in 4:5, proceeds from the throne of God. God is indicating His full support; His authority and power are behind these judgments. We also read that an "earthquake" occurs. After the catastrophic earthquake revealed by the sixth seal (6:12-17), the inhabitants of earth must be filled with fear and anxiety as another one comes, causing them to wonder what terrible judgments must be on the verge of happening again.

The Punishments of Four Trumpets
(8:6-13)

⁶*So the seven angels who had the seven trumpets prepared themselves to sound.*

⁷*The first angel sounded: And hail and fire followed, mingled with blood, and they were thrown to the earth; and a third of the trees were burned up, and all green grass was burned up.*

⁸*Then the second angel sounded: And something like a great mountain burning with fire was thrown into the sea, and a third of the sea became blood;* ⁹*and a third of the living creatures in the sea died, and a third of the ships were destroyed.*

¹⁰*Then the third angel sounded: And a great star fell from heaven, burning like a torch, and it fell on a third of the rivers and on the springs of water;* ¹¹*and the name of the star is Wormwood; and a third of the waters became wormwood; and many men died from the water, because it was made bitter.*

¹²*Then the fourth angel sounded: And a third of the sun was struck, a third of the moon, and a third of the stars, so that a third of them were darkened; and a third of the day did not shine, and likewise the night.* ¹³*And I looked, and I heard an angel flying through the midst of heaven, saying with a loud voice, "Woe, woe, woe to the inhabitants of the earth, because of the remaining blasts of the trumpet of the three angels who are about to sound!"*

These verses continue the dramatic events that bring the trumpet judgments upon the earth. The seven angels now step forward with their trumpets and prepare themselves to sound God's alarms—the day of the Lord has come, the day of God's wrath!

First Trumpet Judgment:
Trees and Grass Burned Up (8:7)

A judgment such as this has enormous effect upon the quality of life and available food supply. Trees not only produce food, they are essential protection from violent storms and flooding. This verse predicts that one-third of all trees on the planet are destroyed by this judgment. It is difficult to conceive what this might mean for human survival.

This judgment is similar to one of the plagues of Egypt involving hail and fire (Exodus 9:22-26). The text of Revelation adds that the hail and fire were "mingled with blood," probably indicating that many people will be killed when this judgment hits. We also remember that God rained hail, fire, and brimstone on the ancient cities of Sodom and Gomorrah and many people were killed. Joel 2:30-31 predicts that God will "show wonders in the heavens and in the earth: Blood and fire and pillars of smoke," right before the coming of the great and terrible day of the Lord.

This judgment destroys "all green grass." That fact alone will affect animal life which depends upon the green grass for food. The appearance of the planet will radically change, and it will seem as though the entire globe has become a virtual wasteland or desert.

Second Trumpet Judgment:
Sea Life and Ships Destroyed (8:8-9)

The first plague of Egypt (Exodus 7:14-25) turned the water of the Nile River into blood. Something similar occurs at the second trumpet judgment of Revelation. Three consequences are described:

One-third of the sea becomes blood. The word "sea" is both singular and preceded by the definite article—it is *"the* sea" which is affected. That would seem to indicate the Mediterranean Sea. The cause behind this disaster is described in symbolic language (note the use of "like"). It is not a literal mountain burning with fire that was thrown into the sea, but something that in John's eyes looked like a burning mountain. Some commentators have suggested a giant meteor; others have seen atomic or nuclear explosions. That the sea became blood suggests that either animal or human life has been destroyed by this supernatural catastrophe.

One-third of sea life is killed. The Mediterranean Sea is filled with fish, supplying the food needs of many countries and peoples. This disaster will have a serious effect upon the peoples of the world, especially those who live in countries dependent upon the fishing industry in the Mediterranean. Similar descriptions of destruction to animal life occur elsewhere in the prophetic Scriptures (Hosea 4:3; Zephaniah 1:2- 3).

One-third of the ships are destroyed. This particular tragedy becomes more significant when one studies the presence of naval vessels in the

Mediterranean. It is not only the permanent location of the United States Sixth Fleet, it is also filled with Soviet vessels as well as ships from many countries of the world. It sometimes seems as though the Mediterranean is the place where most of the ships of the world have decided to be. The sea is covered with naval vessels, cruise ships, and fishing boats of all sizes. One-third of these ships will be destroyed in this one judgment, and of course, many lives will be lost.

Third Trumpet Judgment:
Rivers and Springs Made Bitter (8:10-11)

Many believe this "great star" is a meteorite. That may be, but the results of this tragedy affect one-third of the rivers and springs of water. It is certainly an unusual meteorite if that is in fact what it is.

The star is called Wormwood after the strong bitter taste of the wormwood plant, an Old Testament symbol for bitterness and sorrow. In Lamentations 3:15 we read, "He has filled me with bitterness, / He has made me drink wormwood." Amos 5:7 adds, "You who turn justice to wormwood, / And lay righteousness to rest in the earth!" Jeremiah uses it to describe God's judgment on those who disobey Him (9:13-16; 23:15).

"Wormwood" is God's judgment upon those who disobey Him. Although not itself lethal, wormwood's bitter taste suggests death. This tragic judgment, affecting the water supply of the world and bringing about the death of many, is a consequence upon those who refuse to submit to God's authority in their lives. We all need water; it is basic to human survival. One can only imagine what sort of additional tragedies will occur because of the terrible pollution caused by this third trumpet judgment.

Fourth Trumpet Judgment:
Sun, Moon, and Stars Darkened (8:12)

This judgment causes a reduction of light. The problems arising from this judgment extend to many areas of life that we take for granted. One needs only to experience darkness over an extended period of time in order to appreciate the light. Several years ago my wife was confined to a darkened room for about ten weeks due to an infection of her face and eyes. Her appreciation of light, especially the light of the sun on a clear day, became much more important to her.

The light sources of the universe are all struck by this judgment. God clearly shows us that they are also dependent upon His power and control. The sun, moon, and stars have been consistently used by pagan religions as objects of worship. God shows us in this one judgment that He alone is to be worshiped. As with the first trumpet judgment, this judgment reminds us of one of the plagues in Egypt (Exodus 10:21-23).

Some interpret the 33 percent reduction of light as meaning that the daytime lasts for eight hours and the nighttime for sixteen. However, the wording of this judgment implies an overall reduction of light for these heavenly bodies so that even the daylight hours are darkened to some extent.

Jesus predicted there would be "signs in the sun, in the moon, and in the stars" (Luke 21:25). In addition, several Old Testament prophets foretold this coming day of darkness (Isaiah 13:10; Jeremiah 4:23; Ezekiel 32:7-8; Joel 2:31; 3:15; Amos 5:20). It is clear that the Hebrew prophets knew of this coming judgment of the Lord upon the sun, moon, and stars.

The Proclamation of a Flying Angel (8:13)

Is it really a flying angel? Many interpreters of this verse believe the word "angel" is based on weak manuscript evidence and that the proper word is the word for "eagle." While it is true that there are manuscript variations in this verse, the evidence can support the reading of "angel" instead of "eagle." The use of angels to announce God's plans is well known—why would an exception occur at this point? Angels are blowing the trumpets that announce these judgments—why not an angel to warn the planet that the worst is yet to come?

Three woes to come. The word "woe" is one of those unique words whose sound indicates its meaning. It is a warning of what is to come. The last three trumpets out of the seven trumpet judgments are more severe than the first four. Each of these "woes" corresponds to one of the last three trumpet judgments.

These judgments will fall upon "the inhabitants of the earth," a term referring to unbelievers who take the mark of the beast and do not repent of their deeds. They are the ones who "do not have the seal of God on their foreheads" (cf. 9:4). And what is coming is far more severe than what has already been experienced. What a terrible and tragic period of human history awaits this world!

Chapter 17

Demonic Attack

(9:1-21)

At the end of Revelation 8 we were warned of the terrible judgments remaining to be brought upon the earth. The awesomeness of these catastrophes are now described in chapter 9 as the fifth and sixth trumpets are blown. In the first, an unusual locust plague is described, unlike anything mankind has ever experienced. Following that, and perhaps related to it, is an army of 200 million horsemen who bring death to one-third of the remaining world's population.

Locusts Out of Hell
(9:1-12)

¹Then the fifth angel sounded: And I saw a star fallen from heaven to the earth. And to him was given the key to the bottomless pit. ²And he opened the bottomless pit, and smoke arose out of the pit like the smoke of a great furnace. And the sun and the air were darkened because of the smoke of the pit. ³Then out of the smoke locusts came upon the earth. And to them was given power, as the scorpions of the earth have power. ⁴They were commanded not to harm the grass of the earth, or any green thing, or any tree, but only those men who do not have the seal of God on their foreheads. ⁵And they were not given authority to kill them, but to torment them for five months. And their torment was like the torment of a scorpion when it strikes a man. ⁶In those days men will seek death and will not find it; they will desire to die, and death will flee from them. ⁷And the shape of the locusts was like horses

> *prepared for battle; and on their heads were crowns of*
> *something like gold, and their faces were like the faces of*
> *men.* [8]*They had hair like women's hair, and their teeth*
> *were like lions' teeth.* [9]*And they had breastplates like*
> *breastplates of iron, and the sound of their wings was like*
> *the sound of chariots with many horses running into battle.*
> [10]*They had tails like scorpions, and there were stings in*
> *their tails. And their power was to hurt men five months.*
> [11]*And they had as king over them the angel of the bottom-*
> *less pit, whose name in Hebrew is Abaddon, but in Greek*
> *he has the name Apollyon.* [12]*One woe is past. Behold, still*
> *two more woes are coming after these things.*

One must always remember when studying the book of Revelation that the writer, the apostle John, lived in the first century A.D. and, being Jewish, was well aware of various biblical passages which spoke of the future day of God's wrath. Sometimes he uses illustrations and symbols common to all periods of history; at other times he expresses an event or a judgment from God in the language and knowledge of his day. The prophet Joel spoke of a locust plague as the judgment of God upon His people. It is possible John is thinking of that when he describes this fifth trumpet judgment. But these locusts are highly unusual, to say the least!

The Leader of the Locusts Is the Devil Himself (9:1-2, 11)

Several factors lead us to believe that the leader of these locusts— their so-called "king"—is in reality the devil himself.

His position. This leader is depicted as "a star fallen from heaven to the earth" (9:1), and this "star" is identified by the personal pronoun "him," indicating a real person.

1. This star is an angel. In Revelation 1:20 we are told that "stars" represent "angels" in the symbolism of the book of Revelation. There seems to be no valid reason why that principle of interpretation should not be applied here. Also, in 9:11 this king of the locusts is called "the angel of the bottomless pit."

2. This star is a fallen angel. This "star" had "fallen from heaven to the earth," indicating a moral failure. In Jude 6-7 we learn of angels who have experienced such ruin. The Bible speaks of "unclean spirits" (Mark 5:2, 8, 13) and indicates that they are "demons" (Mark 5:12-13) capable of controlling a person's mind and actions (Mark 5:3-5, 15).

Satan is an angel, an unclean spirit, morally fallen from his original state. He is the head of other demons, dedicated to thwarting the purposes of God and expressing their anger and hostility toward all that is right and good. Isaiah 14:12-15 speaks of the moral fall of Satan and states that it was his pride and ambition that caused it to happen (cf. 1 Timothy 3:6). Jesus identifies him as a liar and murderer (John 8:44). The Bible speaks elsewhere of "the devil and his angels" (Matthew 25:41) and tells us they are "deceiving spirits (1 Timothy 4:1) and "rulers of the darkness of this age" (Ephesians 6:12).

3. This star loses access to heaven. The Bible indicates that Satan has access to God in heaven where he continues to bring accusations against the people of God (Job 1:6-12; Revelation 12:10). One day it will end. Satan will be removed from heaven during the tribulation period; his final destiny is to be cast into the lake of fire where he will be tormented day and night forever and ever (Revelation 20:10).

His power. The power of this fallen star is indicated by two things:

1. A key was given to him. This clearly indicates that his power and authority is limited, being determined and controlled by God Himself. In Revelation 1:18 we were told the "keys of Hades and of Death" are in the hands and control of Jesus Christ. Satan is not the king of hell—he is the chief prisoner. The key that unlocks the chains of those demonic spirits in hell was given to Satan. He obviously did not have it in his control. God allows him to unleash his fury against a world that has rejected the Lord. The Day of God's wrath has come, and, as always, God is using Satan to accomplish His purposes.

The key is for the "bottomless pit," the abyss, described elsewhere as a "place of torment" (Luke 16:19-31). Second Peter 2:4 states that "God did not spare the angels who sinned, but cast them down to hell and delivered them into chains of darkness, to be reserved for judgment." Satan himself will be bound for a thousand years in this bottomless pit (Revelation 20:1-3).

The plague of locusts comes out of the bottomless pit. In Revelation 11:7 the beast comes out of the bottomless pit as well, possibly indicating that this coming world ruler is in fact a demon who enters the body of a human being and eventually deceives the whole world. It is fascinating to note Luke 8:31 where a legion of demons begged the Lord not to command them to go "into the abyss." It is a place of torment, a place where the demons reside and from which they are released during the fifth trumpet judgment to do much harm upon the earth.

2. He is king of the locusts. The power of Satan is clearly revealed in the simple statement, "they had as king over them the angel of the bottomless pit" (9:11). One of the reasons for believing that this locust plague is not referring to actual locusts is that they have a king. Proverbs 30:27 indicates that locusts do not in fact have a king over them.

The devil is the king of the demons. He controls a vast empire of wicked spirits and through them can affect the lives of millions of people. The devil is not omnipresent like God. He cannot be everywhere at once, but through his demons he is able to attack many people at any given moment.

We do not know how many demons there are. The word *legion* is used in the case of one man possessed by demons. The word refers to at least six thousand. In Revelation 12:3-4, the devil is described as a great, fiery red dragon whose tail "drew a third of the stars of heaven and threw them to the earth." Since the "stars" represent angels, this passage suggests that the devil is king over one-third of all the angels God created, a multitude that cannot be counted (5:11).

His purpose. Satan is called *Abaddon* in Hebrew and *Apollyon* in Greek, names that identify him as the destroyer. Satan is out to ruin people's lives (1 Peter 5:8).

The Locusts Are Demons out of Hell (9:3-10)

We have already suggested that these locusts are in fact demons with Satan as their king. In describing these demons, John deals with several important things for our understanding.

Their authority. Verse 3 says "to them was given power." Demons operate under divine permission; their power or authority comes ultimately from God. This underscores again that all things, including demons, are working toward the accomplishment of God's purposes and will (Ephesians 1:11; Romans 11:36).

1. The extent of their authority. We are told several things about the extent of the authority of these demonic hordes from hell. As to *time*, their authority is limited to "five months," no more. As to the *targets* of their destructive acts, they are commanded "not to harm the grass of the earth, or any green thing, or any tree, but only those men who do not have the seal of God on their foreheads" (v. 4). They will cause much *torment*, but they are instructed not to kill (v. 5). They are clearly operating under the control and limitations of God.

2. The effects of their authority. Their torment of unbelievers is described as being "like the torment of a scorpion when it strikes a man" (v. 5). While a scorpion sting is usually not fatal (although children often die from such a sting), it is very painful. The venom affects the veins and the nervous system. Normally the pain and discomfort last for several days. This plague lasts for five months! The intensity of it is clearly seen by the fact that people will want to die because of the horrible suffering they will experience (v. 6). It appears that God will frustrate all attempts to commit suicide. People will try but will be unsuccessful.

Their appearance. Needless to say, their description in verses 7-10 is unlike ordinary locusts. Though it is possible these locusts are some sort of modern military equipment being described by a writer who would have no knowledge of such things, it is better to argue that these locusts are demons whose appearance John is now trying to describe in the language and knowledge of his day. Demons are spirit beings who can manifest themselves in various ways and take up residency in the bodies of human beings.

1. Overall description ("like horses prepared for battle"). It appears from careful reading of the predicted locust plague described in Joel 2 that John is noting similarities from that ancient prophecy. Comparing locusts to horses and the sound of chariots is consistent with Joel's description of the coming "day of the Lord" (2:1):

> Their appearance is like the appearance of horses;
> And like swift steeds, so they run.
> With a noise like chariots
> Over mountaintops they leap,
> Like the noise of a flaming fire that devours the stubble,
> Like a strong people set in battle array (2:4-5).

2. Specific descriptions.

> *heads:* crowns like gold
> *faces:* like men's
> *hair:* like women's
> *teeth:* like lions'
> *breastplates:* like iron
> *wings:* like the sound of chariots with many horses
> *tails:* like scorpions

In each case, the word *like* indicates that a comparison is being made and that something other than a literal description is intended. The "crowns . . . like gold" perhaps reveal that they will be conquerors and achieve some sort of victory in the worldwide conflicts for power during the tribulation period. Their "breastplates" may indicate that they are immune to any attempts by the world's governments and people to resist them.

Demonic Attack

Only the Beginning (9:12)

Many Bible scholars believe the fifth and sixth trumpet judgments describe the same event. However, verse 12 suggests the opposite. The sixth trumpet judgment is another "woe" like the fifth trumpet judgment but distinct from it. The verse says that "two more woes are coming," which makes the attempt to identify what follows with what was just revealed highly unlikely. The verse ends with the words "after these things," a clear statement to the sequential order of things. The details are different as well as the effects upon the world's population. In the fifth trumpet judgment men are tormented but not killed. In the sixth trumpet judgment a third of mankind is killed.

The Infernal Army
(9:13-21)

¹³ Then the sixth angel sounded: And I heard a voice from the four horns of the golden altar which is before God, ¹⁴ saying to the sixth angel who had the trumpet, "Release the four angels who are bound at the great river Euphrates." ¹⁵ So the four angels, who had been prepared for the hour and day and month and year, were released to kill a third of mankind. ¹⁶ Now the number of the army of the horsemen was two hundred million, and I heard the number of them. ¹⁷ And thus I saw the horses in the vision: those who sat on them had breastplates of fiery red, hyacinth blue, and sulfur yellow; and the heads of the horses were like the heads of lions; and out of their mouths came fire, smoke, and brimstone. ¹⁸ By these three plagues a third of mankind was killed—by the fire and the smoke and the brimstone which came out of their mouths. ¹⁹ For their power is in their mouth and in their tails; for their tails are like serpents, having heads; and with them they do harm. ²⁰ But the rest of mankind, who were not killed by these plagues, did not repent of the works of their hands, that they should not worship demons, and idols of gold, silver, brass, stone, and wood, which can neither see nor hear nor walk; ²¹ and they did not repent of their murders or their sorceries or their sexual immorality or their thefts.

While the fifth and sixth trumpet judgments are distinct, there is one major similarity—they both describe the attack of demons upon the world's population.

The Control of This Army (9:13-15)

Demons operate under the control of God. He limits their ability to oppress the human race. The control of these demonic hordes is indicated by several things in these three verses:

The pronouncement that is made. Often John hears a voice near the throne of God. Perhaps it is a special angel who speaks or one of the four living creatures (cherubim) who function as the worship leaders of heaven. It is also possible that it is the voice of God Himself. The connection of this voice with the "golden altar" would lend support to the view that it is the voice of an angel (cf. 8:3).

The place where this army is bound. That this army is "bound" portrays again the control of God upon the demonic world. The mention of "four angels" who are bound and apparently leaders of this infernal army causes us to reflect upon their identity and purpose. There are four living creatures who function as the worship leaders of heaven and four angels who stand at the "four corners of the earth, holding the four winds of the earth" (Revelation 4:6-8; 7:1). God's good and holy angels are never described as being "bound." That only fits wicked angels, the demons of hell (2 Peter 2:4, Jude 6-7).

The fact that these angels were bound "at the river Euphrates" is fascinating indeed. The Euphrates River was one of four rivers which came out of the Garden of Eden. Since it was the place of Satan's original deception of Adam and Eve, it is possible that God has kept the demons in check there as a reminder of the original evil Satan brought into the world.

Another possibility regarding the river Euphrates is its connection with Babylon and the symbolism as "Babylon the Great, the Mother of Harlots and of the Abominations of the Earth" (Revelation 17:5). According to Revelation 18:2, Babylon becomes the "habitation of demons, a prison for every foul spirit, and a cage for every unclean and hated bird."

It is also possible that mention of the river Euphrates implies that the army which invades the world's population and brings death to one-third of the human race comes from the Orient. The Euphrates serves as a natural boundary and barrier between the lands of the East and the Middle Eastern, European, and Western nations.

Demonic Attack

The preparation of these angels. Demons operate under God's authority and time schedules! These angels were prepared by God at some point in past history and continue to be ready for the special moment in history ("the hour") for which God has designed them. Again God's timing and providential control of all things, including Satan and the world of demons, is clearly indicated.

The purpose of these angels. Earlier in the tribulation, one-fourth of the earth's population was eliminated by the fourth seal judgment (6:7-8) and others died from polluted water (8:10-11). Now the population is reduced by one-third. All totaled, over half of the world's population has died before the middle of the tribulation period occurs. The day of God's wrath has indeed come (6:17)!

The Characteristics of This Army (9:16-17)

The four angels (demons) are released and the greatest army in history goes on the attack. The size of the army is incredible—two hundred million strong. It is possible that the number is not to be taken literally but simply suggests an army that is impossible to count and is greater than anything mankind has ever seen.

The symbolism employed in verse 17 needs to be examined carefully. For example, it does not say this army was "like horses"; it says, "I saw the horses in the vision." The riders had "breastplates of fiery red, hyacinth blue, and sulfur yellow." No symbolic words such as *like* or *as* are used.

On the other hand, the heads of the horses were "like the heads of lions." Here symbolic language describes the nature and purpose of such an army, ready to devour like a hungry lion (cf. 1 Peter 5:8). Verse 19 says their tails were "like serpents, having heads." It is possible John is describing military machines. This seems likely when we read in verse 17 that "out of their mouths came fire, smoke, and brimstone." Since these three things result in the death of one-third of mankind, weapons of warfare may be pictured.

The Consequences of This Army (9:18-21)

It is hard to imagine such consequences. At least three results are experienced from this demonic attack:

Their plagues bring death to one-third of the world's population. Specifically, the "fire and the smoke and the brimstone which came out of their mouths" bring death to so many people. Is this the result of military weaponry? Highly possible. All peace attempts that may be promoted in our world and that may be prevalent at the beginning of the tribulation period, will not last. Military equipment and weapons of destruction will continue to be built and financed. Without the Prince of peace, our Lord Jesus Christ, no lasting peace is possible in this terrible and confused world of ours. The problem is in the hearts of mankind. It is not money or new programs that we need—we need changed hearts! Only the gospel of Jesus Christ can bring that kind of change.

Their powers cause great harm to people. This attack brings harm in other ways than death to one-third of the population of the world. Verse 19 says the power of this invading army is not only in what comes out of their mouths but also in what is "in their tails." It is with their tails that "they do harm."

Their actions do not change the hearts of people on earth. The survivors of what appears to be a worldwide war refuse to repent. They will not repent of the "works of their hands" nor of their murders, sorceries, immorality, or thefts. How deceived we are when we think that a change in environment or our circumstances can result in a changed heart.

The "works of their hands" describes the worship of demons and the constructing of idols. When we do not repent and acknowledge the God of creation, we exchange the glory of the Creator for what we ourselves can design (Romans 1:21-23). We are the "godmakers" and deserve the judgment of God for the "works of our hands." We were designed to worship, and when we refuse to worship the God of the Bible, the only alternative is to worship demons.

In their determination to continue their sinful practices and ways, the Bible says the survivors would not repent of four major sins:

1. Murders. Violent crime continues to be portrayed and promoted in movies, television, books, magazines, and newspapers. It almost seems the producers of such media have decided this is what the public wants to see and hear. They are appealing to the depravity of the human heart.

In addition to the killing of people on our streets, we now tolerate the most terrible of all crimes—the murder of the unborn. The horrible sin of abortion has taken the lives of millions of children before they ever had the chance to see life outside their mother's womb. The blood of innocent children is on the hands of an unrepentant generation. Can judgment be far behind?

2. Sorceries. This is not referring simply to fascination and involvement with occultic practices, although that is a part of it. Horoscopes, palm reading, astrology, tarot cards, and so on are certainly forms of "sorceries." However, the word in Greek indicates the use of drugs, which has become a worldwide tragedy. In spite of law enforcement efforts and agencies designed to combat the spread and use of drugs in our society, drugs continue to destroy the lives of millions, to the profit of the few who market and distribute them. In spite of the obvious and well-known judgment of God which comes on the earth, people will not give up their sins.

3. Sexual immorality. No sin so captures and controls our lives as that of sexual immorality. It is treated so lightly today in spite of the danger of sexually-transmitted diseases. We continue to encourage the toleration and involvement of people in sexual immorality by our failure to see it as sin before God and deserving of His judgment.

Immorality destroys individuals, marriages, and families, but no one seems to care. It appeals to our depravity and deep desire for sexual satisfaction and pleasure. We hear the standards of God and may even know that He created sex and desires us to be satisfied in the sexual desires He has given us, but we refuse to believe Him when He tells us this satisfaction comes through marriage alone. Premarital and extramarital sex bring loss of sexual vitality and emotional ruin. Yet in spite of its destructiveness, does anyone really care?

4. Thefts. Stealing is a national and international problem that is literally out of control. Police must often look the other way because they cannot handle all of the reported cases. We have begun to talk of serious theft versus harmless or petty theft. Is there really a difference? Is it not our propensity to place a price tag on everything in life that causes us to categorize theft?

Stealing is wrong if it involves a pencil that does not belong to me or stamps that belong to your employer that you have taken for personal use. Stealing a bike is the same sin as stealing a car. It is just as wrong for a child to steal a few coins from his parents as it is for an executive to embezzle funds from the company for which he works.

What a tragic picture of depravity is presented in this prophecy—a clear reminder to all of us that we need a change of heart that is possible only through the forgiveness and cleansing of God through His Son Jesus Christ, our Lord and Savior.

Chapter 18

The Little Book

(10:1-11)

After describing six terrible trumpet judgments which result in millions of people being killed, John is given a vision of a mighty angel with a little book that prepares him for what is yet ahead. The seventh trumpet is sounded apparently at the middle of the tribulation period and its message contains all the events that remain.

The original scroll (5:1) was sealed with seven seals. Each of those seals has now been broken by Jesus Christ and the message unveiled for all to read. The seventh seal introduced us to seven trumpets (8:1-2), and we are now looking at the seventh trumpet which contains the longest message of all. It covers the last three and a half years of the tribulation period, the most awful holocaust of terror, suffering, violence, and catastrophe the world has ever seen (Matthew 24:21).

The Appearance of a Mighty Angel
(10:1-4)

¹And I saw still another mighty angel coming down from heaven, clothed with a cloud. And a rainbow was on his head, his face was like the sun, and his feet like pillars of fire. ²And he had a little book open in his hand. And he set his right foot on the sea and his left foot on the land, ³and cried with a loud voice, as when a lion roars. And when he cried out, seven thunders uttered their voices. ⁴Now when the seven thunders uttered their voices, I was about to write; but I heard a voice from heaven saying to me, "Seal up the things which the seven thunders uttered, and do not write them."

The Identity of This Angel

In the book of Revelation, angels are angels, not symbols of events, things, places, or persons. Many believe this "mighty angel" is none other than Jesus Christ. Jehovah's Witnesses teach that Jesus Christ is Michael the archangel, but that cannot be true. All the angels of God are told to worship Jesus Christ (Hebrews 1:6), and we are specifically forbidden to worship angels (Revelation 22:8-9). We are to worship God alone, not what He created (Romans 1:25).

However, it is obvious by the description of this mighty angel that divine authority and attributes are being presented. Four things about this mighty angel lead many people to conclude that it is Jesus Christ.

The picture of divine characteristics connected with this angel. The angel is "clothed with a cloud," a symbol of divine presence (Exodus 40:34-38; Psalm 104:3; Daniel 7:13; Revelation 1:7). That this mighty angel was clothed with a cloud gives us reason for connecting him with the Lord Himself.

We are also told that "a rainbow was on his head." Revelation 4:3 revealed that there was "a rainbow around the throne" of God the Father, a picture of His faithfulness (Psalm 89). His promises will be fulfilled.

The statement that "his face was like the sun" reminds us of the description of Jesus Christ that "His countenance was like the sun shining in its strength" (1:16).

When it says that his feet were "like pillars of fire," we cannot help but relate it to the description of our Lord: "His feet were like fine brass, as if refined in a furnace" (1:15). There are similarities—but also differences in the two passages.

So is this a picture of Jesus Christ? Emphatically *no!* Jesus Christ is not described as an angel in the book of Revelation. He is Lord of the angels, using them to execute His judgment and purposes on the earth. Also this angel is described as "another mighty angel" (10:1), which means he is "another of the same kind." In Revelation 5:2 a "strong angel" proclaimed with a loud voice, "Who is worthy to open the scroll and to loose its seals?" Obviously, that strong angel is not Jesus Christ, the "Worthy One" to open the seals. The "strong angel" in chapter 10 is like the one previously mentioned in chapter 5. This angel is not Jesus Christ.

It is possible that this angel is Gabriel, if the one in chapter 5 is not him. Gabriel's name means "strength of God." It is also possible that this angel is Michael, the archangel, who appears in the book of Daniel as a special agent for the nation of Israel (Daniel 10:13; 12:1). Both

Gabriel and Michael are mentioned in the book of Daniel in connection with prophetic events. If the angel of Revelation 5 is Gabriel, then this angel is probably Michael, whose name means "Who is like God." This would explain some of his characteristics. God's presence, authority, and power are being pictured by this "mighty angel."

The presence of the little book open in his hand. The word for the seven-sealed scroll is different from that used for this little book, but that does not necessarily mean this book contains a different message. The size of the book may mean that most of the message has been revealed— only a small portion remains. Yet due to the importance of what remains (seventh trumpet), this dramatic interlude is given to John to impress upon him what is about to be revealed.

The place where the angel was standing. Verse 2 says "he set his right foot on the sea and his left foot on the land," picturing the sovereignty of God's authority and control over the whole earth. It apparently is a preview of the seventh trumpet's message that "the kingdoms of this world have become the kingdoms of our Lord and of His Christ, and He shall reign forever and ever!" (Revelation 11:15). This not only pictures the tremendous size of the mighty angel, but more likely emphasizes that the message that remains will impact the entire world.

The power of the angel's voice. The angel's cry is likened to a lion roaring. God's anger is described as the roaring of a lion, especially when he is ready to devour (Job 4:9-10; Hosea 5:14). He is often referred to as a lion roaring (Isaiah 31:4; Hosea 11:10; Amos 3:8), emphasizing the importance of His message and the power and majesty of His authority and sovereignty over all.

The Instruction about the Seven Thunders

The angel's voice was also accompanied by the sound of seven thunders who "uttered their voices." Such "thunders" do come forth from the throne of God (4:5) and dramatically emphasize the importance of God's message and purposes (cf. 8:5). The number seven could emphasize the completeness of the message or be a symbolic number that points to the voice of God Himself. Psalm 29:3 says the "God of glory thunders," speaking of the power of His voice.

As John prepared to write the message which the seven thunders uttered, another voice stopped him and said: "Seal up the things which the seven thunders uttered, and do not write them." This is quite unusual in that the book of Revelation is designed to reveal, not conceal, God's plans and future events.

171

It is difficult to understand why this message was "off limits" to John and all future readers. Some have speculated that the message deals with the terrible suffering God's people will endure during the last half of the tribulation.

The Announcement of This Mighty Angel
(10:5-7)

⁵And the angel whom I saw standing on the sea and on the land lifted up his hand to heaven ⁶and swore by Him who lives forever and ever, who created heaven and the things that are in it, the earth and the things that are in it, and the sea and the things that are in it, that there should be delay no longer, ⁷but in the days of the sounding of the seventh angel, when he is about to sound, the mystery of God would be finished, as He declared to His servants the prophets.

The Announcement Is Based on
God's Authority

The angel swears by God Who created all things; he could swear by none greater (Hebrews 6:13-18). The angel swears by the Creator, emphasizing God's authority behind what is to take place. The importance of God's character and promises are being illustrated here. God will not lie. The end is coming; God's purposes will be fulfilled on this planet.

The Announcement Is Based on
God's Timing

The angel announces that "there should be delay no longer." God is now ready to complete His predicted plans for judging this world and to answer the prayers of the saints (6:9-11). Human history operates according to Divine plan. Although at times we wonder if God knows or cares about what is taking place on earth, the Bible assures us that He does. Psalm 135:6 says, "Whatever the LORD pleases He does, / In heaven and in earth."

The events remaining on God's calendar, which are described in the little book, will happen "in the days of the sounding of the seventh angel." These days will cover the last three-and-a- half years of the tribulation period. Revelation 11:15 announces the sounding of the seventh trumpet, but the words "it is done" do not appear until the seventh and last plague (16:17).

The Announcement Is Based on God's Promise

The promise of God is described as "the mystery of God," that which "He declared to His servants the prophets" (10:7). The long-standing promise of God is about to be fulfilled. No longer mysterious and hidden, God now reveals what He will do.

It is a mystery about God Himself as well as His plans. The prophets knew portions of this mystery, but did not understand it in its complete fulfillment. According to Revelation 11:15, this mystery of God includes the fact that the kingdoms of this world will become the kingdom of our Lord and of His Christ. The mystery involves the establishment of God's kingdom on earth with His Son, Jesus Christ our Lord, ruling and reigning over all. The mystery includes how this will all take place. The prophets predicted it would come, but did not have all the details which the book of Revelation will now give us.

The Application of the Angel's Message to John (10:8-11)

> ⁸*Then the voice which I heard from heaven spoke to me again and said, "Go, take the little book which is open in the hand of the angel who stands on the sea and on the earth."* ⁹*And I went to the angel and said to him, "Give me the little book." And he said to me, "Take and eat it; and it will make your stomach bitter, but it will be as sweet as honey in your mouth."* ¹⁰*And I took the little book out of the angel's hand and ate it, and it was as sweet as honey in my mouth. But when I had eaten it, my stomach became bitter.* ¹¹*And he said to me, "You must prophesy again about many peoples, nations, tongues, and kings."*

The Message Illustrates a Previous Revelation

The unusual action John took in eating the little book is similar to the experience of the prophet Ezekiel:

> Now when I looked, there was a hand stretched out to me;
> and behold, a scroll of a book was in it. Then He spread it
> before me; and there was writing on the inside and on the
> outside, and written on it were lamentations and mourning
> and woe.
>
> Moreover He said to me, "Son of man, eat what you find;
> eat this scroll, and go, speak to the house of Israel." So I
> opened my mouth, and He caused me to eat that scroll.
> And He said to me, "Son of man, feed your belly, and fill
> your stomach with this scroll that I give you." So I ate it,
> and it was in my mouth like honey in sweetness (2:9-3:3).

Although the message of the scroll Ezekiel was instructed to eat
contained lamentations, mourning, and woe, it was sweet to his taste.
God's Word is like that (Psalm 19:10; Jeremiah 15:16).

In Ezekiel's day, God's judgment fell upon the people of Israel;
Babylon destroyed Jerusalem and the temple of Solomon in 586 B.C.
The symbol of eating the scroll pictures the complete assimilation of
the message of the Lord. The prophet who proclaims the message is
not unrelated to its impact. It becomes a part of him.

The Message Involves a
Twofold Response

Unlike Ezekiel's response, John experiences both sweetness and bitterness. To hear God's Word and to know that He will fulfill His promises and judge this sinful world is sweet news to the believer's ears.
But the longer we contemplate what God will do, the more we see
that the bitter is mixed with the sweet. God's people will suffer greatly
during the tribulation period. We rejoice that God's plan is fulfilled
and His righteous judgment executed, but we also grieve to see what
His people will suffer.

Perhaps the full impact of what John experienced is a reminder to
all who proclaim God's wonderful Word and speak of His coming
judgment and wrath. We must speak it with a measure of sorrow and
bitterness. A broken heart is a prerequisite to the proclamation of
God's judgment and wrath.

The Message Indicates a
Special Responsibility

John is told that he must continue (v. 11). His hesitation no doubt came from his bitter stomach as he realized the awful suffering the tribulation will bring. But the angel now orders him to continue.

The words "You *must* prophesy" remind all preachers of God's Word that we cannot compromise. God's Word must be proclaimed no matter how it affects or offends people. We should speak God's truth in love, of course, but there is too much compromise in the pulpits of our churches. The Bible's message on judgment, God's wrath, and hell is rarely heard or understood by today's culture. Yet there is no message more important for our world than that which Revelation clearly presents. May God help us to be faithful to it and to heed what it says.

Chapter 19

The Two Witnesses and the Temple of God

(11:1-19)

This chapter is crucial to the various interpretations of the book of Revelation. It is a part of the sixth trumpet judgment, the second woe (cf. 11:14 with 9:13). After John was told that he must prophesy again (10:11), chapter 11 opens with a strange request for John to measure the temple, its altar, and its worshipers. Before the seventh angel sounds his trumpet, John is given a picture of what will happen in the city of Jerusalem during the tribulation period. The discussion centers around the ministry of two witnesses.

The Two Witnesses and the Temple of God
(11:1-14)

[1] Then I was given a reed like a measuring rod. And the angel stood, saying, "Rise and measure the temple of God, the altar, and those who worship there. [2] But leave out the court which is outside the temple, and do not measure it, for it has been given to the Gentiles. And they will tread the holy city underfoot for forty-two months. [3] And I will give power to my two witnesses, and they will prophesy one thousand two hundred and sixty days, clothed in sackcloth." [4] These are the two olive trees and the two lampstands standing before the God of the earth. [5] And if anyone wants to harm them, fire proceeds from their mouth and devours their enemies. And if anyone wants to harm them, he must be killed in this manner. [6] These have power to shut heaven, so that no rain falls in the days of their prophecy; and they have power over waters to turn

them to blood, and to strike the earth with all plagues, as often as they desire.

[7]Now when they finish their testimony, the beast that ascends out of the bottomless pit will make war against them, overcome them, and kill them. [8]And their dead bodies will lie in the street of the great city which spiritually is called Sodom and Egypt, where also our Lord was crucified. [9]Then those from the peoples, tribes, tongues, and nations will see their dead bodies three and a half days, and not allow their dead bodies to be put into graves. [10]And those who dwell on the earth will rejoice over them, make merry, and send gifts to one another, because these two prophets tormented those who dwell on the earth.

[11]Now after the three and a half days the breath of life from God entered them, and they stood on their feet, and great fear fell on those who saw them. [12]And they heard a loud voice from heaven saying to them, "Come up here." And they ascended to heaven in a cloud, and their enemies saw them. [13]In the same hour there was a great earthquake, and a tenth of the city fell. In the earthquake seven thousand men were killed, and the rest were afraid and gave glory to the God of heaven. [14]The second woe is past. Behold, the third woe is coming quickly.

The Measuring of the Temple of God (11:1-2)

Two major questions face us as we begin our study of chapter 11: (1) Will a temple be rebuilt in Jerusalem during the tribulation? and (2) Why were the temple, its altar, and the worshipers measured?

The word for "temple" refers to the holy place where only the priests could go. It does not refer to the entire temple complex. The "altar" could refer to the brazen altar which stands outside the holy place or the altar of incense, the only altar inside the holy place.

The current situation in Jerusalem as it relates to this prophecy (11:1-2) is not clear. There are rumors and reports constantly from both Jewish and Christian circles about efforts to restore the temple. There are great arguments and debates over the exact location of the Holy of holies into which only the high priest could go once a year on the day of atonement (Yom Kippur). Jews have a holy and awesome fear of accidentally stepping on such sacred ground.

An additional problem is that a Moslem shrine, the Dome of the Rock, sits upon the temple mount. Though perhaps not the exact ancient site of the Holy of holies, it is obviously quite near it, and any efforts to build a Jewish temple close to it would be met with great resistance by Arab nations.

Does the Bible teach that a temple will be rebuilt in Jerusalem during the tribulation period? Daniel 9:27 implies that a temple will be rebuilt and be in existence during the tribulation period, though it could be built many years before the tribulation period begins:

> "Then he [Antichrist] shall confirm a covenant
>   with many for one week [seven years];
> But in the middle of the week
> He shall bring an end to sacrifice and offering.
> And on the wing of abominations
>   shall be one who makes desolate,
> Even until the consummation, which is determined,
> Is poured out on the desolate."

Jesus referred to this verse when He said, "Therefore when you see the *'abomination of desolation,'* spoken of by Daniel the prophet, standing in the holy place . . . then let those who are in Judea flee to the mountains" (Matthew 24:15-16).

The "abomination of desolation" is referring to a coming world ruler who makes an agreement with the nation of Israel to restore their ancient temple sacrificial system and then breaks his agreement halfway through its time frame of seven years.

Daniel 12:11 adds further proof that a temple will be rebuilt and the ancient sacrificial system restored when it says, "And from the time that the daily sacrifice is taken away, and the abomination of desolation is set up, there shall be one thousand two hundred and ninety days."

Second Thessalonians 2:4 adds conclusive proof that a temple will be rebuilt when it says this coming world leader "opposes and exalts himself above all that is called God or that is worshiped, so that he sits as God in the temple of God, showing himself that he is God." This world ruler, who appears initially to be on Israel's side, will set himself up as one worthy of worship and will literally desecrate the holy temple of the Jews by going into its Holy of holies, an act reserved only for the high priest. Such blasphemy and arrogance will come as a shock to the Jewish people who have supported his efforts and encouragement to rebuild their temple and restore their ancient sacrificial system.

The Two Witnesses and the Temple of God

Why measure the temple? It is possible the instruction to measure the temple suggests what the last part of verse 2 reveals. The Gentiles will once again take control of Jerusalem and its holy sites. Because of the reference to the temple worshipers, the measurement indicates God's protection of His people during such a Gentile takeover. As Israel was uniquely separated from the Egyptians' suffering under the plagues in Moses' day, so the godly Jews of the tribulation period will be set apart by God and divinely protected. The act of measuring the temple circumscribes an area that uniquely belongs to God. Similar incidents occur elsewhere in Scripture (Zechariah 2, Ezekiel 40, Revelation 21).

The Gentiles take Jerusalem. Jesus predicted that Jerusalem would be in Gentile hands until the "times of the Gentiles" were fulfilled or ended (Luke 21:24). The times of the Gentiles end with the coming of the Messiah (at the end of the tribulation period) to set up His kingdom on earth, thus fulfilling the promise of God to His people Israel.

Israel maintains control over the city of Jerusalem at the present time. Their control requires a delicate balance between their own desires and their relationships with the nations of the world who seem to desire Jerusalem as an international city, open and available to all nations and religions. In order to maintain peace with their Arab neighbors, Israel must tolerate conditions they personally find quite undesirable. According to the Bible, it will take an agreement by a great Western power to secure the peace of this strategic part of the world. After three and a half years, this leader will break the terms of the agreement, and Gentiles will once again control the city and its holy places.

The "forty-two months" of Revelation 11:2 refer to the last half of the tribulation period, a time described by ancient Hebrew prophets as a time of trouble and distress for the people of Israel. They will be persecuted and will escape to the mountains and wilderness for protection. (More about that when we come to Revelation 12.)

The Message of the Two Witnesses (11:3)

I love to preach and proclaim the Bible to people. It is the great joy of my life, and it is exciting to see what God does through the simple presentation of His truth. The Bible *is* the power of God (Romans 1:16)—I don't make it powerful. The Bible is the incorruptible seed that produces spiritual life (1 Peter 1:22-25).

When we examine the powerful preaching of these two witnesses in the tribulation period, we must conclude that this is a ministry unlike anything we have seen. They are able to do things we cannot do, and the whole world becomes much aware of their abilities and the seriousness of their message. In unbelief, the world will rejoice when they are dead, no longer troubling them with their message and miracles.

According to verse 3, they will prophesy for 1260 days, or forty-two months, or three and a half years. Their preaching takes place in the first half of the tribulation period. We are not told much about people's response to their message, but we do know that 144,000 Jews will also put their faith in the Messiah, be protected by God during the days of the tribulation, and proclaim His message to the whole world. It is possible this group of Jews respond to the preaching of the two witnesses. Perhaps their message will also influence many Gentiles to become believers in the Messiah (cf. Revelation 7).

The message the two witnesses preach is a message of repentance. They are clothed in sackcloth, the garment worn by the prophets of God who preached repentance. It is the garment that suggests the need to mourn and lament over our sins and to get right with God. John the Baptist and Jesus Himself preached a message of repentance saying, "repent for the kingdom of heaven is at hand."

**The Meaning of the
Two Witnesses (11:4)**

Verse 4 is a reference to Zechariah 4, the clue we need to determine the identity and purpose of the two witnesses. The prophet Zechariah preached a message of repentance to the people of Israel during the days of the Babylonian captivity. His inspired proclamations and visions encouraged the people to return to the land of Israel and to rebuild the temple destroyed by Babylon in 586 B.C. In his vision recorded in Zechariah 4, he saw a lampstand of solid gold with a bowl on top of it. There were seven lamps with seven pipes connected to the bowl of oil. On either side of the lampstand were two olive trees from which two gold pipes carried oil to the bowl on top of the lampstand.

John's reference to the "two olive trees and the two lampstands" is an allusion to Joshua and Zerubbabel in Zechariah's vision. Joshua and Zerubbabel were the leaders (one civic and one religious) who would take the people back to Israel and inspire them to rebuild the fallen ruins of the temple. Zerubbabel would lay the foundation of the temple and also finish it (Zechariah 4:9). When the final stone would be set in place, there would be shouts of "Grace, grace" to emphasize that God's Spirit enabled them to achieve this tremendous goal (vv. 6-7).

This historical incident points to a future day when the temple would be rebuilt. Just as Zerubbabel and Joshua were used by the Lord to challenge the people to return and rebuild the temple, it is possible the two witnesses of Revelation 11 will have the same impact upon the Jewish people of the tribulation period. Perhaps it is their preaching that motivates the Jews to rebuild the temple once again.

Revelation 11:4 calls the two witnesses "two lampstands" as well as "two olive trees." There was only one lampstand in the prophecy of Zechariah 4. This distinction reveals that we are not to make the two passages identical, but rather to see that the one illustrates the other.

Just as the oil provides the resources to make the lampstand shine brightly, so the Holy Spirit causes our lives to bear witness effectively. The two witnesses of Revelation 11 are the means God uses to bring His message to the world, and perhaps in a restricted sense to the nation of Israel and the 144,000 Jews, during the tribulation period.

Who are these two witnesses? Attempts to identify these two witnesses have led to a wide variety of interpretations, including a symbolic approach that sees them as representatives of Israel and the church or Israel and the Word of God. Some believe that these witnesses are two unique individuals who have never before existed. Others connect them with leaders from Israel's past. Suggestions include the reappearance of Zerubbabel and Joshua (obvious connection with the prophecies of Zechariah), Enoch and Elijah (two men who were taken to heaven by unusual circumstances), and Moses and Elijah (based on statements in v. 6).

A strong case can be made for Moses and Elijah, the one representing the law and the other the prophets. The miraculous powers mentioned in 11:6 certainly point to these two men. It was Moses and Elijah who appeared with Jesus Christ on the mount of transfiguration (Matthew 17:3). Two witnesses told the women at the tomb of Jesus that He had risen from the dead (Luke 24:4-7). Two men in white apparel also appeared to the disciples at the ascension of Jesus into heaven, reminding them of His second coming (Acts 1:9-11). It is possible these two witnesses who appear on several occasions are the same two individuals in Revelation 11.

The prophet Elijah is to appear on the scene of human history before the Messiah returns to the earth:

> "Behold, I will send you Elijah the prophet
> Before the coming of the great and dreadful day
>   of the LORD.

And he will turn
The hearts of the fathers to the children,
And the hearts of the children to their fathers,
Lest I come and strike the earth with a curse."

(Malachi 4:5-6)

The angel who announced the coming birth of John the Baptist makes mention of Malachi's prophecy when describing the ministry of John, who would come "in the spirit and power of Elijah" (Luke 1:17). Jesus said in Matthew 11:14, "And if you are willing to receive it, he [referring to John the Baptist] is Elijah who is to come." If the people of Israel had repented and received the message of the coming King and His kingdom, then John the Baptist would have fulfilled the prophecy concerning Elijah's ministry before the coming of the Lord. Since they did not, we still wait for the return of the Messiah and the coming of the prophet Elijah before that glorious day arrives. At a Jewish passover celebration, a young child is sent to the door to see if Elijah has come yet. That symbolic action reminds us of Malachi's prophecy.

The Protection of the
Two Witnesses (11:5)

One would not want to harm these witnesses! God supernaturally protects them by giving them awesome power. Death will come to anyone who even wants to harm them. Another reason for believing these two witnesses are Moses and Elijah is the fact that a similar fate befell their enemies in the Old Testament (Numbers 16:35; 2 Kings 1:10-12).

The Power of the
Two Witnesses (11:6)

One cannot help but associate the two witnesses' demonstrations of power with the work of Elijah and Moses. The witnesses' power to "shut heaven, so that no rain falls in the days of their prophecy," reflects the same kind of power displayed by Elijah the prophet (James 5:17-18). And it was Moses who struck the waters of Egypt so that they "were turned to blood" (Exodus 7:20). Moses was involved in the plagues of Egypt, and the words of verse 6 forcefully remind us of him.

The Killing of the
Two Witnesses (11:7-10)

The person who kills them. This is the first of thirty-six references in Revelation to "the beast." Some Bible teachers believe this beast is Satan. They speak of three kinds of beasts: Satan, the beast out of the bottomless pit (11:7); the Antichrist, the beast out of the sea (13:1); and the false prophet, the beast coming up out of the earth (13:11). While interesting to see this unholy trinity in such a light, it seems better to understand the beast out of the bottomless pit as the Antichrist who is energized by Satan himself. According to Revelation 17:8, the "beast that you saw was, and is not, and will ascend out of the bottomless pit." Here is a clear reference to the coming world ruler we call the Antichrist.

That the Antichrist kills the two witnesses is amazing indeed since they are able to destroy their enemies with fire from their mouths. But the Antichrist is empowered by Satan, and in God's will and plan, their testimony is completed. Other events will yet take place following their restoration to life.

The place their bodies are displayed. The term "great city" appears ten times in Revelation. It is used of the new Jerusalem, the heavenly city (21:10) as well as the city of Babylon (14:8; 16:19; 17:18; 18:10, 16, 18, 19, 21). The Lord has His great city and Satan has one as well. Satan's will fall, and God will honor His city by bringing a new Jerusalem out of heaven to the earth, the most beautiful city ever designed.

The city depicted here is the earthly Jerusalem, the place "where also our Lord was crucified." It is interesting that Jerusalem is also called "Sodom and Egypt" during the tribulation period. The word "spiritually" indicates that the spiritual condition of the city is like that of Sodom, with all of its wickedness and immorality, and Egypt, a symbol of oppression and slavery. How sad that Jerusalem has become that by the middle of the tribulation period. In some respects, the city is becoming like that today.

The publicity the two witnesses receive. For three and a half days all the peoples, tribes, tongues, and nations of the world will see their dead bodies. Before television and satellites, this prediction seemed impossible. People will be so thrilled to see them dead no burial will be allowed.

The reason for all this celebration is simply stated—"these two prophets tormented those who dwell on the earth" (v. 10). Unbelievers are "tormented" by a message of repentance. The prophets of God have been killed throughout history. The world is no friend to God or to His messengers. Hebrews 11:35-38 speaks of the way the prophets of God have been treated in the past and concludes "the world was not worthy" of them.

The Resurrection of the Two Witnesses (11:11-13)

The witnesses preached for three and a half years, and their bodies lay in the street for three and a half days. In the midst of the world's celebration of their deaths, God miraculously intervenes (the "breath of life from God entered them"). What a wonderful encouragement to all of us today. We too shall rise; resurrection day is coming (Romans 8:11)! The two witnesses remind us that the harvest, of which Jesus Christ was the firstfruits, is about to be reaped (1 Corinthians 15:23).

The "loud voice from heaven" gives the same command as was given to John in 4:1—"Come up here." Their ascension was much like the ascension of Jesus Christ in that it was visible to those present. When believers are resurrected at the rapture, it will happen "in a moment, in the twinkling of an eye" (1 Corinthians 15:52). The loud voice is probably the voice of God Himself or possibly the voice of the archangel (1 Thessalonians 4:16).

The results upon earth are interesting indeed—a great earthquake kills seven thousand men, and those that remain are fearful and give glory to God. The earthquake dramatizes this event as truly an action of God. It is also interesting to see that a great earthquake occurs at the sixth seal judgment, the sixth trumpet judgment, and the last plague judgment.

Bible teachers disagree about the meaning of "the rest were afraid and gave glory to the God of heaven." Does this indicate that a remnant of Jewish people in Israel will believe in the Messiah because of this event? Is this reverential fear and worship of the Lord or merely human fright over the terrible earthquake and the loss of lives?

I believe the phrase "gave glory to the God of heaven" implies a fear that leads to salvation. In Revelation 14:6-7, an angel preaches the everlasting gospel to all the world and says, "Fear God and give glory to Him, for the hour of His judgment has come; and worship Him who made heaven and earth, the sea and springs of water." This usage of the phrase "fear God and give glory to him" is clearly associated with worship. Thus I believe the resurrection of the two witnesses and the subsequent earthquake causes a remnant of Jewish people in Jerusalem to believe in the Lord and give him glory.

The Two Witnesses and the Temple of God

We were all designed to glorify God (Revelation 4:10-11). Where do we really stand? Have we committed our lives and futures to Him? Do we purpose in our hearts to glorify God in all we say and do (1 Corinthians 10:31)?

The Third Woe Is Coming (11:14)

Much has transpired since the sixth trumpet was blown. It all started in Revelation 9:13 with the invasion of a great army that kills one-third of the human race. Now the announcement comes that the seventh and last of the trumpets is to be blown. According to Revelation 10:7 it will be "in the days of the sounding of the seventh angel" that the "mystery of God would be finished."

Seventh Trumpet Judgment: The Majesty of God and His Plan (11:15-19)

[15] Then the seventh angel sounded: And there were loud voices in heaven, saying, "The kingdoms of this world have become the kingdoms of our Lord and of His Christ, and He shall reign forever and ever!" [16] And the twenty-four elders who sat before God on their thrones fell on their faces and worshiped God, [17] saying:

"We give You thanks, O Lord God Almighty,
The One who is and who was and who is
to come,
Because You have taken Your great power
and reigned.
[18] The nations were angry, and Your wrath
has come,
And the time of the dead, that they should
be judged,
And that You should reward Your servants
the prophets and the saints,
And those who fear Your name, small and
great,
And should destroy those who destroy the
earth."

[19] Then the temple of God was opened in heaven, and the ark of His covenant was seen in His temple. And there

were lightnings, noises, thunderings, an earthquake, and great hail.

The sounding of the seventh trumpet continues over the last three and a half years of the tribulation period. Its message covers all that transpires during the last half of the tribulation, right up to the great and long-awaited event of the second coming of Jesus Christ.

The Extent of His Majesty (11:15)

What a marvelous statement to begin the events of the seventh trumpet and the last half of the tribulation period. God announces that He is taking over! The prophets spoke of the "kingdoms" of this world being conquered by the coming kingdom of the Messiah (Daniel 2:44; 7:14; Zechariah 14:9).

The kingdom is jointly held by the Lord and His Christ, and 1 Corinthians 15:24 speaks of the time when the Messiah will deliver the kingdom to God the Father.

The Exaltation of His Majesty (11:16-18)

Upon hearing the "loud voices" announcing that God is taking over and the kingdom of the Messiah will come to earth, the twenty-four elders in heaven (representing the church of Jesus Christ) respond with praise and adoration to God.

The response that is given. The number one priority of every believer should be the worship and praise of Almighty God. We were created to worship the God Who made us. The action of falling down on their faces demonstrates a clear understanding of God's greatness and the believer's humility before God. The worship they expressed was a giving of thanks. Thanksgiving is the sacrifice God wants from our lips (Hebrews 13:15). We need more of that attitude and response in our lives today. God is to be glorified, not man.

The reasons for their exaltation of God. The reasons for praising and worshiping God are clearly given here and serve as a constant reminder to all believers of what God truly wants from us.

1. God's power is being proclaimed (17b). Revelation 13:7 says of the coming Antichrist, "And authority was given him over every tribe, tongue, and nation." But according to Revelation 19:20 he will be captured and along with the false prophet be thrown into the lake of fire. Revelation 20:6 reminds us that believers shall reign with Jesus Christ for a thousand years. Here the twenty-four elders give thanks to the Lord that He will reign over the entire earth, a kingdom that will be set up immediately following the great tribulation.

2. God's plan is being accomplished (18a). Here is a reference to the rebellion of the nations during the coming tribulation period, a fulfillment of Psalm 2:1-6. Revelation 19:15 says Jesus Christ Himself will tread "the winepress of the fierceness and wrath of Almighty God."

The reference to the judging of the dead reminds us all of the ultimate accountability we have to God. One day even the unbelievers of this world will stand before God to be judged (Revelation 20). It is possible verse 18 is referring to the resurrection of the righteous dead, including Old Testament believers (Daniel 12:1-3) and tribulation believers (Revelation 20:6). However, since the next phrase speaks of rewarding the servants of God, it is best to consider this a reference to the judgment of the wicked dead.

3. God's promise is being fulfilled (18b). The reward of God is a great reason to give thanks! Believers will be rewarded by God, and that fact alone should cause us to give thanks to Him (Hebrews 6:10; Matthew 25:21-23, 34-40; Mark 10:29-31; Revelation 22:12).

4. God's punishment is being declared (18c). The wicked do not escape the judgment of God. No one gets away with anything. God will punish unbelievers for what they have done (2 Thessalonians 1:8-9).

The Expression of His Majesty (11:19)

How fascinating to observe that Revelation 11 opens with a temple on earth and ends with the temple of God in heaven. Revelation 15:5 tells us "the temple of the tabernacle of the testimony in heaven was opened." Out of this temple come the seven angels with the seven last plagues. In the new Jerusalem, there will be no temple (Revelation 21:22). Hebrews 8 and 9 tell us that the earthly temple was a copy of the heavenly.

Notice two things that express the majesty of God from this final verse of chapter 11:

A visual reminder of God's sovereignty and faithfulness. The temple of God was opened in heaven, reminding us that heaven is a place of worship and the place from which God rules and reigns in the events of this planet. The ark of His covenant reminds us of His faithfulness and abiding presence (Psalm 89) and that His long-awaited promises are now about to be fulfilled. Any earthly replicas fade into insignificance in the light of this heavenly ark. Inside the ark were three items: the law written on tablets of stone, a reminder of God's holy and righteous character; Aaron's rod that budded, an item pointing to the resurrection; and a pot of manna, reminding us that our Lord is the Bread of Life.

A dramatic response to emphasize God's power and judgment that will come upon the earth. In chapter 4 there were "lightnings, thunderings, and voices" that came from the throne of God the Father. In chapter 8 there were "noises, thunderings, lightnings, and an earthquake" just preceding the seven angels with the seven trumpets announcing the judgments of God. In chapter 16 there were "noises and thunderings and lightnings; and there was a great earthquake" when the last plague is brought to the earth. This remarkable display of the forces of nature is clearly a sign that God's judgment has come.

Revelation 11 is a crucial chapter. It marks a dividing point between the first half and the second half of the tribulation period. It reveals that the Jewish people will rebuild the temple in Jerusalem. It reminds us all that God is in control and that the kingdoms of this world are under His direction. The remaining chapters will show how God is going to bring His final judgments upon the earth and set up His kingdom and eternal reign through the return of His Son Jesus Christ, our Lord and Savior. Have you made your personal commitment to Him? We are closer to His return today than we were yesterday!

Chapter 20

Satan's War against Israel

(12:1-17)

The nation of Israel has a prominent place in God's plan for human history. In one respect, all human history is vitally related to the history and destiny of the people of Israel. God's promise to Abraham (Genesis 12:1-3) reveals that all nations of the world will be blessed through the descendants of Abraham.

According to the Bible, Satan has a deep hatred of the Jewish people and has sought by many means to destroy them. God has never allowed that to happen, though some political leaders have dedicated themselves to eliminating Israel from the face of the earth. Those leaders have perished as will all who curse Abraham's descendants (Genesis 12:3). God is committed to their survival and future glory. He will one day restore the kingdom to Israel, and a Jewish Messiah will rule from Jerusalem over the entire world. Naturally, many Gentiles do not appreciate such words nor do they believe that such a prophecy will ever be fulfilled.

In Revelation 12, details about Israel's troubles and survival during the tribulation period are given. The nation is represented by a woman with a special child, who is none other than the Messiah Himself.

The Woman, the Child, and the Dragon
(12:1-6)

¹Now a great sign appeared in heaven: a woman clothed with the sun, with the moon under her feet, and on her head a garland of twelve stars. ²Then being with child, she cried out in labor and in pain to give birth. ³And another sign appeared in heaven: behold, a great, fiery red

> *dragon having seven heads and ten horns, and seven diadems on his heads. [4]His tail drew a third of the stars of heaven and threw them to the earth. And the dragon stood before the woman who was ready to give birth, to devour her Child as soon as it was born. [5]And she bore a male Child who was to rule all nations with a rod of iron. And her Child was caught up to God and to His throne. [6]Then the woman fled into the wilderness, where she has a place prepared by God, that they should feed her there one thousand two hundred and sixty days.*

The Sign of the Woman (12:1-2, 5-6)

Her connection with religion. A woman is often used to symbolize a religious system or set of beliefs. In Revelation 2, a woman named Jezebel is used to picture false teaching and immorality. In Revelation 17, "the great harlot" is used to picture the false religious system that will dominate the world in endtimes. Believers in Jesus Christ are referred to as the "wife" of the Lamb (19:7), and the heavenly city, the new Jerusalem, is described as "the bride, the Lamb's wife" (21:9). Likewise Israel is described as the wife of the Lord and often as a wife who has departed from her husband (Jeremiah 3). It is, therefore, quite reasonable for this woman to refer to Israel or at least to stand as a symbol of some religious system or group of people.

Verse 1 says this is "a great sign in heaven," the first of seven "signs" that occur in the book of Revelation (12:1, 3; 13:13-14; 15:1; 16:14; 19:20). That is further reason for seeing this woman as symbolic. It becomes clear from what follows that she symbolizes the nation of Israel.

Her clothing. Unusual attempts have been made in the past to identify this woman. The Roman Catholic Church has stated that the woman represents the Virgin Mary. Mary Baker Eddy, founder of Christian Science, claimed she was the woman of Revelation 12, and the child the religious system of Christian Science.

However, the description of the sun, moon, and twelve stars makes the identification clear. It is a reference to Joseph's dream in which the sun, moon, and stars—representing Joseph's father, mother, and brothers—bowed down to him (Genesis 37:9-11). Jacob had twelve sons, including Joseph, representing the heads of the twelve tribes of Israel. The woman of Revelation 12 is the nation of Israel.

Her cries of labor pain. At the time of the birth of Jesus Christ, Israel was in a great deal of pain. They were under the heel of Rome, and they had suffered much under Rome's rule. It is understandable why some consider the woman to be the Virgin Mary in that she indeed did give birth to the Messiah. But this refers to the nation's travail, not to Mary's. The Messiah is the child of the nation Israel as well as the child of Mary.

Her Child.

1. The Child's authority. The statement that the Child will "rule all nations with a rod of iron" clearly identifies Him as the promised Messiah. In Psalm 2 we read of the kings and rulers taking counsel against the Lord and His Anointed (Messiah). The Lord says to His Anointed (vv. 7-9):

> "You are My Son,
> Today I have begotten You.
> Ask of Me, and I will give You
> The nations for Your inheritance,
> And the ends of the earth for Your possession.
> You shall break them with a rod of iron;
> You shall dash them in pieces like a
>   potter's vessel."

Revelation 19:15 says specifically that Jesus Christ "will rule [the nations] with a rod of iron" when He returns to the earth at the end of the tribulation. A shepherd carries a rod and a staff (Psalm 23:4); one is for correction (rod) and the other for protection (staff). The rod is a symbol of judgment and correction. When God judges Israel He says, "I will make you pass under the rod" (Ezekiel 20:37).

2. The Child's ascension. Some object to the usage of the word "caught up" as referring to the ascension. The Greek word used here means "to seize" or "to rescue from danger." Can that apply to His ascension to heaven? It appears so. In 1 Thessalonians 4:17, this same word is used for the rapture of believers when the church is caught up to heaven. It is also used of Paul being caught up to paradise or the third heaven (2 Corinthians 12:2, 4).

That the Child was "caught up to God and His throne" settles the question. Who else would be caught up to the very throne of God? It implies an honor and position that could only be given to our Lord Jesus Christ, the true Messiah of Israel.

Her care by God during the tribulation.

1. The place. Jesus said in Matthew 24:16, "let those who are in Judea flee to the mountains." As any traveler in Israel knows, the Judean wilderness is full of mountains.

The fascinating point about the place is that it is "prepared by God." This phrase appears only one other time—when Jesus said, "I go to prepare a place for you" (John 14:2-3). There it is a reference to the "mansions" (dwelling-places) of our "Father's house," heaven itself. God's loving care for Israel is unmistakable. He has prepared a place for His people in the wilderness—a place of protection and provision during the awful days of the tribulation which will bring much suffering to Israel.

2. The purpose. The Lord took care of Israel in the wilderness in the days of Moses by providing food (manna) from the sky. God will once again take care of His people when they flee to the wilderness to hide from satanic pressure and attacks during the last half of the tribulation.

The Sign of the Dragon (12:3-4)

The identity of the dragon. The *context* leaves no doubt as to the dragon's identity. Verse 9 says he is "that serpent of old, called the Devil and Satan, who deceives the whole world." The "serpent of old" reminds us of Genesis 3 and proves conclusively that the talking serpent of that chapter was none other than the Devil himself.

The dragon's fiery red *color* reveals his real character. No doubt this pictures his murderous motivations. Jesus said in John 8:44 that the devil was a "murderer from the beginning." According to Revelation 9:11, this angel of the bottomless pit is a destroyer, as his names in Hebrew and Greek clearly indicate. He has murdered the people of God throughout history and has used wicked men to accomplish that purpose.

His *connection* with the beast—"having seven heads and ten horns" (cf. 13:1)—shows his involvement in the nations and governments of this world. Second Corinthians 4:4 calls him the "god of this age," and Ephesians 2:2 says he is "the prince of the power of the air, the spirit who now works in the sons of disobedience." The beast reveals Satan's involvement in the nations and governments of this world. Revelation 13:2 says "the dragon gave [the beast] his power, his throne, and great authority."

The *crowns* on his seven heads show Satan's power and authority over the major empires of the world. These "heads" represent the empires of world history, as we shall learn later. These heads belong in some sense to Satan Himself, though both he and the heads are allowed to function and exist under the overall direction and sovereignty of God Himself.

The influence of the dragon. The stars the dragon hurls down represent the angels who were cast out with Satan (12:9). As we've noted previously, the symbolism of "stars" representing angels is consistent throughout the book of Revelation. It is remarkable that Satan could influence one-third of all the angels to join him in his diabolical schemes. There are millions of angels, too many to count, and one-third of them are evil spirits! No wonder the Bible warns us about them and the need to be strong in the Lord (Ephesians 6:10-18).

The intent of the dragon. Satan's attempt to destroy the Child is a matter of historical record. Herod's murder of all the male children in Bethlehem who were two years old and under was a fulfillment of prophecy (Matthew 2:16-18), and represents the suffering of the Jewish people under Gentile domination, motivated by Satan himself.

The continual conflict between Satan and the Messiah was predicted in Genesis 3:15. God spoke these words directly to the serpent or Satan himself:

> "And I will put enmity
> Between you and the woman,
> And between your seed and her Seed;
> He shall bruise your head,
> And you shall bruise His heel."

This prophecy points to the death of Jesus Christ on the cross. Satan's apparent victory turned out to be his ultimate defeat. Jesus' death on the cross struck the fatal blow since our sins were paid for by His substitutionary atonement, a fact assured by our Lord's resurrection. What a wonderful salvation we enjoy!

Satan Thrown Out of Heaven
(12:7-12)

7And war broke out in heaven: Michael and his angels fought against the dragon; and the dragon and his angels fought, 8but they did not prevail, nor was a place found for them in heaven any longer. 9So the great dragon was cast out, that serpent of old, called the Devil and Satan, who deceives the whole world; he was cast to the earth, and his angels were cast out with him. [10] *Then I heard a loud voice saying in heaven, "Now salvation, and strength, and the kingdom of our God, and the power of His Christ have come, for the accuser of our brethren, who accused them before our God day and night, has been cast down.* [11] *And they overcame him by the blood of the Lamb and by the word of their testimony, and they did not love their lives to the death.* [12] *Therefore rejoice, O heavens, and you who dwell in them! Woe to the inhabitants of the earth and the sea! For the devil has come down to you, having great wrath, because he knows that he has a short time."*

The Struggle in Heaven (12:7-9)

Angels at war! It seems so incredible, and yet it makes sense if you know the teaching of the Bible regarding good and evil spirits. Evil angels or spirits (demons) are trying to defeat and destroy believers while good angels or spirits are defending and protecting them (Hebrews 1:14). In the tribulation, one great final battle settles the issue forever.

A fulfillment of prophecy. Daniel 12:1-2 speaks of the day when this battle would come:

> "At the time Michael shall stand up,
> The great prince who stands watch
>   over the sons of your people;
> And there shall be a time of trouble,
> Such as never was since there was a nation,
> Even to that time.
> And at that time your people shall be delivered,
> Every one who is found written in the book.

Michael has been in conflict with the devil in previous history (Jude 9) and a staunch defender of Israel (Daniel 10:13, 21). Furthermore, as we argued in our study of Revelation 10, he is the strong angel announcing God's plans to complete the mystery of God. Michael is the archangel of God connected with the rapture of the church when the Lord returns for the believers of this present age (1 Thessalonians 4:16-17).

The failure of satanic forces to overcome the plans and purposes of our God. Two things happened to Satan and his angels: They lost, and they were cast to the earth. Satan has had access to heaven until this moment.

God has tolerated his presence and accusations throughout history, but no more—he and his angels are cast out forever!

Satan is a conquered enemy (Romans 16:20; 1 John 4:4). His defeat was fully accomplished when Jesus died on the cross (John 12:31; Hebrews 2:14).

The fall of Satan and his angels. Many arguments have been given as to why and when Satan was cast out. Some say this event occurred between Genesis 1:1 and 1:2 and explains the chaotic condition of the earth and the age of dinosaurs, huge reptiles, and grotesque birds. It is often referred to as the "gap theory," and it connects Revelation 12:7-9 with Isaiah 14 and Ezekiel 28.

While the moral fall of Satan is implied by those two Hebrew prophets, a geographical relocation from heaven to earth does not occur until Revelation 12. In the book of Job, Satan still had access to the presence of the Lord; he had not yet been cast out. Based on Revelation 12:9, I believe Satan was not cast to the earth until the tribulation period. Satan and his angels fell into sin long before the events of Revelation 12, but it is here and only here that we learn of their removal from heaven to earth and access to heaven is denied forever (v. 8).

We discover three additional things about Satan from 12:9—he was directly involved in the temptation of Adam and Eve ("that serpent of old"), he is a slanderer and an adversary ("called the Devil and Satan"), and he deceives the whole world.

The Secret of Victory over the Devil (12:10-12)

Victory is based on the coming of the messianic kingdom. At the sounding of the seventh trumpet the pronouncement was made: "The kingdoms of this world have become the kingdoms of our Lord and of His Christ, and He shall reign forever and ever!" (11:15). The coming kingdom of the Messiah is the stone that crushes and destroys all the kingdoms of this world (Daniel 2:44-45). His kingdom is an everlasting kingdom that will never be destroyed. Satan's activity will be brought to an end when he is bound for a thousand years while Jesus Christ reigns on the earth (cf. 20:1-4).

Victory is based on the cleansing of the blood of Jesus Christ. What wonderful assurance comes as we read, "they overcame him by the blood of the Lamb and by the word of their testimony." The martyrs of the tribulation period are among those being assured in this text ("and they did not love their lives to the death"). But it is a promise that applies to all who have been accused by the devil.

The devil accuses the brethren and does so continually ("day and night"). He is the prosecuting attorney before the throne of God. But we have a defense attorney there who pleads our case, interceding for us—"Jesus Christ the righteous" (1 John 2:1-2). He is our Advocate and the propitiation for our sins. He satisfied the righteous demands and wrath of a holy God by paying the penalty for our sins with His own precious blood!

Victory is based on God's control of Satan and his wrath. The heavens rejoice over the removal of Satan and his angels, but earth is warned. The devil's wrath will be allowed to explode during the last half of the tribulation, and the people of God will suffer greatly with many suffering martyrdom. His wrath will be great because he knows his time is limited. What depravity this fallen angel possesses. He is not in control—God is!

The Suffering of the Jews
(12:13-17)

¹³ Now when the dragon saw that he had been cast to the earth, he persecuted the woman who gave birth to the male Child. ¹⁴ But the woman was given two wings of a great eagle, that she might fly into the wilderness to her place, where she is nourished for a time and times and half a time, from the presence of the serpent. ¹⁵ So the serpent spewed water out of his mouth like a flood after the woman, that he might cause her to be carried away by the flood. ¹⁶ But the earth helped the woman, and the earth opened its mouth and swallowed up the flood which the dragon had spewed out of his mouth. ¹⁷ And the dragon was enraged with the woman, and he went to make war with the rest of her offspring, who keep the commandments of God and have the testimony of Jesus Christ.

Israel has suffered greatly throughout history, having been the object of hatred by many nations and peoples. This anti-Semitism has been promoted and unleashed by Satan himself. Christian involvement in such persecution cannot be defended or justified in any way; such actions are deplorable and inexcusable.

The holocaust is a vivid memory for many Jewish people and is kept alive by the displays in the Yad Hashem memorial in Jerusalem. Many rabbinical interpretations have been given concerning that awful period of suffering, persecution, and death. Some believe it to be the fulfillment of the prophecies of Israel's final suffering, the "time of Jacob's trouble." This is understandable. Who wants to face such persecution and suffering again? But this passage indicates that a greater persecution is coming, instigated directly by Satan himself.

The Persecution Is Connected to the Messiah (12:13)

As was argued earlier, the woman here represents the nation Israel; Mary was never persecuted like this. That the nation "gave birth to the male child," the Messiah, is evidently the reason the devil is unleashing his fury against the Jewish people. It is a part of what Genesis 3:15 predicted, the constant enmity between the devil and the seed of the woman, the Messiah.

The Protection of God Will Be Given to the Jews (12:14-16)

God will "nourish" his people just as He cared for them during the days of their wilderness wanderings. God's protection of His people is a constant theme throughout the psalms of David.

The eagle of God's protection. This beautiful picture of the "wings of a great eagle" reminds the Jewish people of the past protection and care of the Lord (Exodus 19:4; Deuteronomy 32:10-12). God's care of Israel is like the eagle who takes care of its young ones. The Lord provides for His people.

The "wilderness" to which the Jewish people will flee is sometimes connected with the region of ancient Edom, Moab, and Ammon. Daniel 11:41 suggests these regions will "escape" from the conquest of the land of Israel in tribulation times. Perhaps it is for this reason that the people of Israel will hide in these regions from the terrible persecution that is coming.

The extent of God's protection. The word "nourished" is the same Greek word translated "feed" in verse 6, where we are told that the woman will be fed by God for 1260 days. Therefore, the phrase "a time and times and half a time" is a reference to three and a half years, the last half of the tribulation period. This same phrase appears in Daniel 7:25 and 12:7.

The example of God's protection. Does Satan cause a literal flood? Some believe so; others see it as a symbol of satanic attack. Under the symbolic view, the earth that swallows up the flood represents the difficult circumstances and terrain which must be faced when trying to pursue people in the wilderness. What is undisputed is that Satan is unleashing this effort to destroy the nation of Israel, and God in return is thwarting his attempts.

The Purposes of Satan Are Clearly Revealed (12:15, 17)

Satan begins his attack on the whole nation of Israel (v. 15). When this campaign is thwarted by the protection and intervention of God, he then turns his fury against the believers, "the rest of her offspring." This phrase would apply to Jewish believers in the tribulation but could also apply to Gentile believers. The martyrs of Revelation 6:9 are killed "for the word of God and for the testimony which they held." Revelation 14:12 speaks of the "patience of the saints" and describes them as "those who keep the commandments of God and the faith of Jesus." Since the ones mentioned in 12:17 "keep the commandments of God and have the testimony of Jesus Christ," they must be believers in Jesus Christ, either Jewish or Gentile. All Gentile believers are a part of the "offspring" of Israel. We are sons of Abraham by faith (Galatians 3:6-9).

The signs in heaven, the war in heaven, the persecution of Israel by Satan, all point to the last half of the tribulation period. Satan is in a rage toward God and His people. The next chapters will reveal the tools and people Satan will use to carry out his wrath. Nothing is a surprise to God, however. It is all taking place according to His plan and will accomplish His purposes.

Chapter 21

The Coming World Leaders

(13:1-18)

In Revelation 12, the dragon was described as having seven heads and ten horns. That description was a prelude to what we discover in chapter 13. It is Satan himself who brings two world leaders to power, one political and the other religious. Both are called "beasts," one "rising up out of the sea" (13:1) and the other "coming up out of the earth" (13:11). Some commentators add to these two "the beast that ascends out of the bottomless pit" (11:7) to form an unholy trinity. The line-up looks like this:

> First Beast (out of the bottomless pit): *Satan*
> Second Beast (out of the sea): *Antichrist*
> Third Beast (out of the earth): *False prophet*

While this provides an interesting analysis of these passages, Revelation 17:8 declares that the beast with seven heads and ten horns that becomes the final world ruler is also "out of the bottomless pit." They all, in fact, originate from the bottomless pit, demons of hell energized by Satan himself.

The World Political Leader
(13:1-10)

¹Then I stood on the sand of the sea. And I saw a beast rising up out of the sea, having seven heads and ten horns, and on his horns ten crowns, and on his heads a blasphemous name. ²Now the beast which I saw was like a leopard, his feet were like the feet of a bear, and his mouth like the mouth of a lion. And the dragon gave him his power,

his throne, and great authority. [3]*I saw one of his heads as if it had been mortally wounded, and his deadly wound was healed. And all the world marveled and followed the beast.* [4]*So they worshiped the dragon who gave authority to the beast; and they worshiped the beast, saying, "Who is like the beast? Who is able to make war with him?"* [5]*And he was given a mouth speaking great things and blasphemies, and he was given authority to continue for forty-two months.* [6]*Then he opened his mouth in blasphemy against God, to blaspheme His name, His tabernacle, and those who dwell in heaven.* [7]*And it was granted to him to make war with the saints and to overcome them. And authority was given him over every tribe, tongue, and nation.* [8]*And all who dwell on the earth will worship him, whose names have not been written in the Book of Life of the Lamb slain from the foundation of the world.* [9]*If anyone has an ear, let him hear.* [10]*He who leads into captivity shall go into captivity; he who kills with the sword must be killed with the sword. Here is the patience and the faith of the saints.*

The Identity of the Beast (13:1-3)

In Revelation 17:15 the word *waters* represents the sea of humanity. Some apply this symbolic language to chapter 13 to argue that the Antichrist comes up out of the nations of the world and therefore would be Gentile, not Jewish. However, the language describing this beast in 13:2 more accurately reflects Daniel 7 where the sea refers to the Mediterranean Sea. This sea more likely symbolizes the abyss, the source of demonic opposition to God.

The association of this beast with the dragon. In Revelation 12:3 the dragon was described as "having seven heads and ten horns." The only difference between the dragon and the beast is that the dragon had crowns on his heads and the beast has crowns on his horns. Verse 2 tells us the dragon gave the beast "his power, his throne, and great authority." The "beast" is a man who comes to power and influence in the world through the direct help of Satan himself.

Satan is behind the overall presentation of a beast with seven heads and ten horns. In Revelation 17 a harlot rides on the beast indicating her domination of the beast. This woman represents "that great city which reigns over the kings of the earth" (17:18). Therefore, I believe the beast represents the "kings of the earth." It is a picture of world history, the nations and leaders of the past and present. The heads represent seven world empires, and the horns represent the final kingdom out of which will come the world ruler we call "the Antichrist." All of this will be discussed in more detail when we come to chapter 17.

Satan is allowed by God to work out his diabolical plans in the history and affairs of this world. He is "the god of this age" (2 Corinthians 4:4), and "the prince of the power of the air, the spirit who now works in the sons of disobedience" (Ephesians 2:2).

The authority of this beast. The crowns were on the "heads" of the dragon (12:3) but on the "horns" of this beast. A beast usually has one head. The fact that this beast has seven heads implies at least seven empires or kingdoms in past history, all dominated by Satan himself. The "horns" represent ten kings of the end times (17:12) who rule for a short time but eventually give up their power to one man—the Antichrist.

The attitude of this beast. He will blaspheme God and His name, His tabernacle, and those who dwell in heaven (cf. 2 Thessalonians 2:4). One of the major ways past rulers have blasphemed is by demanding the worship of those under their domain. In their lust for power and domination, rulers invariably force their constituents to worship them in some fashion.

The appearance of this beast. The imagery of a leopard, bear, and lion comes directly from Daniel 7:3-8, although the order is reversed. Daniel 7 adds a fourth beast with ten horns that seems identical to Revelation's symbolic description of the final government, a confederacy of ten kings out of which comes the Antichrist. Consider carefully what the ancient Hebrew prophet Daniel had to say:

> "And four great beasts came up from the sea, each different from the other. The first was like a lion, and had eagle's wings. I watched till its wings were plucked off; and it was lifted up from the earth and made to stand on two feet like a man, and a man's heart was given to it. And suddenly another beast, a second, like a bear. It was raised up on one side, and had three ribs in its mouth between its teeth. And they said thus to it: 'Arise, devour much flesh!' After this I looked, and there was another, like a leopard, which had on its back four wings of a bird. The beast also had four heads, and dominion was given to it. After this I saw in the night visions, and behold, a fourth beast, dreadful and terrible, exceedingly strong. It had huge iron teeth; it was devouring, breaking in pieces, and trampling the residue

with its feet. It was different from all the beasts that were before it, and it had ten horns. I was considering the horns, and there was another horn, a little one, coming up among them, before whom three of the first horns were plucked out by the roots. And there, in this horn, were eyes like the eyes of a man, and a mouth speaking pompous words."

What a fascinating portion of the Bible! The connection with Revelation is unmistakable. The prophet Daniel is looking forward from the empire of Babylon, while the apostle John is looking backward from the empire of Rome.

1. The lion. Daniel speaks of a great beast like a lion with eagle's wings that were eventually plucked off. The result of that action was that the lion began to stand on two feet like a man, and a man's heart was given to it. The lion is a symbol of the empire of Babylon, and in particular of one of its greatest kings, Nebuchadnezzar. John refers to the mouth of the lion. A beast can be a symbol of a kingdom as well as a king.

2. The bear. The bear in Daniel's vision was raised up on one side and had three ribs in its mouth. The bear symbolized the Medo-Persian empire.

3. The leopard. Daniel saw a leopard that had four wings of a bird on its back. The leopard was a symbol of the Grecian empire, and the four wings spoke of the four kings and kingdoms into which the Grecian empire was divided after the time of Alexander the Great.

John sees this beast with seven heads and ten horns as characteristic of all three empires from the time of Daniel until the time of John. The beast boasted of great things like Babylon, the lion; it had the feet of the Persian empire, the bear—strong, well-organized, and apparently stable; it was like a leopard as well, manifesting the swiftness at which the Grecian empire conquered the world. This beast would communicate arrogantly, control extensively, and conquer swiftly.

The attraction of the beast. The world marvels at and follows this beast with the healed head wound. The words "mortally wounded" are the same as those in 5:6 describing the Lamb Who appeared "as though it had been slain." Two major viewpoints are expressed by Bible scholars over this wound of the beast that was healed:

1. It refers to a particular person. Attempts to identify this person have been numerous, and have included Judas Iscariot, Nero, Mussolini, Hitler, and Stalin. The primary view is that the "head" that received the fatal wound which was healed refers to the Antichrist, the coming world political leader. The evidence for this view is rooted in the fact that the beast is worshiped and referred to as an individual (13:4-8). However, the passage does not speak of people worshipping the "head" that was healed, but rather the "beast" with the seven heads and ten horns.

2. *It refers to a nation or empire.* This view seems more plausible as it fits better the overall teaching of Revelation concerning the beast with the seven heads and ten horns. According to 17:10, five of the heads had fallen by the time of John, one head was in power when he wrote, and the seventh head "had not yet come." The Antichrist appears to be the "eighth" who will come out of the seven heads (17:11).

The wounded head would apparently be the sixth head which was in power when John wrote. That would no doubt refer to the Roman empire. It would be healed or come back to life as a ten-nation confederacy which would comprise the seventh head. In other words, the ten horns of the beast are on the seventh head. Out of this ten-nation confederacy, the seventh world empire, will come the world political leader the Bible describes as the Antichrist. According to the prophecies of Daniel, this leader will arise as "a little horn" among the ten horns or the ten-nation confederacy.

I believe "the beast" is world government, and it appears in many forms. The last major world government was the Roman Empire. That empire will be revived in a ten-nation confederacy attracting the peoples of the world who are tired of international conflicts and economic difficulties. They will readily accept any attempt to solve the world's tensions and bring peace and order to this troubled planet. They will once again worship the "beast" of world government.

It does not require a great deal of intelligence to see the possibility of this happening in a relatively short period of time. In place now are institutions such as the World Bank, the World Court, and the United Nations. There are many leaders who proclaim the virtues of a world economy and order.

The Influence of the Beast (13:4-8)

The adoration he will receive. Consider the following:

> "all the world marveled and followed the beast"
> "they worshiped the dragon . . . and they
> worshiped the beast"
> "all who dwell on the earth will worship him"

The Coming World Leaders

It is not simply a world government or empire that is being worshiped—it is an individual. This individual will come to power and world leadership by infiltrating the future ten-nation confederacy.

It is possible this individual's ability to command such adoration and respect will result from the defeat of the northern confederacy that invades the Middle East (Ezekiel 38 and 39). The removal of such a threat to world peace would pave the way for the ten-nation confederacy and its future world leader.

Revelation 13:4 states, "Who is like the beast? Who is able to make war with him?" Apparently there will be reasons for such claims and such allegiance. A series of victories over hostile forces would certainly endear this government to the peoples of the world.

The arrogance he will manifest. Daniel 7:8 says this coming world leader will have "a mouth speaking pompous words," and will ultimately direct those pompous words "against the Most High" (7:25). Second Thessalonians 2:4 implies that his boasts have a religious tone; he claims to be divine and seeks the worship of people. He evidently will attack the concept of the one true God and deny His existence.

The anger he will display toward believers. This coming world leader's blasphemy against "those who dwell in heaven" (13:6) could refer to all the believers of the past who have died and are in heaven awaiting the resurrection. It is possible this leader will attack that viewpoint, arguing that there is no such place nor are dead believers with the Lord. Another possibility is that this world leader is blaspheming those who are raptured. Why would this leader find it necessary to blaspheme those who dwell in heaven? Could it not be that the mysterious disappearance of thousands of believers needs to be explained?

In any case, we learn this world leader will "make war with the saints" (13:7). These are the tribulation believers introduced to us in chapter 7. The text says he will "overcome them," indicating that these believers are killed (cf. 11:7). Revelation 13:15 says that "as many as would not worship the image of the beast" would be "killed," and Revelation 20:4 speaks of the "souls of those who had been beheaded for their witness to Jesus and for the word of God, who had not worshiped the beast or his image, and had not received his mark on their foreheads or on their hands." It is clear from this that believers in the tribulation period are killed. Exceptions would include the 144,000 Jewish believers and a believing Jewish remnant who will turn to the Lord at the end of the tribulation period. Apparently all Gentile believers in the tribulation period are, in fact, killed.

The affiliation of those who worship the beast. No true believers will be worshiping the coming world leader. He will be worshiped by those whose names are not written in the Book of Life, all those who will one day be cast into the lake of fire (20:15). The only people able to enter the heavenly city, the New Jerusalem are "those who are written in the Lamb's Book of Life" (21:27). Revelation 13:8 tells us this Lamb was slain "from the foundation of the world." The death of Jesus Christ for our sins was in the mind and plan of God from the beginning. This is truly cause for rejoicing (Luke 10:20)!

The Instruction to Us (13:9-10)

The invitation "if anyone has an ear, let him hear," is reminiscent of the messages to the seven churches (2:7, 11, 17, 29; 3:6, 13, 22) and of similar remarks by our Lord (Matthew 11:15; 13:9, 43). It is a challenge to all of us who read these remarkable prophecies. Are they having any effect upon us now? Are we listening carefully? Have we committed all to Jesus Christ, or are we tempted to follow the ways of unbelievers?

The words "he who leads into captivity shall go into captivity; he who kills with the sword must be killed with the sword" speak of divine retribution and revenge. Sin will be paid for; no one gets away with anything. Judgment day is coming. It is also an encouragement to believers who will be taken into captivity and killed.

The statement "here is the patience and the faith of the saints" can be understood as an exhortation not to take revenge or seek to retaliate. Patience refers to bearing up under a load or a burden, and faith would emphasize the importance of confidence in God and His purposes. Both will be greatly needed by believers during the tribulation period as well as in any period of history before that awful time of persecution.

The World Religious Leader
(13:11-18)

[11] *Then I saw another beast coming up out of the earth, and he had two horns like a lamb and spoke like a dragon.* [12] *And he exercises all the authority of the first beast in his presence, and causes the earth and those who dwell in it to worship the first beast, whose deadly wound was healed.* [13] *He performs great signs, so that he even makes fire come down from heaven on the earth in the sight of men.* [14] *And he deceives those who dwell on the earth by*

> *those signs which he was granted to do in the sight of the beast, telling those who dwell on the earth to make an image to the beast who was wounded by the sword and lived.* [15] *He was granted power to give breath to the image of the beast, that the image of the beast should both speak and cause as many as would not worship the image of the beast to be killed.* [16] *And he causes all, both small and great, rich and poor, free and slave, to receive a mark on their right hand or on their foreheads,* [17] *and that no one may buy or sell except one who has the mark or the name of the beast, or the number of his name.* [18] *Here is wisdom. Let him who has understanding calculate the number of the beast, for it is the number of a man: His number is 666.*

Two leaders are prominent in the tribulation period; one is political and the other religious. World government is represented by the beast, but upon the beast sits a harlot (Revelation 17) who represents world religion, and in particular "that great city which reigns over the kings of the earth (17:18)." The leader of the world religious system in its final form is called "the false prophet" (19:20), and his destiny is the lake of fire!

The Description of This
Religious Leader (13:11-12)

His association with the world political leader. The word "another" means "another of the same kind." The word "beast" is the same used of the first leader. This religious leader has the same beastlike character and attitudes as the world political leader. They are two of a kind. That he comes "out of the earth" is in contrast with heaven. The first beast came out of the sea (13:1).

His appearance. The lamb is a religious symbol, used in sacrifices. This second beast's likeness to a lamb simply confirms his religious character. It is interesting to compare the two horns of this false prophet with the Lamb of God, our Lord Jesus Christ. According to Revelation 5:6, the Lamb of God has seven horns, not two. Since lambs do not have horns, the horns are symbols of authority. The two horns on this false prophet possibly indicate that he exercises authority in two realms (political and religious), or as we sometimes say, he "wears two hats."

His attitude. This beast spoke like a dragon. The primary communication of the dragon is deception (12:9). It is important to realize that the devil is not against religion. He uses it for his own ends and purposes. He deceives us with religion as surely as with any other method or device. This religious leader, the false prophet, will speak as the dragon does, deceiving people with his brand of false religion (2 Corinthians 11:3).

His authority. The wording here implies that world government is in control of world religion at this stage of world history. According to Revelation 13:2, the dragon gave the first beast his authority. Now, satanic authority is given by the first beast to the second beast, the false prophet. This religious leader does nothing without approval from the political leader. He exercises his authority "in his presence," that is, in the presence of the first beast.

His aim. The religious leader will promote the worship of world government. His purpose is to get people to support and follow the world government and its special leader, the Antichrist. We should be wary of all attempts to promote world government, either through economics, politics, or religion. According to Bible prophecy, it is satanic. Without the rule of the Messiah, world government is doomed to failure. It is Satan's plan and will result in the persecution and death of believers.

The only world government blessed and approved by God is the one Messiah Himself will set up during the millennium, the thousand years of Messiah's reign over the whole earth. There will be no real peace and justice for all until the Prince of Peace and Righteousness sets up His kingdom (Isaiah 9:6-7).

The Deception of This Religious Leader (13:13-15)

The performance of miraculous signs. The devil can perform the miraculous and, as a result, deceive many people. The performance of miracles is no proof that the one doing them is from God. Jesus said "false christs and false prophets will arise and show great signs and wonders, so as to deceive, if possible, even the elect" (Matthew 24:24). Jesus' prediction of "great signs" fits exactly what the false prophet will do (Revelation 13:15).

Our culture is being prepared for this deception, and many so-called Christians are involved and do not realize it. We are making claims about miracles today that directly contradict the teaching and warnings of the Bible. We do not deny that God can perform miracles, but the methods and purposes of most miracles being performed in public meetings today simply do not meet biblical requirements. The deception has already begun!

The source is Satan himself; the purpose—"deception" (2 Thessalonians 2:9-10). The miraculous "signs" and "wonders" include healings, casting out demons, and speaking in tongues. Satan will counterfeit all these miraculous acts which were performed by the apostles of New Testament times.

One of the key miraculous signs the false prophet will perform is making fire fall from heaven to the earth. Perhaps this is a counterfeit Pentecost or an attempt to duplicate the miracle of Elijah and make people believe this false prophet is the Elijah who would come before the return of the Messiah. It may also be an attempt to demonstrate the same kind of power that shall accompany the return of the Messiah "in flaming fire" (2 Thessalonians 1:8).

The purpose of these miraculous signs. The general purpose is to deceive the people of earth; the specific purpose is to encourage those who dwell on the earth to make an image to the beast. It is either a monument to world government or to its world leader, the Antichrist. The state now becomes the god.

The deception becomes very powerful as the false prophet, working under the power of Satan himself, causes the image of the beast to speak (13:15). Computers can be programmed to talk, but this appears to be a convincing miracle causing the people of the world to respond with worship and allegiance.

The persecution that will result. One cannot help but relate the killing of those who refuse to worship the image of the beast to a similar incident in Daniel's prophecy. Nebuchadnezzar made an image of gold and required all the people to worship it or be killed in the fiery furnace (Daniel 3:1-7). It is the height of depravity to change the glory of the incorruptible God into an image made like corruptible man (Romans 1:18-23). All who worship such man-made images deserve the judgment of God (Exodus 20:3-5; Romans 1:32).

All those who refuse to worship the image of the beast are to be killed. While this is a decree and does not necessarily imply that all *were* killed, it seems clear from Revelation 20:4 that this is what will take place. Apart from the 144,000 Jews and the believing Jewish remnant, all believers are killed because they do not take the mark of the beast or worship its image.

The Demand of This Religious Leader (13:16-18)

Many attempts have been made in the past to identify the number 666 with a particular individual. Suggestions have included Roman emperors such as Nero and Caligula, and leaders of the twentieth century such as Mussolini, Hitler, and Stalin. Likewise, attempts to identify the Antichrist by assigning numerical equivalents to Hebrew, Greek, and Latin letters have proven futile. The key phrase seems to be "for it is the number of a man."

The extent of this demand. The entire world is subject to the demand of this religious leader; everyone must receive the mark or the name of the beast. This demand requires complete allegiance to the world government. True believers will refuse the mark and lose their lives.

The evidence of this demand. Back in Revelation 7 we learned that God put His mark or seal on the foreheads of the 144,000 Jews. Revelation 14:1 reminds us that these Jewish believers have the "Father's name written on their foreheads." Once again, Satan and his cohorts, the Antichrist and false prophet, try to counterfeit the work of God.

It will be clear to all what the mark of the beast is and why it must be put on the hand or forehead. Believers will not be caught by surprise; they will have the opportunity and wisdom to refuse such a mark. It appears from Revelation that all believers refuse the mark. Only non-believers take the mark and go along with the demands of world government and its leadership.

The effect of this demand. The false prophet imposes economic control on behalf of world government. One can easily see how our present credit card systems could bring such a situation to our world. A credit card number based on the social security system would be one way to bring such control. Perhaps a worldwide census will bring it to pass. We simply do not know how it will be achieved, but there is no doubt it could take place in a relatively short period of time.

What Is the Mark of the Beast?

While some religious groups claim to know what it is, the truth is, no one does. We just know that such an identification mark will be imposed by the world's leaders during the tribulation. The mark is the number of the beast, and the beast represents world government and its leader, the Antichrist.

Chapter 22

Visions of the Tribulation

(14:1-20)

After visions of the dragon's persecution of Israel during the tribulation and his diabolical influence over the two beasts, it is time for a change! John is now given a panoramic picture of the tribulation period from the standpoint of the Messiah's victory. We now view the ultimate triumph of God, the Lamb, and all His followers, the true believers. It is a preview of coming attractions on the movie screen of history.

Vision of Victory
(14:1-5)

¹*Then I looked, and behold, a Lamb standing on Mount Zion, and with Him one hundred and forty-four thousand, having His Father's name written on their foreheads. ²And I heard a voice from heaven, like the voice of many waters, and like the voice of loud thunder. And I heard the sound of harpists playing their harps. ³And they sang as it were a new song before the throne, before the four living creatures, and the elders; and no one could learn that song except the hundred and forty-four thousand who were redeemed from the earth. ⁴These are the ones who were not defiled with women, for they are virgins. These are the ones who follow the Lamb wherever He goes. These were redeemed from among men, being firstfruits to God and to the Lamb. ⁵And in their mouth was found no guile, for they are without fault before the throne of God.*

In chapter 7 we learned that the 144,000 are "servants of our God," and represented "all the tribes of the children of Israel." We were told they were "sealed" by God "on their foreheads." Now we are given additional information about these sealed servants of God.

The words, "Then I looked, and behold," appear for the eighth time in the vision of Revelation. They always introduce a key or major vision of the book. It is critical that we understand God's ultimate triumph over all that is taking place during the tribulation period.

Three things (at least) are presented to us concerning this special group of 144,000 believers: The protection, praise, and purpose of God.

The Protection of God (14:1)

It involves the presence of the Lamb. Jesus said in Matthew 28:20, "and lo, I am *with you* always, even to the end of the age" (cf. Hebrews 13:5). His presence with the 144,000 is indeed reassuring, not only to them, but also to all of us to whom His words of comfort were intended.

It involves the place where they are standing. The Lamb of God is presently in heaven at the right hand of the throne of God (Hebrews 1:3; Revelation 5) where He continues to intercede for us (Hebrews 7:24-25). This picture is not of heaven, though Hebrews 12:22 uses the term "Mount Zion" to refer to the heavenly city, the new Jerusalem. This is a picture of the Lamb's ultimate triumph at the end of the tribulation. "Mount Zion" is used symbolically of the Messianic age, the Jewish hope of all its history—a kingdom promised to the people of Israel with Messiah as its King, reigning in Jerusalem, in fulfillment of God's promise to king David long ago (Psalm 2; 48; 132; Isaiah 2:2-4; 24:23; Joel 2:32; Obadiah 17, 21; Micah 4:1-7).

The place where the 144,000 Jewish believers stand with the Lamb of God is indeed symbolic and thrilling. It is wonderful assurance to all the people of God that His plans will be achieved and His promises will be fulfilled.

It involves the print of God's name on their foreheads. The seal of God upon the foreheads of these Jewish believers is a reminder that they belong to God and to the Lamb. This mark of God's name is an obvious contrast to the "mark of the beast" (13:17). Is the name of world government on you? Are we going along with secular society and its viewpoints, fully embracing all this world's system teaches and believes? Or are we claiming the Name that is above every name (Acts 4:12; Ephesians 1:21)?

The Praise of God (14:2-3)

It was a "voice" that John heard, not "voices." This could refer to God's voice, for it is like "many waters" and "loud thunder" (Psalm 29:3). However, it could also refer to the combined praise of the 144,000 (cf. Revelation 5:11-12). The idea of people playing harps in heaven is not foreign to the Bible (14:2; Psalm 144:9; 147:7; 149:3; 150:3). The harp is a beautiful instrument and a delight to hear when played with skill. Revelation 15:2 mentions those who have been victorious over the beast, his image and his mark, as "having harps of God" and singing the song of Moses and the song of the Lamb. Certainly the 144,000 would be included in that harp orchestra.

What is the new song? This group of 144,000 Jewish believers sing "a new song" in front of the four living creatures and the elders, "and no one could learn that song except the hundred and forty-four thousand who were redeemed from the earth." What is the point behind the fact that only the 144,000 could sing this song? Do not the redeemed ones of Revelation 5:9 sing a "new song"?

In chapter 5, the twenty-four elders who sing the "new song" of praise for their redemption represent the church-age believers who are in heaven during the tribulation. They are redeemed by the precious blood of Jesus Christ. The 144,000 who sing this "new song" in front of the twenty-four elders are "redeemed" as well. They represent the "redeemed from the earth," presumably out of the great tribulation. They alone, having experienced deliverance through their suffering and death, are able to sing its praise.

The Purpose of God (14:4-5)

Their moral purity. Some argue that they are celibates, singles unencumbered by family responsibilities and uniquely set apart for the preaching of the gospel during this time of trouble (Matthew 24:19). Paul's discussion in 1 Corinthians 7:25-35 is often used to demonstrate the importance of the single state during times of great distress and persecution.

But if that is the case for the 144,000, would it not also be advisable for the rest of the believers during the tribulation period? Jesus mentioned "virgins" in his parable of Matthew 25:1-13. The five wise virgins certainly represent the believers of the tribulation period who are ready when the Bridegroom comes. But to identify the 144,000 with these five virgins does not seem likely; the five virgins represent all tribulation believers, not just the 144,000.

It is better to understand the word *virgins* here as a reference to moral purity and possibly undefilement from idolatry. They have remained faithful to Christ (2 Corinthians 11:2-3). Since they are Israelites, there is probably a connection as well with passages where Israel is described as "the virgin, the daughter of Zion" (2 Kings 19:21; Isaiah 37:22; Lamentations 2:13) or "the virgin of Israel" (Jeremiah 18:13; 31:4, 21). Appeals for moral purity before God are made to His people by the use of the word *virgin*.

Their faithful practice. There is no doubt that a primary concern of our Lord Jesus Christ is that we be followers of Him (Matthew 4:19; John 21:15-22). The commitment of these followers of the Lord is revealed when it says they "follow the Lamb wherever He goes." They were willing to go anywhere the Lord wanted them to go and to do whatever He wanted them to do. What marvelous examples they are to all of us who seek to follow Jesus Christ.

Their spiritual position. The 144,000 were "redeemed from among men." While a broad and general definition of "redeemed" could be used, it seems more likely this indicates a specific group of people who became believers. It is possible they responded to the preaching of the two witnesses. We do know that when the two witnesses ascended to heaven and the great earthquake hit Jerusalem, a remnant of people (presumably Jewish) "were afraid and gave glory to the God of heaven" (11:13).

The term "firstfruits" is well known to Jewish people for it is the name of one of the seven feasts they are to celebrate each year (Leviticus 23). The Feast of Firstfruits always falls on a Sunday, and follows the week in which Passover occurs. The "firstfruits" are an indication of the harvest to come. First Corinthians 15:23 refers to Jesus Christ as "the firstfruits," a reference to the promised resurrection. He was the first to arise from the dead and not die again. More will follow at His second coming.

The 144,000 are the "firstfruits" of those to be saved during the tribulation. More will come. A major portion of the Jewish people will turn to the Lord at the end of the tribulation when the Messiah returns in power and great glory. Zechariah 13:8-9 suggests that the remnant will consist of one-third of all the Jewish people. Zechariah 12:10 indicates that their response to the Lord will be the result of "the Spirit of grace and supplication" being poured out upon them. Ezekiel 39:29 prophesies a time when God will pour out His Spirit on the house of Israel.

Today, the Holy Spirit is being poured out upon Gentiles. From the Day of Pentecost (Acts 2) until now, God has been pouring out His Spirit upon all nations. It refers to salvation. It will continue throughout "the last days," which began on that Day of Pentecost and will continue until the end of the tribulation period.

It is also possible that the 144,000 Jews will be the evangelists God will use in the tribulation period to bring a multitude of Gentiles to Himself, and "the fullness of the Gentiles" will be completed (Romans 11:25). Perhaps the miracle of Pentecost will be repeated and the 144,000 Jewish evangelists will be able to speak in all the languages of the world without any previous knowledge of them (Acts 2). The prophecy of Joel 2, which began to be fulfilled on the Day of Pentecost, will find its ultimate fulfillment in the tribulation period when the sun will be darkened and the moon turned to blood. Joel 2:32 ends with this marvelous prophecy:

> "And it shall come to pass
> That whoever calls on the name of the LORD
> Shall be saved.
> For in Mount Zion and in Jerusalem there
>   shall be deliverance,
> As the LORD has said,
> Among the remnant whom the LORD calls."

How fascinating to see the prophecy "in Mount Zion and in Jerusalem there shall be deliverance" in light of the 144,000 who stand with the Lamb of God, our Lord Jesus Christ, "on Mount Zion" (14:1).

A summary of the 144,000. The words "no guile" mean there was nothing false in them. This could mean they had nothing to do with the false religion of the tribulation promoted by the false prophet. It is also a clear statement of their relationship to God. Revelation 21:27 and 22:15 use this word to indicate that falsehood will not be present in God's eternal city.

The words "without fault" reemphasize their moral purity. The same root word is used in 2 Peter 2:13 of false prophets and teachers when it says they are "spots and blemishes." True believers are to be the opposite, and the term is used several times of believers (Ephesians 1:4; 5:27; Colossians 1:22; Jude 24) and of our Lord Jesus Christ as the Lamb of God (1 Peter 1:19).

What a wonderful group of people, these 144,000 Jewish believers of the tribulation period! May God help us all to follow their example.

Vision of Judgment
(14:6-13)

After the vision of victory, picturing the triumph of 144,000 Jewish believers standing with the Lamb on Mount Zion, the apostle John receives another vision introduced by an angel proclaiming the gospel and warning of the coming judgment of God.

Three Angels and God's Judgment
(14:6-13)

Early in our study we mentioned an important phrase signaling the visions John was given. Those words "I looked" or "I saw" help us put the book together with order and design. The first vision of chapter 14 was marked by the words "Then I looked" (v. 1); the second vision by the words "Then I saw" (v. 6); and the third by the words "And I looked" (v. 14). Three angels announce God's messages in vision two (14:6-13).

> [6]*Then I saw another angel flying in the midst of heaven, having the everlasting gospel to preach to those who dwell on the earth—to every nation, tribe, tongue, and people—*[7] *saying with a loud voice, "Fear God and give glory to Him, for the hour of His judgment has come; and worship Him who made heaven and earth, the sea and springs of water."* [8]*And another angel followed, saying, "Babylon is fallen, is fallen, that great city, because she has made all nations drink of the wine of the wrath of her fornication."* [9]*Then a third angel followed them, saying with a loud voice, "If anyone worships the beast and his image, and receives his mark on his forehead or on his hand,* [10]*he himself shall also drink of the wine of the wrath of God, which is poured out full strength into the cup of His indignation. And he shall be tormented with fire and brimstone in the presence of the holy angels and in the presence of the Lamb.* [11]*And the smoke of their torment ascends forever and ever; and they have no rest day or night, who worship the beast and his image, and whoever receives the mark of his name."* [12]*Here is the patience of the saints; here are those who keep the commandments of God and the faith of Jesus.* [13]*Then I heard a voice from heaven saying to me, "Write: 'Blessed are the dead who die in the Lord from now on.'"*

"Yes," says the Spirit, "that they may rest from their labors, and their works follow them."

The Proclamation of the Gospel (14:6-7)

The words "another angel" perhaps connects with Revelation 8:13 where an angel was seen "flying through the midst of heaven" warning about three more of God's judgments to come. Once again an angel is seen "flying in the midst of heaven" (v. 6). Here the emphasis is upon the preaching of the gospel, not simply announcing the coming judgments.

Is this the same gospel of God's grace and salvation which we are to believe? Some think not because of the emphasis here upon judgment. However, this verse connects the gospel with the phrase "to every nation, tribe, tongue, and people," indicating the great multitude who will be saved out of the great tribulation (7:9-17). Their robes were washed and made white in the blood of the Lamb. That is true of all believers.

Several things are emphasized by this angel's proclamation:

The gospel is an "everlasting" gospel. The "good news" has always been a part of God's plan. There is nothing new here. The gospel is eternal, not localized to certain points of human history.

The gospel will reach all nations by the end of the tribulation period. Christians speak of fulfilling the Great Commission of our Lord Jesus Christ, Who told us to make disciples of all nations or preach the gospel to every creature (Matthew 28:19; Mark 16:15). In Matthew 24:14, Jesus predicted: "And this gospel of the kingdom will be preached in all the world as a witness to all the nations, and then the end will come." The "end" is the end of the tribulation period. The gospel will reach all nations, languages, tribes, and peoples before the end of the tribulation period. As we noted earlier, the 144,000 Jewish believers will have a part in that great fulfillment.

The gospel is a message that brings men to God. That simple statement contains a world of meaning for the believer. The gospel is not simply a way of feeling better about yourself or getting your life in order. The gospel brings you to God. The angel's message emphasized three things: "Fear God . . . give glory to Him . . . worship Him." That is the gospel and always has been. God's ultimate purpose is that He might receive worship and praise from all He has created (4:10-11). A gospel that falls short of bringing men to God to give Him glory and worship is insufficient.

Two reasons are given for such a response to God: (1) The hour of His judgment has come; and (2) He made heaven and earth, the sea and springs of water. God's judgment and God's creation become the major reasons for urging us to turn to God and be saved. Much of today's preaching of the gospel falls short on two accounts. First, the appeal to people to be saved is not based on God's coming judgment but upon personal benefits that may come as a result of believing in Jesus Christ. Second, by not urging people to be saved on the basis of God's creation of all things, the purpose and intention of God behind our salvation is set aside. Romans 1 presents the tragic account of people who are "without excuse" because they reject the God of creation.

The Prediction of the Fall of Babylon (14:8)

The word *Babylon* appears here and in chapters 16, 17, and 18, and is frequently called "the great city." According to 17:5, the name "Babylon the Great" was written on the forehead of the harlot who sits on the beast with seven heads and ten horns. If the beast represents world government, then the woman called "Babylon the Great" represents false religion and is centered in a place described as "that great city" (17:18). We will study the identity of Babylon the Great in later chapters, but at this point it might be well to list the major viewpoints concerning "the great city" called "Babylon."

It refers to the city of Jerusalem. This view connects Revelation 11:8 with the other passages using the term "the great city" and sees the earthly city of Jerusalem becoming the international headquarters of the major religious systems of the world. It is certainly possible. Proponents of this view also connect the earthly Jerusalem with the heavenly one mentioned in 21:10, pointing out that both are called "the great city." Obviously they are "great" in much different ways.

It refers to the rebuilt city of Babylon. This view has interested Bible prophecy students for many years. The basic problem with such an argument is not only that the city has not been rebuilt and thus does not hold a prominent place among the nations of the world like Revelation 18 describes, but the symbolic character of the discussion concerning Babylon the Great also makes such a view highly unlikely.

It refers to the city of Rome. This was the view of the early church fathers and has been the majority view among premillennialists. The major religious system that seems to include the doctrines and practices of ancient Babylon as well as represent the kind of influence over the nations of the world that Revelation 17 and 18 present, would be the Roman Catholic Church.

In Revelation 14 we simply have the prediction of Babylon's ultimate destruction. The twice repeated description ("is fallen, is fallen") parallels Isaiah's prophecy of doom for the city (Isaiah 21:9).

The reason for Babylon's fall. The reason for her fall is clearly given— "she has made all nations drink of the wine of the wrath of her fornication." This point is emphasized in Revelation 17:2 where she is described as one "with whom the kings of the earth committed fornication, and the inhabitants of the earth were made drunk with the wine of her fornication." In 17:5 this same woman is called "the mother of harlots and of the abominations of the earth." Political leaders throughout history have committed fornication with this woman, the false religious system, and the people of earth have accepted it. But God's judgment will come. The details are graphically portrayed for us in Revelation 18.

The Punishment of Those Who Worship the Beast (14:9-11)

The evidence that such punishment is deserved. Worshiping the beast and his image is a demonstration of loyalty and allegiance, whereas receiving the mark is a matter of economic survival. According to Revelation 13:16-18, one cannot buy or sell without the mark of the beast. The state will be god in that day, demanding support and wielding total control over the lives of its citizens.

The explanation of this punishment upon those who worship the beast. In verse 8, all nations drink of "the wine of the wrath of [Babylon's] fornication." Now we read that those who worship the beast will drink the wine of the wrath of God (cf. Psalm 75:7-8). The cup out of which they drink is described as the "indignation" of God Himself.

The extent of this punishment. No passage is more clear on the eternal punishment of the wicked than this one. Though many attempts have been made to eliminate the concept of eternal retribution, this passage and others make it quite clear (Matthew 25:41; Jude 6-7; Revelation 20:10). All who refuse to put their faith and trust in the Lord and His Messiah will be "cast into the lake of fire" (Revelation 20:15). The consequences of the gospel are indeed frightening and awesome! No wonder people laugh at such ideas or try to reinterpret the meaning of these words.

But does God punish people *forever*? It appears that His holiness, justice, and righteous character demand it. If we refuse His offer of salvation from sin, death, and hell, what else could He do and remain a holy God? His love, mercy, and forgiveness become totally meaningless if there is no retribution for our rebellion and sin. If there is eternal life for the believer then there is also eternal punishment for the unbeliever (Matthew 25:46). Revelation 14:9-11 leaves us no alternative—the punishment of those who worship the beast is an unending torment allowing no sleep or rest.

The Patience of the Saints (14:12-13)

What a contrast to the previous verses concerning the punishment of those who worship the beast. Patience, the ability to endure difficult times, is rooted in the rewards one can expect for enduring. God's people can be patient if they know how things will ultimately turn out.

The primary characteristic of the saints. Keeping the commandments of God is a frequent description of believers (12:17). It refers to our allegiance or loyalty to the teachings of the Bible, and specifically to the doctrine of salvation as found in Jesus Christ. Those believers who have been persecuted and killed for their faith were described in Revelation 6:9 as those who had been "slain for the word of God and for the testimony which they held."

The future condition of the saints. This beatitude ("Blessed are the dead who die in the Lord"), like those in the Sermon on the Mount (Matthew 5), describes the spiritual condition of true believers. We are truly blessed if we know the Lord. The death of unbelievers is not a blessing but a great tragedy; the judgment of hell will follow. This is a reminder to all who will suffer martyrdom in the tribulation period that better things will follow after their death. Death can be a blessing when we understand that it is a sweet release into the presence of God.

Two things make the future condition of dead believers a blessing:

1. Their eternal rest. "We work now . . . we rest in heaven," a wonderful Chinese believer told me when discussing how tired one can become in the work of the Lord. There will be no more struggles after death— no more pain or suffering, no more exhaustion. We will finally *rest* forever!

2. Their eternal reward. Nothing we have done for the Lord will be overlooked. All acts in His Name and for His glory shall be rewarded. The rewards will be much greater than the effort expended (1 Corinthians 3:5-17; 15:58; Colossians 3:24). The words of Hebrews 6:10 appear on a plaque my wife made for my office and are of great encouragement to me:

> For God is not unjust to forget your work and labor of love which you have shown toward His name, in that you have ministered to the saints, and do minister.

Yes, God will reward His servants! Their works do follow them.

Vision of the Final Harvest
(14:14-20)

The first vision of this chapter dealt with the 144,000 Jewish believers standing with the Lamb on Mount Zion. The second vision, the proclamation of the three angels, spoke of God's judgment. Now, beginning in verse 14, John describes a third vision of three angels and the appearance of the Son of Man with a sharp sickle in His hand. The harvest is ripe; God's wrath has come upon the earth.

> *14 And I looked, and behold, a white cloud, and on the cloud sat One like the Son of Man, having on His head a golden crown, and in His hand a sharp sickle. 15 And another angel came out of the temple, crying with a loud voice to Him who sat on the cloud, "Thrust in Your sickle and reap, for the time has come for You to reap, for the harvest of the earth is ripe." 16 So He who sat on the cloud thrust in His sickle on the earth, and the earth was reaped.*

> *17 Then another angel came out of the temple which is in heaven, he also having a sharp sickle. 18 And another angel came out from the altar, who had power over fire, and he cried with a loud cry to him who had the sharp sickle, saying, "Thrust in your sharp sickle and gather the clusters of the vine of the earth, for her grapes are fully ripe." 19 So the angel thrust his sickle into the earth and gathered the vine of the earth, and threw it into the great winepress of the wrath of God. 20 And the winepress was trampled outside the city, and blood came out of the winepress, up to the horses' bridles, for one thousand six hundred furlongs.*

Notice four things about this One on the white cloud:

His human personality. Jesus Christ was called "the Son of Man" throughout the Gospels. It was the title He most often used for Himself. It is a reminder that our coming Judge is One Who knows what we are like. His humanity gives Him valid credentials for judging mankind. John 5:27 says the Father "has given Him authority to execute judgment also, because He is the Son of Man."

His moral purity. The harlot sits on the waters of earth (17:1, 15), but the Son of Man sits on the clouds of heaven (Daniel 7:13; Revelation 1:7)! The "cloud" was a symbol of the divine and holy presence of God. The word *white* emphasizes moral purity and pictures the righteousness of God made possible by the blood of Jesus Christ (7:14; 19:8).

His great power. The "golden crown" is the mark of a king—a conqueror. Revelation 19:12 says that "on His head were many crowns." His name is "King of kings and Lord of lords" (19:16).

His awesome purpose. The presence of "a sharp sickle" suggests the reaping of a harvest. It is an unusual picture of the Son of Man, our Lord Jesus Christ, but it is the picture of Him in judgment. Matthew 13:37-43 gives us a parable that parallels Revelation 14. The harvest symbolism is the same. The time is the same—"the end of the age." The reapers are the angels (14:17-20). The conclusion of the Matthew 13 parable is the angels "will gather out of His kingdom all things that offend, and those who practice lawlessness, and will cast them into the furnace of fire."

The Instruction about the Sharp Sickle (14:15-18)

Instruction is given to the Son of Man and then to another angel, each one carrying a sharp sickle. The judgment is ordered by Jesus Christ but executed by angels.

The reason for this instruction. God's judgments will come according to His time schedule. Though many would question the wisdom of God in allowing the world to continue as it has with all its misery, corruption, and rebellion, Revelation makes it abundantly clear that God will bring His vengeance upon the earth in due time (Hebrews 9:27; Revelation 6:17; 10:6-7). Everything will be brought to a grand climax that will fulfill the purposes of Almighty God.

It is highly significant that the reaping of the harvest is placed into the hands of the Son of Man (14:15). He is the Judge of all the earth, being given that responsibility by God the Father. The same One Who died on the cross to judge our sins is the One Who will judge those who refuse to accept His payment. His blood flowed from the cross as a ransom for all who will believe in Him. If we do not put our trust in His shed blood for the forgiveness of our sins, then at His final judgment our blood will flow as we are trampled like grapes in the winepress of God's wrath.

Notice two things about this time of reaping:

1. *The condition of the harvest.* Verse 15 says the "harvest of the earth is ripe." The Greek word for "ripe" speaks of being overly ripe to the point of being rotten or withered. When the judgment of God finally falls upon the unbelieving world, it will come as a judgment long overdue. No one can accuse God of acting too rashly or judging without just cause (Romans 1:32; 2:5). God's judgment is always righteous.

2. *The connection with Bible prophecy.* The picture of God's judgment being like a sharp sickle reaping a harvest comes from Joel 3:12-16:

> "Let the nations be wakened, and come up to
>   the Valley of Jehoshaphat;
> For there I will sit to judge all the
>   surrounding nations.
> Put in the sickle, for the harvest is ripe.
> Come, go down;
> For the winepress is full,
> The vats overflow—
> For their wickedness is great."
>
> Multitudes, multitudes in the valley of
>   decision!
> For the day of the LORD is near in the
>   valley of decision.
> The sun and moon will grow dark,
> And the stars will diminish their brightness.
> The LORD also will roar from Zion
> And utter His voice from Jerusalem;
> The heavens and earth will shake;
> But the LORD will be a shelter for His people,
> And the strength of the children of Israel.

The sickle being thrust into the harvest symbolizes God's judgment on the nations who come against Jerusalem and the people of Israel. This judgment occurs in the Valley of Jehoshaphat, adjacent to the city of Jerusalem. It is there that all nations will come against Jerusalem, and it is there where their blood will flow. That it is called the "valley of decision" does not refer to this multitude's opportunity to believe but to the fact that there God will decide the fate of all who reject His Messiah and His salvation.

The relationship of the two harvests. In verses 14-16, the Son of Man thrusts in His sickle to harvest the over-ripe grain. In verses 17-20, an angel thrusts in the sickle to harvest fully ripe grapes. Are these two different events? Some see the ingathering of believers in the first harvest and the judgment of unbelievers in the second. However, the parallel passage in Joel 3 suggests the same event is being symbolized— the judgment of unbelieving nations. All nations will be judged, and it appears one of the criteria for this judgment is how these nations have treated the Jewish people (Matthew 25:31-46).

The role of the angel who came out from the altar. Verse 18 speaks of a special angel "who had power over fire," a likely reference to the angel with the golden censer (8:3-5). This is a reminder that the judgment of God upon unbelievers is in answer to the prayers of His people and particularly the martyrs who cried, "How long, O Lord, holy and true, until You judge and avenge our blood on those who dwell on the earth?" (6:10). The "fire" represents God's judgment (cf. Matthew 3:11-12).

The Impact of This Judgment (14:19-20)

All true believers are designed by God to bear the fruit of God's righteousness (Galatians 5:22-23; Philippians 1:9-11). In a similar manner, unbelievers are described as a vine that bears fruit, not the fruit of God's character, but the fruit of wickedness and rebellion against God.

The place where the grapes are thrown. The grapes of the final harvest are thrown into "the great winepress of the wrath of God." One can visualize workers tramping the grapes with their feet, causing the juice to flow to the wine vats underneath. In this instance, Jesus Christ Himself will tread "the winepress of the fierceness and wrath of Almighty God" (Revelation 19:15). His personal involvement in the final judgment of the nations who come against Jerusalem is unmistakable. The Son of Man has blood all over His garments (Isaiah 63:1-6; Revelation 19:13).

God's righteous anger is unleashed against all unbelievers, the nations of the world who have lived in opposition to His purposes and have rejected His Messiah. Now, at the end of the tribulation, they will taste His personal wrath. The consequences are awesome!

> For He is coming to judge the earth.
> With righteousness He shall judge the world,
> And the peoples with equity.
>
> (Psalm 98:9)

The picture the winepress presents. The final verse of Revelation 14 presents a graphic picture of what Messiah's wrath will accomplish when He judges the nations of the world. Is this gory scene literal or symbolic? Probably both. Messiah *will* judge the nations of the world who come against Jerusalem, and their blood *will* be shed, revealing a terrible massacre. The blood "up to the horses' bridles" probably indicates the great multitude who will be killed rather than a literal flood of blood that reaches that height. It is possible, however, that a literal flood is intended.

The mention of "one thousand six hundred furlongs" has intrigued Bible students throughout history. It describes a distance of about two hundred miles. Does this refer to a radius around Jerusalem where the nations of the world will be gathered? The length of the land of Israel is about two hundred miles. It is possible this reference is to Israel as the site of the final destruction of the nations by the Messiah.

Some Bible teachers believe the two hundred miles refers to the distance between the valley of Armageddon (which separates Galilee from Samaria) and the city of Bozrah, former capital of Edom (located southeast of the Dead Sea). Since both areas are a part of the final destruction by the Messiah (Isaiah 63:1; Revelation 16:16), some see the two hundred miles as the total area between those points and visualize it covered with the blood of those unbelieving nations judged by the Messiah.

What an awesome, horrible sight Revelation 14 gives us of the final harvest of God's judgment upon the unbelieving nations of the world. It is a reminder that all who refuse to put their faith and trust in the Messiah and His salvation will one day face Him as their Judge. Where do you stand?

Chapter 23

Vision of the
Seven Last Plagues

(15:1-16:21)

The scroll containing God's program for the future has seven seals. The seventh seal was broken (8:1), and we were introduced to seven angels with seven trumpets. The seventh trumpet message is the longest and began with the great announcement of Revelation 11:15. Within that seventh trumpet message are several signs and visions.

The Signs of the Seventh Trumpet Message:
    Sign of the woman (12:1)
    Sign of the dragon (12:3)
    Sign of the seven last plagues (15:1)

The Visions of the Seventh Trumpet Message:
    Vision of the beast with seven heads (13:1)
    Vision of the beast with two horns (13:11)
    Vision of the 144,000 (14:1-5)
    Vision of the gospel and judgments (14:6-13)
    Vision of the final harvest (14:14-20)
    Vision of the heavenly temple and the
       seven last plagues (15:1-16:21)

Additional visions in the seventh trumpet message are recorded in chapters 17-22 and will be discussed later.

Preparation for the Seven Last Plagues
(15:1-8)

[1]*Then I saw another sign in heaven, great and marvelous: seven angels having the seven last plagues, for in them the wrath of God is complete.* [2]*And I saw something like a sea of glass mingled with fire, and those who have the victory over the beast, over his image and over his mark and over the number of his name, standing on the sea of glass, having harps of God.* [3]*And they sing the song of Moses, the servant of God, and the song of the Lamb, saying:*

> *"Great and marvelous are Your works,*
> *Lord God Almighty!*
> *Just and true are Your ways,*
> *O King of the saints!*
> [4]*Who shall not fear You, O Lord,*
> *and glorify Your name?*
> *For You alone are holy.*
> *For all nations shall come and worship*
> *before You,*
> *For Your judgments have been manifested."*

[5]*After these things I looked, and behold, the temple of the tabernacle of the testimony in heaven was opened.* [6]*And out of the temple came the seven angels having the seven plagues, clothed in pure bright linen, and having their chests girded with golden bands.* [7]*Then one of the four living creatures gave to the seven angels seven golden bowls full of the wrath of God who lives forever and ever.* [8]*The temple was filled with smoke from the glory of God and from His power, and no one was able to enter the temple till the seven plagues of the seven angels were completed.*

The Sign in Heaven (15:1-2)

The importance of the sign. It is called "another" sign, meaning it is like others that preceded it. The signs preceding this one were the sign of the woman (representing Israel) and the sign of the dragon with seven heads and ten horns (Satan's control of world empires and governments). The adjectives "great and marvelous" suggest a connection with the works of the Lord God Almighty (15:3).

1. The plagues reveal the importance of the sign. Previous judgments were also plagues from God, but here we have the final judgments of God upon planet earth. The completion of His wrath has come.

2. The plan behind the plagues reveals the importance of this sign. God is angry, and the seven last plagues will bring to completion His anger against a rebellious world. His anger will not continue forever (Psalm 103:9). The word "complete" indicates that a plan is being carried out, a goal is being accomplished (cf. 10:7; 16:17).

The identity of those standing on the sea of glass. John wants us to understand the significance of this vision of the seven last plagues. What he saw (vv. 1, 2) is for us to see and understand. John saw the following two things:

1. A sea of glass mingled with fire. This "sea of glass" is different from the sea of glass described in chapter 4 in that it is "mingled with fire." This may indicate that those standing on it have gone through the fire (perhaps a reference to the tribulation period) or it may simply symbolize the judgment of God.

2. Those standing on the sea of glass. Who do these represent? Do they include the believers of all history, all who have put their trust in the Messiah? From the description of them in verse 2, I think it is clear we are looking at the martyrs of the tribulation period, the great multitude of Revelation 7:9-17 who come out of that terrible time as believers in Jesus Christ, ones who refuse to worship the beast or take his mark. As a result, they suffer greatly and ultimately lose their lives for their allegiance and loyalty to Him (Revelation 13:15; 20:4). Their position of "standing" implies victory and conquest through resurrection. They were killed for their faith; they now stand victorious in heaven. What great encouragement to us all! The Lord has a special ministry for these martyrs of the tribulation period. They will form a marvelous orchestra of harps, a symphony of praise to our God, rejoicing in His ultimate victory over all His enemies and ours.

The Song of Moses and the Lamb (15:3-4)

What a wonderful song of praise to our God! There is much for us to learn from these glorious words, the music of heaven itself, sung by those who have not only tasted deeply of the grace of God and His forgiveness and cleansing (7:14), but who also know what it means to suffer and to give their lives for the Lord (20:4). This is a song of martyrs, and an exhortation to the living about praise and worship.

The connection to previous songs. Moses and the children of Israel sang a song to the Lord after the armies of Pharaoh were destroyed in the Red Sea (Exodus 15:1-18). It is a song of victory over the enemies of God's people and a reminder of God's protection of those who put their trust in Him. In Deuteronomy 32, Moses composed a song recounting the experiences of God's people and the victories they had witnessed. The song of the Lamb in Revelation 5 speaks of God's redemption and the final victory of His people. Both the song of Moses and the song of the Lamb carry the same theme as this song which the tribulation believers will sing—the ultimate victory of the Lord over all the nations of the world.

The content of this song. The message of this song centers in the praise of God. The focus is on Who He is and what He can and will do. It is a grand reminder to all believers.

1. They praise the works of God, emphasizing His power. These judgments demonstrate the mighty power of God Himself—what He can do (Psalm 145:10-13).

2. They praise the ways of God, emphasizing His plan . The Lord is right and just in all He does (Psalm 145:17). He is faithful to his promises, totally reliable. We may not always understand the plan of God, especially as it relates to justice and the future, but we can be assured there is a plan and that it is the correct plan because of Who God is and how He works His ways in human history.

3. They praise the worthiness of God, emphasizing His perfection. He is "holy," completely separate from all He has created, a distinction uniquely His. Only He deserves the glory and praise (Psalm 29:2; 96:8).

4. They praise the worship of God, emphasizing His purpose. God's ultimate purpose for all nations and all creation is to worship and praise Him (Psalm 66:4; 72:11; Isaiah 66:23; Revelation 4:10-11). Yes, all nations and all creation shall worship the Lord. Everyone, believers and unbelievers alike, shall bow the knee to Him and confess that He is Lord (Philippians 2:9-11).

The Scene in Heaven (15:5-8)

The vision John saw in heaven is often debated. Is there a literal temple in heaven? That's what the Bible seems to indicate by this passage and others. Hebrews 8 and 9 seem to argue for the earthly tabernacle and temple being a "copy" of the heavenly (cf. 8:2, 5; 9:23-24).

The appearance of the seven angels. These are probably the same seven angels mentioned throughout the book of Revelation, chosen by God to execute His purposes upon this world. Notice two things about their appearance here.

1. Their coming out of the temple reminds us of the faithfulness of God. The "temple" is called "the temple of the tabernacle of the testimony in heaven." The "testimony" refers to the law, the commandments of God that were placed within the ark of the covenant. God's covenant with His people will be kept. He will honor His holy and high standards; His judgment will fall upon those who reject Him and His principles. God will be faithful to what He has said and revealed to His people.

2. Their clothing reminds us of the righteousness and majesty of God. They were "clothed in pure bright linen," a picture of righteousness (19:8). What these angels will do in pouring out God's wrath upon the earth in the seven last plagues is a demonstration of the holy and righteous character of God Himself. They were also "having their chests girded with golden bands." It could be a symbol of the priests who ministered in the temple or, more likely, a picture of the majesty and greatness of our God. It is fascinating to compare their clothing with that of our resurrected Lord for He was "girded about the chest with a golden band" (1:13). It is the apparel of a sovereign ruler, a picture of majesty.

The assignment they were given. One of the worship leaders of heaven (one of the four living creatures) gave the seven golden bowls to the seven angels. These bowls are "full of the wrath of God Who lives forever and ever." God's anger is at the boiling point as the seven last plagues are poured out upon the earth. The description of God as the One "Who lives forever and ever" may suggest the eternal consequences of these seven last plagues upon those who receive their fury.

The atmosphere in the temple. What an awesome display of God's presence and power! Two things are emphasized in this one verse:

1. The intensity of God's power. When Isaiah had his vision of the Lord of hosts, "the posts of the door were shaken by the voice of him who cried out, and the house was filled with smoke" (Isaiah 6:4). God's presence was often pictured by a cloud or smoke (Exodus 40:34).

2. The importance of God's plan. God's wrath is a part of His plan, and it will be "completed." Until it is, no one could enter the temple in heaven, dramatically emphasizing the importance of these seven last plagues in the overall plan of God. The tribulation is a demonstration of God's wrath against all who refuse to put their trust in Him. God's day of vengeance is coming (Revelation 6:17)!

The Seven Last Plagues
(16:1-21)

These seven last plagues or judgments complete the wrath of God against a world that has rejected Him and His message of salvation.

¹Then I heard a loud voice from the temple saying to the seven angels, "Go and pour out the bowls of the wrath of God on the earth."

²So the first went and poured out his bowl upon the earth, and a foul and loathsome sore came upon the men who had the mark of the beast and those who worshiped his image.

³Then the second angel poured out his bowl on the sea, and it became blood as of a dead man; and every living creature in the sea died.

⁴Then the third angel poured out his bowl on the rivers and springs of water, and they became blood. ⁵And I heard the angel of the waters saying:

> *"You are righteous, O Lord,*
> *The One who is and who was and who is*
>   *to be,*
> *Because You have judged these things.*
> *⁶For they have shed the blood of saints*
>   *and prophets,*
> *And You have given them blood to drink.*
> *For it is their just due."*

⁷And I heard another from the altar saying, "Even so, Lord God Almighty, true and righteous are Your judgments."

⁸Then the fourth angel poured out his bowl on the sun, and power was given to him to scorch men with fire. ⁹And men were scorched with great heat, and they blasphemed the name of God who has power over these plagues; and they did not repent and give Him glory.

¹⁰Then the fifth angel poured out his bowl on the throne of the beast, and his kingdom became full of darkness; and they gnawed their tongues because of the pain. ¹¹And they blasphemed the God of heaven because of their pains and their sores, and did not repent of their deeds.

[12] Then the sixth angel poured out his bowl on the great river Euphrates, and its water was dried up, so that the way of the kings from the east might be prepared. [13] And I saw three unclean spirits like frogs coming out of the mouth of the dragon, out of the mouth of the beast, and out of the mouth of the false prophet. [14] For they are spirits of demons, performing signs, which go out to the kings of the earth and of the whole world, to gather them to the battle of that great day of God Almighty. [15] "Behold, I am coming as a thief. Blessed is he who watches, and keeps his garments, lest he walk naked and they see his shame." [16] And they gathered them together to the place called in Hebrew, Armageddon.

[17] Then the seventh angel poured out his bowl into the air, and a loud voice came out of the temple of heaven, from the throne, saying, "It is done!" [18] And there were noises and thunderings and lightnings; and there was a great earthquake, such a mighty and great earthquake as had not occurred since men were on the earth. [19] Now the great city was divided into three parts, and the cities of the nations fell. And great Babylon was remembered before God, to give her the cup of the wine of the fierceness of His wrath. [20] Then every island fled away, and the mountains were not found. [21] And great hail from heaven fell upon men, every hailstone about the weight of a talent. And men blasphemed God because of the plague of the hail, since that plague was exceedingly great.

The Command to the Seven Angels (16:1)

Loud (or great) voices are mentioned twenty times in the book, and when used in the singular, it could be a reference to the voice of God or one of His mighty angels. This loud voice originates from the "temple" which was "filled with smoke from the glory of God and from His power" (15:8). The seven angels have already received the seven "bowls of wrath of God," and they are now commanded by God to pour them out upon the earth.

Make no mistake about it—our God is a God of wrath and power. His holiness and justice require Him to execute judgment upon those who refuse to bow the knee to Him and receive His message of salvation.

235

Vision of the Seven Last Plagues

First Plague: Malignant Sores (16:2)

The target of this plague is the people on earth who have received the mark of the beast and worshiped his image. The beast represents the world governments of mankind, and the image is dedicated to the final stage of that governmental history. A ten-nation confederacy will be the immediate arena in which a world leader will emerge. This world leader (Antichrist) will become in and of himself the final government of man before the coming kingdom of Jesus Christ.

The judgment attacks the health of these earth-dwellers causing tremendous emotional upheaval for a culture obsessed with outward appearance and physical well-being. The affliction is described as "a foul and loathsome sore." It appears that all who worship the beast and go along with the new world government will be struck by this plague. Its effects will be enormous upon the health and personal well-being of those afflicted.

Second Plague: The Sea Turns to Blood (16:3)

Similar words were spoken at the announcement of the second trumpet judgment (8:8-9), but the results are different. The second trumpet judgment is caused by what appears to be a meteor crashing into the sea (probably the Mediterranean). One-third of the sea became blood and one-third of its creatures died. In this second plague, the results are more catastrophic—this bowl of wrath causes the death of every living creature in the sea, one of the major food sources of the world. The first bowl of wrath affected the health of those who worship the beast and his image; this plague attacks the food supply of the world.

What an awesome display of God's power and wrath! Imagine the stench alone that will come from these polluted waters. The blood of a dead man is what the text describes, underscoring the horrible consequence of this judgment. It is not merely a different color of the sea that is being pictured; it is the death of millions of sea creatures. What will the world of that day think about such a tragedy?

Third Plague: The Waters Turn to Blood (16:4-7)

The similarity to previous plagues is noteworthy, but the magnitude here is what strikes us. In the third trumpet judgment of chapter 8, one-third of the springs and rivers were affected. In this judgment, all of the world's springs and rivers are affected. The results are catastrophic. The drinking water of mankind is now polluted, causing worldwide panic. The health problems accompanying such a disaster will increase the agony of life. Undoubtedly, people will be aware that the end of the world has come.

Such tragedies could be caused by man's own pollution of the environment, but these are special, supernatural, and unique catastrophes that truly reveal the awesome power and wrath of Almighty God. Nothing in previous history will compare to these plagues from God Himself.

The response of the angels. The angel of the waters proclaims the righteousness of God and another angel comes from the altar and expresses similar praise. While people often question the ways of the Lord and debate His concern and justice in this world, the angels of heaven do not.

The reason for their praise. These angels proclaim the righteousness of God over this judgment in particular because it is a just response to those who have killed the saints and prophets. The world sheds the blood of God's people, and God judges them by turning the water supply of the world into blood. God is answering the prayers of the martyred saints by avenging their blood with this plague (6:9-11).

Fourth Plague: Men Are Scorched (16:8-9)

While it is true that the fourth trumpet judgment affected the sun, the two judgments are not the same. The trumpet judgment in chapter 8 strikes the sun, moon, and stars, reducing their light by one-third of their normal output. Here, only the sun is affected, and its impact is not a reduction in light but an increase in its capacity to bring heat to the earth. What is normally a blessing becomes a curse as men are scorched by the sun's burning rays.

The persons affected by this plague. The text may imply that only those who worship the beast and his image are affected by this plague (cf. 16:2). We, of course, do not know how believers will escape such a judgment. It is possible the areas to which they will escape and hide will be supernaturally protected by God.

The power of this plague. When the text says that "power was given to him," it is referring to the sun, not the angel or to God. God has power over all the plagues. The sun's heat is intensified and that particular star of God's original creation, often worshiped by mankind, now becomes an enemy. The last plagues strike at the heart of humanity's security and survival. This is no late summer heat wave. The earth will be scorched with "great heat" causing severe burning.

The purpose of this plague. Since the unbelievers of this world will blaspheme the name of God because of this plague, it is obvious they are aware of the source of this judgment. One of the purposes of this plague is to demonstrate the power and wrath of Almighty God and to make sure that humanity knows it is coming from God.

Another purpose is to prove that the problem with humanity is not the environment but the human heart. Mankind's depravity will not be altered by knowledge that God is bringing judgment, contrary to what many people think. This plague proves once and for all that humanity has a serious problem with sin. It blinds us to our need and refuses to acknowledge what we know to be true. That those afflicted by this plague "did not repent and give Him glory," exposes their continuing willful rebellion against God.

Fifth Plague: Darkness and Pain (16:10-11)

This is not merely a dark night when clouds cover the moon and the stars are not visible. This is a supernatural judgment that blackens so extensively people cannot see each other and no one dares to move.

The result of this plague. Verse 10 tells us the kingdom of the beast became "full of darkness." The darkness is so intense, pain is experienced and people express their anguish by gnawing their tongues. In Matthew 25:30 Jesus spoke of the awful consequence of eternal punishment, describing it as "outer darkness" where there will be "weeping and gnashing of teeth." The darkness of the fifth plague is a preview of hell itself.

The response of those who worship the beast and his image. Those afflicted by this plague continue to blaspheme God "because of their pains and their sores." Evidently the darkness intensifies the suffering they already were experiencing. The "sores" refer back to the first plague and confirm that those who blaspheme are "the men who had the mark of the beast and those who worshiped his image" (v. 2).

The refusal to repent. No more tragic words could be written than the final words of verse 11—"and did not repent of their deeds." In the final analysis, repentance demands change in lifestyle. These beast worshipers know the plagues are coming from the God of heaven, but they refuse to repent because they want to continue their sinful lifestyles (cf. 9:20-21). It is indeed amazing that under such circumstances people will continue to rebel and will not repent of their wicked ways. What a graphic reminder of our need for God's grace and power to break the shackles of sin that so strongly bind us and keep us from turning to the only One Who can save us!

Sixth Plague: Euphrates Dried Up (16:12-16)

The preparation for battle. When the sixth bowl of wrath is poured out by the angel, a fascinating event takes place—the river Euphrates, one of the great rivers of the world, is dried up! This occurs "so that the way of the kings from the east might be prepared." If the Euphrates were to dry up, it would make it possible for great land armies from the east to come into the Middle East. The text speaks of "kings," implying that several nations will be involved. Since "all nations" are gathered against Jerusalem during the battle of Armageddon, we would expect that all the nations from the east will invade the Middle East. The armies of the orient will be drawn into this final conflict along with the other nations of the world.

Some Bible teachers connect this passage with Revelation 9:14-16 where the river Euphrates and an army of horsemen numbering two hundred million is mentioned. However, that passage is describing a demonic attack that occurs earlier in the tribulation period, whereas the sixth plague is the preparation for the final battle or campaign of Armageddon in which all nations of the world are gathered against Jerusalem, the great battle the Hebrew prophets of old predicted would take place at the end of the age (Zechariah 12:1-9; 14:1-15). This is not yet the final rebellion. Revelation 20:7-10 records that at the end of the thousand-year reign of Jesus Christ, Satan will be released and attempt to deceive the nations to attack Jerusalem. God will destroy with fire those who rebel, and the devil will be cast into the lake of fire where he will join the beast and the false prophet.

The presence of demonic forces. "Three unclean spirits like frogs" is John's description of the ugly, diabolical creatures who infest and pollute the world. We are told clearly that these are "spirits of demons." They come out of the dragon (Satan), the beast (world political leader), and the false prophet (world religious leader). This vision reveals the wicked and demonic activities of those who are world leaders in the tribulation period; they are inspired by demons. These spirits of demons are capable of "performing signs," a reminder of the "great signs" the false prophet will be able to perform in order to deceive the inhabitants of the earth (13:13-14; cf. 2 Thessalonians 2:9).

When miraculous signs are performed, many people believe God is behind them. The Bible teaches otherwise. While it is possible that

God is performing the signs, it is also possible they are being done through the power of Satan or demons. Miraculous signs are used to persuade people that God is doing great things today in most cultures and countries of the world. Many Christians are persuaded that these signs are from the Lord. However, often there are questions in the minds of mature and discerning believers when these signs do not measure up to the miracles of Jesus Christ. Christians need to be alert to the claims of people who say they are able to perform miraculous signs. The Antichrist, the false prophet, and the devil himself are all capable of doing amazing things intended to deceive people and to draw them away from the Lord.

The purpose of these demonic forces. The simple purpose is "to gather them to the battle of that great day of God Almighty." Anti-Semitism is the work of Satan and demons. Why will all nations gather in the Middle East to wipe out the Jews? They will be influenced by demons.

The promise of the second coming. The One Who claims He "is coming as a thief" (v. 15) is none other than Jesus Christ. That is clear from the last chapter of Revelation where we are told He is "coming quickly" (22:7, 12, 20). The second coming of Christ will be a surprise to many, but not to those who are watching and ready (Matthew 24:42-44; 1 Thessalonians 5:1-6; 2 Peter 3:10).

One of the sober passages upon which all of us should meditate are these words from our Lord's lips in the Sermon on the Mount (Matthew 7:21-23):

> "Not everyone who says to Me, 'Lord, Lord,' shall enter the kingdom of heaven, but he who does the will of My Father in heaven. Many will say to Me in that day, 'Lord, Lord, have we not prophesied in Your name, cast out demons in Your name, and done many wonders in Your name?' And then I will declare to them, 'I never knew you; depart from Me, you who practice lawlessness!'"

A lifestyle of "lawlessness" and sinfulness is evidence of unbelief, not salvation. We may profess to be Christian, but the proof is found in the way we live. Moral purity will be the result of those who anticipate the second coming of Christ and have this hope resting upon them (1 John 3:2-3).

Verse 15 gives us the third beatitude in the book of Revelation:

> 1:3—"*Blessed* is he who reads and those who hear the words of this prophecy, and keep those things which are written in it; for the time is near."

240

14:13—"'*Blessed* are the dead who die in the Lord from now on.'" "Yes," says the Spirit, "that they may rest from their labors, and their works follow them."

16:15—"*Blessed* is he who watches, and keeps his garments, lest he walk naked and they see his shame."

The place where the nations are gathered. The place bears a Hebrew name—*Armageddon.* The exact meaning is not clear. Some believe the word simply means "mountain or hill of slaughter," and is a symbolic term. Others believe it is a literal place where many great battles of Old Testament times occurred. The first part of the word is the Hebrew word for mountain or hill; the second part could refer to Megiddo and thus be a reference to the enormous and beautiful valley which separates Galilee from Samaria. It was often the place where ancient armies would gather to do battle. The city of Megiddo was an important fortress, guarding the road which leads in and out of the valley on the southwest edge.

The area is not sufficient for all the armies of the world, but it may represent the central focus of all these invaders who intend to attack Jerusalem and destroy the Jewish people. It appears from the account of Revelation 14:20 that the armies are gathered in an area covering at least two hundred miles. We know from the biblical record that some of the armies are going to be at Jerusalem (Zechariah 14:1-3).

Seventh Plague: A Great Earthquake (16:17-21)

The last of the seven plagues will finish God's wrath upon the earth. It will be the most catastrophic and terrible judgment ever to hit this planet. At least three things are clear from this passage about this judgment of God:

It will be the completion of God's plan. In 10:7 we were told of the day when "the mystery of God would be finished." In 15:1 we read that in the seven last plagues "the wrath of God is complete."

It will be the greatest catastrophe of all time. Four things clearly reveal that this is the greatest catastrophe of all human history:

1. The magnitude of the earthquake. Earthquakes are frightening. They can also cause much property damage and loss of life. This earthquake is the big one—there has never been one like it in human history. It will cause panic on a massive scale. Revelation 6 introduced us to a terrible and awesome earthquake announcing that the great day of God's wrath had come. Now a more frightening and much more extensive earthquake will end the day of God's wrath. The whole world will be affected (cf. Isaiah 24:18-20).

2. *The destruction of the world's cities.* The major capitals of the world are all destroyed. This is a worldwide disaster of incredible proportions! Verse 19 says, "the great city was divided into three parts." This is probably not a reference to Jerusalem but to Babylon, the center of world government and religions during tribulation times. The statement, "and great Babylon was remembered before God," supports this view.

3. *The disappearance of mountains and islands.* Great changes in the topography of the earth will occur because of this final judgment of God. The earthquake that begins the tribulation caused the mountains and islands to be moved out of their places (6:14), but this one causes the disappearance of the islands and mountains!

4. *The dropping of giant hailstones.* Though a similar plague hit ancient Egypt (Exodus 9:22-24), the hail of Revelation 16 is the worst in the history of the world. These hailstones weigh about a hundred pounds. Can you imagine hailstones that weigh a hundred pounds each falling out of the sky?

It will be the consequence God will bring on those who worship the beast and his image. This is the third time those who worship the beast and his image (v. 2) have blasphemed God (16:9, 11, 21). The severity of the plague does not drive them to their knees; it only intensifies their hatred of God. Once again, the depravity of the human heart is manifest.

The Seven Last Plagues

Where do you stand? If you have not yet committed your life to Jesus Christ as your only Savior from sin, death, and hell, why not do it now? There is no more important decision in your life than this one. You must believe on the Lord Jesus Christ! His death on the cross for your sins almost two thousand years ago is the sufficient payment and the only sacrifice God accepts for our sin and rebellion. He is not a dead Savior. He arose from the dead, and because of His resurrection we shall arise form the dead as well. Jesus Christ is coming back! Are you ready to meet Him?

Chapter 24

The Mystery of Babylon the Great

(17:1-18)

In chapter 12 we were introduced to the beast with seven heads and ten horns, a manifestation of the dragon, the devil himself. In chapter 13 a beast comes out of the Mediterranean Sea and has seven heads and ten horns. One of its heads received a deadly wound and was brought back to life. We believe the sixth head is the one that received the fatal blow. It came back to life as a ten-nation (ten horns) confederacy, making it the seventh head, out of which will come a world dictator.

Chapter 17 introduces us to a woman who sits on the beast with seven heads and ten horns. She is called "the great harlot," and the name on her forehead is: "MYSTERY, BABYLON THE GREAT, THE MOTHER OF HARLOTS AND OF THE ABOMINATIONS OF THE EARTH."

In chapter 18 we will see the fall of Babylon the Great. It appears this chapter is a detailed account of what is described in the closing verses of chapter 17. Many Bible teachers see the destruction of the woman as a removal of the world religious order, and the destruction of the city called "Babylon the Great" as the end of the political system that controls the entire world. That is difficult to prove. A simple reading of the text suggests that the fall of Babylon the Great is the destruction of the woman; she is Babylon the Great.

The beast is destroyed by the return of Jesus Christ (19:11-21). The beast and the false prophet are cast into the lake of fire (19:20). The woman is destroyed by the ten kings (horns) who form the political alliance through which the beast ascends to power.

The woman pictures a false religion that will dominate the world in the tribulation period, whereas the beast symbolizes the world government of the last half of the tribulation period. Both symbols illustrate the past as well as the present. Past history has demonstrated the awful reality of both systems—religious and political—as they have been corrupted by human depravity and moral degradation. The religious system of the end times will be led by the false prophet (13:11-18) whereas the political system will be led by the beast we know as the Antichrist (13:1-10).

The Woman on the Beast
(17:1-18)

[1] *Then one of the seven angels who had the seven bowls came and talked with me, saying to me, "Come, I will show you the judgment of the great harlot who sits on many waters,* [2] *with whom the kings of the earth committed fornication, and the inhabitants of the earth were made drunk with the wine of her fornication."* [3] *So he carried me away in the Spirit into the wilderness. And I saw a woman sitting on a scarlet beast which was full of names of blasphemy, having seven heads and ten horns.* [4] *The woman was arrayed in purple and scarlet, and adorned with gold and precious stones and pearls, having in her hand a golden cup full of abominations and the filthiness of her fornication.* [5] *And on her forehead a name was written:*

MYSTERY,
BABYLON THE GREAT,
THE MOTHER OF HARLOTS AND OF
THE ABOMINATIONS OF THE EARTH.

[6] *And I saw the woman, drunk with the blood of the saints and with the blood of the martyrs of Jesus. And when I saw her, I marveled with great amazement.*

[7] *But the angel said to me, "Why did you marvel? I will tell you the mystery of the woman and of the beast that carries her, which has the seven heads and the ten horns.* [8] *The beast that you saw was, and is not, and will ascend out of the bottomless pit and go to perdition. And those who dwell on the earth will marvel, whose names are not written in the Book of Life from the foundation of the world, when they see the beast that was, and is not, and*

yet is. *⁹Here is the mind which has wisdom: The seven heads are seven mountains on which the woman sits. ¹⁰There are also seven kings. Five have fallen, one is, and the other has not yet come. And when he comes, he must continue a short time. ¹¹ And the beast that was, and is not, is himself also the eighth, and is of the seven, and is going to perdition. ¹²And the ten horns which you saw are ten kings who have received no kingdom as yet, but they receive authority for one hour as kings with the beast. ¹³These are of one mind, and they will give their power and authority to the beast. ¹⁴These will make war with the Lamb, and the Lamb will overcome them, for he is Lord of lords and King of kings; and those who are with Him are called, chosen, and faithful." ¹⁵And he said to me, "The waters which you saw, where the harlot sits, are peoples, multitudes, nations, and tongues. ¹⁶And the ten horns which you saw on the beast, these will hate the harlot, make her desolate and naked, eat her flesh and burn her with fire. ¹⁷For God has put it into their hearts to fulfill His purpose, to be of one mind, and to give their kingdom to the beast, until the words of God are fulfilled. ¹⁸And the woman whom you saw is that great city which reigns over the kings of the earth."*

The Definition of the Woman (17:1-6, 15)

The announcement of judgment. When John is invited to see this great harlot who sits on many waters, he is told he will be viewing her judgment. The description of her as the *"great* harlot" emphasizes the all-pervasive influence of this woman throughout history and the seriousness of that influence in the eyes of God. This is not to be taken lightly.

Revelation 19:2 is the response of a great multitude in heaven over the fall of the harlot, Babylon the Great. This praise honors God because "He has judged the great harlot," avenging the blood of His servants which the harlot has shed throughout history.

The authority of the woman. The influence of this harlot is quite extensive; she "sits on many waters," representing "peoples, multitudes, nations, and tongues" (vv. 1, 15). Her influence has invaded all nations of the world.

John saw the woman "sitting on a scarlet beast which was full of names of blasphemy, having seven heads and ten horns" (17:3). It was in a desolate place that John viewed this woman on the beast, reminding us that death not life is the environment in which the harlot and the beast thrive. The woman sits on the beast, exercising authority and influence over it. Whatever the woman represents, she has dominated all the great empires of the world and will be prominent in the tribulation as well.

Perhaps the most fascinating statement of all concerning her authority and influence is the statement of verse 2: "With whom the kings of the earth committed fornication, and the inhabitants of the earth were made drunk with the wine of her fornication." Fornication is sexual immorality. Symbolically, this harlot has used sex and drunkenness to entice and seduce world leaders and the inhabitants of the world (cf. 18:3, 9, 23; 19:2). What a graphic picture of deception, manipulation, and seduction. Throughout history, the story has been repeated. This harlot has affected all nations, and God will judge her for it and destroy her once and for all.

The appearance of the woman. It is tempting to relate the appearance of this woman with the lavish wealth of the Roman Catholic Church. That viewpoint was the strong opinion of the Reformers, as we might expect. It was also the view of Tertullian, Jerome, Augustine, and most Bible commentators throughout medieval church history. Protestant Bible scholars have been strongly influenced to identify this woman as the Roman church. That may be the case—time will tell. However, it is important to see that the woman sits on the beast whose heads represent the empires of past and future world history.

The Roman Catholic Church is a part of the problem but cannot be the only problem in this prophetic puzzle. False religion is found among Protestants as well as Catholics. False religion has permeated all the cultures of the world and has produced a variety of beliefs and practices incompatible with orthodox Christianity. Organized religion has never been a friend to true believers in the one true God and His Messiah, Jesus Christ our Lord. Devotion to God has often been set aside by those who prefer pomp and lavish display. Spiritual commitment has never been the "bottom line" for those dedicated to power and wealth.

Notice three things about this woman's appearance:

1. Her apparel. The simplicity of a godly lifestyle stands in stark contrast to the appearance of this harlot. The garments of royalty and prosperity are displayed on her. One cannot help contrasting her apparel with that of a godly woman described in 1 Timothy 2:9-10.

2. Her adornment. Revelation 18:16 says the "great city" was "adorned with gold and precious stones and pearls." Religion is big business! The wealth accumulated by religion throughout human history is awesome indeed. Again, quite a contrast to the qualities of the godly woman (1 Timothy 2:9; 1 Peter 3:3).

3. Her abominations. This woman is "full of abominations." She has done it all, and is ripe for the judgment of God (18:5-6). That judgment is graphically portrayed in Jeremiah 51:7-8 where the symbolism of "a golden cup" is also used:

> Babylon was a golden cup in the LORD's hand,
> That made all the earth drunk.
> The nations drank her wine;
> Therefore the nations are deranged.
> Babylon has suddenly fallen and been destroyed.

The "golden cup" is filled with wine that the nations have drunk. This cup is "full of abominations." False religion and its methods and practices are abominations to God.

Israel's abominations usually consisted of immorality and idolatry (1 Kings 14:22-24; 2 Kings 21). God confronted Israel during the Babylonian captivity about her abominations (Ezekiel 20:30-31).

The association of this woman with Babylon. The name written on the forehead of this harlot is: "MYSTERY, BABYLON THE GREAT, THE MOTHER OF HARLOTS AND OF THE ABOMINATIONS OF THE EARTH." Two things are clear from this name:

1. She is a mystery. This suggests that neither ancient Babylon nor its site is intended. It teaches us to look deeper and to see it figuratively rather than literally. A mystery is not something mysterious but something previously unknown that is now being revealed to those given understanding.

2. She is a mother. The woman represents that which began with Babylon and has continued throughout history. She is the "mother of harlots" and the "mother of the abominations of the earth." She is the source from which much evil and spiritual adultery has come. She has been instrumental in seducing multitudes and using other women ("harlots") to accomplish her objectives.

This fact alone would control any attempts to limit the meaning of this harlot to one particular religious system. The "mystery" of Babylon the Great is not a reference to ancient Babylon, nor merely the Roman Catholic church. The false religion symbolized by her has permeated all history from the time of Babylon until the present day. Satan's counterfeits have appeared in many countries and cultures, and they will reach their climax of sinister methods, evil practices, and deceptive teachings during the tribulation period.

The accusation against this woman. Apostate Christianity has always persecuted true Christianity. In the name of religious zeal, many have been slaughtered. That the harlot is "drunk" suggests a continual carnage, not just one historical moment in which a few believers were killed unjustly. "Saints" and "martyrs of Jesus" may be synonymous or they may indicate two distinct groups of believers—those before the time of Jesus and those after His time. This woman would then picture a religious system both before and after the time of Christ. One thing is certain—the woman has been persecuting believers in Jesus Christ (cf. 6:10; 16:5-6; 18:24)!

The Description of the Beast (17:7-14)

John is amazed at all that he is seeing. He was a victim of the political persecution of his day, and now he is granted a vision that shows how Christianity will become corrupt and the persecutor of the faithful and true believers. No wonder he is amazed!

Not only is the woman a "mystery" but so is the beast, which is now described with some details we have not seen in previous passages. And what a description! Put yourself in the place of the apostle John, and you will have a greater appreciation of this passage.

The impact the beast will have. The beast with seven heads comes "out of the bottomless pit." In Revelation 9, the "bottomless pit" was opened and a plague of locusts whose king is "the angel of the bottomless pit," none other than the devil himself, was released. The "bottomless pit" is the habitat of demonic spirits. The beast is of satanic origin, and as we learned in chapter 13, it is "the dragon" who "gave him his power, his throne, and great authority."

This beast will have enormous impact ("those who dwell on the earth will marvel"). The unbelievers of the tribulation will be impressed with the restoration of world government which appeared to end with the fall of Rome. It will come back to life as a ten-nation confederacy around the Mediterranean Sea.

These unbelieving earth-dwellers are those "whose names are not written in the Book of Life from the foundation of the world." That statement implies that names are not written in the Book of Life during the course of human history, but rather before the foundation of the world. It also implies that names are not erased. Names are either written down in the Book of Life or not written down, and this occurs before the creation of the world. Those whose names are written down in the Book of Life are believers, and those who do not have their names in that Book are unbelievers. A difficult teaching, but nevertheless an accurate reflection of biblical statements. While it may go beyond our finite human capacity to understand, it rests securely in the counsels and foreknowledge of God, to Whom belongs all the glory and praise!

The destiny of the beast is "perdition" (destruction), and the final form of the beast will also go to perdition (v. 11). Second Thessalonians 2:8 says that the Antichrist, the lawless one, will be consumed by the Lord "with the breath of His mouth." The Lord will "destroy" this coming world leader "with the brightness of His coming."

The identity of the seven heads. Verse 9 begins with the words, "Here is the mind which has wisdom" (cf. 13:18). This passage takes spiritual understanding and careful study of the biblical record. The difficulty of interpreting it is revealed by the many ways it has been explained throughout church history.

To identify the seven heads as the seven hills ("mountains") of the city of Rome is ignoring the clear statement of verse 10 that the seven mountains are seven kings. The seven kings can represent political empires or kingdoms as well as individual rulers. When an attempt is made to identify these kings as Roman emperors in the first century A.D., the five emperors before the exile of John under Domitian are usually seen as those who "have fallen" (v. 10). The one who "has not yet come" is some unknown ruler, whether in the immediate future of John's day or in the distant future extending beyond our present time.

The view that the seven kings refer to individual Roman rulers is not convincing. It does not explain adequately the seventh head with ten horns (ten kings). It also does not connect well with the prophecies of Daniel which imply that world empires or extensive kingdoms are being suggested, rather than individual leaders. The use of "king" to refer to a kingdom better fits both Old and New Testament prophecies. The beast with seven heads represents world government throughout human history and should not be relegated to the time of the apostle John.

The following points summarize what I believe to be the best interpretation of these verses:

1. The beast with seven heads represents world government at seven moments of history.

2. The five empires that have controlled the world before John's day are Egypt, Assyria, Babylon, Medo-Persia, and Greece.

3. The world government existing in John's day was the Roman empire, and there has not been a true world empire since. This sixth head or empire is the one that received the fatal wound, but will be brought back to life as the seventh empire of the world.

4. The seventh empire will not last long and will develop from a ten-nation confederacy around the Mediterranean Sea. It will be a revived Roman Empire.

5. Out of this seventh empire of ten nations will arise a world leader (Antichrist) who will in himself become the eighth empire of the world.

The introduction of the eighth head of the beast. One of the problems with the description of the beast is the reference in verse 11 to it becoming the eighth head. Let's look at that verse again: "And the beast that was, and is not, is himself also the eighth, and is of the seven, and is going to perdition."

The key is the phrase, "and is of the seven." It appears that the past six world empires, and the coming ten-nation confederacy which will become the seventh world empire, are all summarized or revealed in a person who will become in and of himself the eighth world empire. It is possible that this person, who is a beast also, is the coming Antichrist, the "little horn" of Daniel 7:8 who arises from within the final ten-nation confederacy.

The beast is world government and has seven periods of history in which to be manifested. The beast is also revealed in all of its characteristics and policies in one future world leader—the Antichrist!

The involvement of the ten horns. The "beast" in verses 12 and 13 is the coming world leader, the Antichrist. The ten horns (cf. Daniel 7:7-8, 23-25) are ten kings or nations who were not in existence in John's day ("who have received no kingdom as yet"). Their confederacy will not last long ("for one hour as kings with the beast") before they surrender their authority and power to the beast who comes into their midst and quickly assumes control by affecting three of them (Daniel 7:8).

The impossibility the ten horns will face. The final ten-nation confederacy under the leadership of the coming world ruler, the Antichrist, will go to war against the Lamb of God, our coming Messiah and Lord. It is a hopeless struggle for "He is Lord of lords and King of kings"! What a powerful and thrilling statement for every true believer; we are on the victory side of human history!

Psalm 2 speaks eloquently of this final conflict and the Lord's victory:

Why do the nations rage,
And the people plot a vain thing?
The kings of the earth set themselves,
And the rulers take counsel together,
Against the LORD and against His
    Anointed, saying,
"Let us break Their bonds in pieces
And cast away Their cords from us."

He who sits in the heavens shall laugh;
The LORD shall hold them in derision.
Then He shall speak to them in His wrath,
And distress them in His deep displeasure:
"Yet I have set My King
On My holy hill of Zion."

"I will declare the decree:
The LORD has said to Me,
'You are My Son,
Today I have begotten You.
Ask of Me, and I will give You
The nations for Your inheritance,
And the ends of the earth for Your
    possession.
You shall break them with a rod of iron;
You shall dash them in pieces like a
    potter's vessel.'"

Now therefore, be wise, O kings;
Be instructed, you judges of the earth.
Serve the LORD with fear,
And rejoice with trembling.
Kiss the Son, lest He be angry,
And you perish in the way,
When His wrath is kindled but a little.
Blessed are all those who put their trust
    in Him.

What a powerful statement of our Lord's final victory over all the nations of the world who gather against Him!

Notice that Revelation 17:14 speaks of "those who are with Him" who are "called, chosen, and faithful." These are the ones described as "the armies in heaven, clothed in fine linen, white and clean" (19:14). Believers are the "called" (Romans 1:6-7; 8:28; 1 Corinthians 1:2), the "chosen" (Ephesians 1:4; 1 Peter 2:9), and the "faithful" (Colossians 1:2; 1 Peter 5:12; Revelation 2:10).

The Destruction of the Woman (17:16-18)

The manuscript evidence favors the words "and the beast" in verse 16 instead of the words "on the beast." This matches with what verse 13 has already declared: "they will give their power and authority to the beast." Along with the beast, and no doubt under his leadership, the ten nations will destroy the woman who represents false religion. The world government of the future will use religion to promote its goals and achieve its purposes. When religion is no longer useful, it will be destroyed.

The means by which she is destroyed. The graphic description of the ten nations' hostility to religion ("hate the harlot") reminds us that political powers will tolerate religious beliefs and systems but essentially have no regard for them. In the tribulation we will see this truth displayed in what the confederacy does to the woman.

The statement "make her desolate and naked" reveals that the massive wealth of the woman (17:4) will be stripped away and taken by the government. The words "eat her flesh and burn her with fire" describe the extent to which the government will go in completely eliminating all forms and institutions of religion throughout the world.

It is possible that the destruction of the woman will come at the middle of the tribulation period or shortly thereafter. This would explain the terrible persecution by the Antichrist in the last half of the tribulation. During the first half, religious freedom will exist, allowing for the preaching of the gospel by the two witnesses and the 144,000 Jewish evangelists. This also explains the Jewish temple sacrifices being restored. A measure of freedom will exist for all religions during the first half of the tribulation. However, the coming world leader, will break his covenant with the nation of Israel and begin to persecute believers during the last half of the tribulation.

The motivation behind her destruction. All history is unfolding the plan of Almighty God. Nothing happens outside His direction and will. The real reason the ten-nation confederacy will destroy the religious system that originally supported it is that God will cause them to do so. His words are being fulfilled, reminding all of us that the plan of God is being fulfilled according to what He has declared (cf. Matthew 5:17-18).

The meaning of the woman. The woman "is that great city which reigns over the kings of the earth." The name written on her forehead is "BABYLON THE GREAT." Since this is not the literal historical site of ancient Babylon, it must represent something else. Many throughout church history have identified the "great city" as the city of Rome, where the Roman Catholic Church has its international headquarters. Interestingly so, the Roman church has also stated that the harlot of Revelation 17 represents the city of Rome. Some of the art works of the Vatican are paintings of the harlot with a golden cup in her hand, representing the church of Rome.

The Roman Catholic Church may well be the final dominant religious system of the world in the tribulation period, but the harlot has reigned over all the governments of the world in past history. The city could be Jerusalem as an international center for all religions (cf. 11:8), or a city which remains unknown at the present but will become the major religious center of the tribulation period. We simply do not know.

There are many lessons to be learned in the study of this chapter. One obvious lesson is that the existence of a world religious system is not to be supported by true believers in Jesus Christ. This system is no friend of true believers. The false religious systems of this world have killed the saints and the prophets.

Chapter 25

The Fall of
Babylon the Great

(18:1-24)

Is this chapter describing the destruction of the harlot or the destruction of the political and commercial system of the Antichrist's world government? The opening phrase "after these things" suggests to some Bible scholars that the events of chapter 18 are not synonymous with those in chapter 17. They see the political and economic system of world government collapsing in chapter 18, whereas the religious system falls in chapter 17.

However, it is not necessary to interpret the phrase "after these things" as indicating a time sequence. It could be simply a phrase indicating additional remarks about what was just said in chapter 17. Many commentators of the past and present do not see a distinction between chapters 17 and 18. They believe the destruction of the woman, called "MYSTERY, BABYLON THE GREAT" (17:5), is exactly what is described in chapter 18 as the fall of Babylon. There are several reasons for such a view.

The usage of the word "Babylon." The harlot is called "Babylon the Great" (17:5) and "that great city which reigns over the kings of the earth" (17:18). It is not directly used to refer to the beast with seven heads or the world government of the end time. It refers to the woman.

The context before and after Revelation 18. At the end of chapter 16 we have a clear reference to the fall of "great Babylon" (16:19). Revelation 17:1 begins with the words of one of the seven angels (perhaps the seventh one that poured out the judgment on Babylon): "Come, I will show you the judgment of the great harlot who sits on many waters." John is being shown the judgment of the great harlot, not the judgment of the beast and his armies. The end of chapter 17 makes that abundantly clear—it is the woman's destruction that is being revealed.

Chapter 18 then describes the fall of Babylon, continually using words, phrases, and sentences that apply to the harlot. Then at the beginning of chapter 19, we read about the praise of heaven over the fact that the Lord our God "has judged the great harlot who corrupted the earth with her fornication."

The statements of Revelation 18. Many statements about Babylon in chapter 18 are the same as what was said about the harlot in chapter 17. The use of the feminine pronoun throughout chapter 18 suggests that the woman's destruction is being described in great detail.

Verse 3 says "all the nations have drunk of the wine of the wrath of her fornication, the kings of the earth have committed fornication with her." This is an obvious reference to the harlot's widespread immorality (cf. 14:8; 17:2; 18:9). In addition to these references about her "fornication" with "the kings of the earth," we have the clear statement in 18:24 as to the reason for the judgment: "and in her was found the blood of prophets and saints, and of all who were slain on the earth." From the cry of the martyrs under the altar (6:9-11) to the triumphal voice of the great multitude in heaven (19:1-10), it is clearly the judgment of the woman that is being pictured.

There is no mention of the harlot in the descriptions of the final conflict between "the beast, the kings of the earth, and their armies" and the One Who "sat on the horse . . . and His army" (19:19). She has possibly been destroyed already by the kings of the ten-nation confederacy. Revelation 19:20 does mention that the beast and the false prophet are captured and cast into the lake of fire. The existence of the false prophet at this point, who is the world leader of false religion in the tribulation, might lead us to doubt that the woman has already been destroyed, but such an argument is far from conclusive.

The Fall of Babylon
(18:1-24)

¹*After these things I saw another angel coming down from heaven, having great authority, and the earth was illuminated with his glory. ²And he cried mightily with a loud voice, saying, "Babylon the great is fallen, is fallen, and has become a habitation of demons, a prison for every foul spirit, and a cage for every unclean and hated bird! ³For all the nations have drunk of the wine of the wrath of her fornication, the kings of the earth have committed fornication with her, and the merchants of the earth have*

become rich through the abundance of her luxury." [4] And I heard another voice from heaven saying, "Come out of her, my people, lest you share in her sins, and lest you receive of her plagues. [5] For her sins have reached to heaven, and God has remembered her iniquities. [6] Render to her just as she rendered to you, and repay her double according to her works; in the cup which she has mixed, mix for her double. [7] In the measure that she glorified herself and lived luxuriously, in the same measure give her torment and sorrow; for she says in her heart, 'I sit as queen, and am no widow, and will not see sorrow.' [8] Therefore her plagues will come in one day—death and mourning and famine. And she will be utterly burned with fire, for strong is the Lord God who judges her.

[9] "And the kings of the earth who committed fornication and lived luxuriously with her will weep and lament for her, when they see the smoke of her burning, [10] standing at a distance for fear of her torment, saying, 'Alas, alas, that great city Babylon, that mighty city! For in one hour your judgment has come.' [11] And the merchants of the earth will weep and mourn over her, for no one buys their merchandise anymore: [12] merchandise of gold and silver, precious stones and pearls, fine linen and purple, silk and scarlet, every kind of citron wood, every kind of object of ivory, every kind of object of most precious wood, bronze, iron, and marble; [13] and cinnamon and incense, fragrant oil and frankincense, wine and oil, fine flour and wheat, cattle and sheep, horses and chariots, and bodies and souls of men. [14] And the fruit that your soul longed for has gone from you, and all the things which are rich and splendid have gone from you, and you shall find them no more at all. [15] The merchants of these things, who became rich by her, will stand at a distance for fear of her torment, weeping and wailing, [16] and saying, 'Alas, alas, that great city that was clothed in fine linen, purple, and scarlet, and adorned with gold and precious stones and pearls! [17] For in one hour such great riches came to nothing.' And every shipmaster, all who travel by ship, sailors, and as many as trade on the sea, stood at a distance [18] and cried out when they saw the smoke of her burning, saying, 'What is like this great city?' [19] And they threw dust on their heads and

cried out, weeping and wailing, and saying, 'Alas, alas, that great city, in which all who had ships on the sea became rich by her wealth! For in one hour she is made desolate.' [20]*Rejoice over her, O heaven, and you holy apostles and prophets, for God has avenged you on her!"*

[21]*Then a mighty angel took up a stone like a great millstone and threw it into the sea, saying, "Thus with violence the great city Babylon shall be thrown down, and shall not be found anymore.* [22]*The sound of harpists, musicians, flutists, and trumpeters shall not be heard in you anymore. And no craftsman of any craft shall be found in you anymore. And the sound of a millstone shall not be heard in you anymore.* [23]*And the light of a lamp shall not shine in you anymore. And the voice of bridegroom and bride shall not be heard in you anymore. For your merchants were the great men of the earth, for by your sorcery all the nations were deceived.* [24]*And in her was found the blood of prophets and saints, and of all who were slain on the earth."*

The Prediction of the Fall of Babylon (18:1-3)

The angel of verse 1 has "great authority" and may be the "mighty angel" who throws the stone into the sea and announces the violent overthrow of the great city of Babylon (v. 21). The stunning appearance and authority of this angel is, of course, a clear indication that God Himself is announcing His judgment upon Babylon. God backs up His messenger with a dramatic display so no one can doubt Who is behind this destruction.

The results of the fall of Babylon. The angel announces that Babylon has become "a habitation of demons, a prison for every foul spirit, and a cage for every unclean and hated bird." What a terrible place it will be! This threefold description reminds us of previous prophecies about the unsurpassed destruction of the Babylonian empire that existed in the sixth century before Christ (Isaiah 13-14; Jeremiah 50-51). Babylon was once a world empire and it was destroyed, never to be inhabited again. The mystery side of Babylon's influence, both political and religious, has continued throughout history and will culminate in the tribulation period with a world government and a world religious system, both of which will fall by the judgment of God Himself.

The reason for the fall of Babylon. The reason is stated several times in this book—"all the nations have drunk of the wine of the wrath of her fornication."

1. The extent of her influence. Any view of the harlot that does not include her influence over all the nations of the world is inadequate. The harlot has influenced every nation on the face of the earth, including those from the past.

2. The explanation of her seductive ways. The kings of the earth have been seduced by her wine. It was common in the ancient world (and today!) to use wine to manipulate or seduce a person to do something he or she would not normally do. Her wine is described as being her "wrath." This "wrath" is directed toward the prophets, apostles, and saints. She seduces the leaders of the world to murder true believers. The extent of that seduction will be most severe during the tribulation period.

3. The effect of her seductive ways. The "bottom line" is money. People have become rich by relating to this symbol of false religion. First Timothy 6:10 says "the love of money is a root of all kinds of evil." How true! Many have been the injustices and crimes of this world for the sake of money. The commercial enterprises in which religion has engaged are endless.

The Plea to God's People (18:4-5)

The command for God's people to "come out of her" comes from Jeremiah's prophecies to the people of Israel to get out of ancient Babylon (50:8-10; 51:45). It is clear from these two passages that God desires to protect His people, and He desires to punish Babylon. God's protection of His people demands their withdrawal from the embrace of the harlot. This assumes that true believers will be caught within her web. Otherwise, there is no need for such an appeal.

It is indeed amazing how true believers can continue their affiliations and relationships with apostate organizations. Separation from apostate Christianity has always been the requirement of God. Do not stay within the membership of any organization that no longer believes and teaches the fundamental and historic doctrines of salvation as taught in the Bible (1 Timothy 6:3-5; 2 Timothy 3:1-5).

God will not forget! Revelation 18:5 says the harlot's "sins have reached to heaven," a possible wordplay on the situation of the Tower of Babel (Genesis 11), and that "God has remembered her iniquities." This has obvious connection with the outpouring of the seventh plague when

The Fall of Babylon the Great

"Babylon was remembered before God, to give her the cup of the wine of the fierceness of His wrath" (16:19). The harlot woman's cup was filled with the wine of her wrath by which she seduced the nations and leaders of the world. God will reward her with a drink from His own cup of wrath!

The Payment Babylon Will Receive (18:6-8)

In spite of what people often think, no one is getting away with anything. Payday someday! God's vengeance will be revealed, even against false religion in whose name and under whose influence millions have suffered and died. God's judgment will fall and vindicate His people (Deuteronomy 32:35; Romans 12:19; Revelation 6:10).

The extent of Babylon's payment. The law of retribution is applied; what we sow, we shall reap. It is doubled to emphasize the enormity of the woman's sins and the justice behind her judgment and fall. The "cup which she has mixed," containing the wine of her wrath against the people of God, is now mixed for her with a double portion of God's wrath (14:10).

The experience of Babylon's sorrow. Like so many unbelievers today, this woman believes she will never experience sorrow or torment for her lifestyle and luxurious living. She boasts "I sit as queen, and am no widow." After all, she reasons, the kings of the earth are her lovers. But she is a widow in that God has forsaken her. These words are taken from Isaiah's prophecy concerning the "virgin daughter of Babylon":

> "Therefore hear this now, you who are given
>   to pleasures,
>   Who dwell securely,
>   Who say in your heart,
>   'I am, and there is no one else besides me;
>   I shall not sit as a widow,
>   Nor shall I know the loss of children';
>   But these two things shall come to you
>   In a moment, in one day:
>   The loss of children, and widowhood.
>   They shall come upon you in their fullness
>   Because of the multitude of your sorceries,
>   For the great abundance of your enchantments.

"For you have trusted in your wickedness;
You have said, 'No one sees me';
Your wisdom and your knowledge have warped you;
And you have said in your heart,
'I am, and there is no one else besides me.'
Therefore evil shall come upon you;
You shall not know from where it arises.
And trouble shall fall upon you;
You will not be able to put it off.
And desolation shall come upon you suddenly,
Which you shall not know" (Isaiah 47:8-11).

What a graphic picture of the fall of ancient Babylon. It now finds its completion in the harlot in Revelation 18, the woman who arises out of the past history of Babylon and becomes the "mystery" aspect of Babylon's influence throughout the history of the world, culminating in the religious system of the tribulation times.

Two things characterize the harlot's lifestyle: self-glorification and sensuous living. For this, she will receive torment and sorrow. So will all who choose to follow her path.

The evidence of her judgment. Here is a reminder of the fall of ancient Babylon. God's judgment was swift; the great nation came to a sudden end (Daniel 5). So will the woman we know as "Babylon the Great." Her "plagues" will come "in one day," and she "will be utterly burned with fire" (18:8).

The execution of her judgment. The Lord God brings His judgment upon the harlot and does so through the ten-nation confederacy of the tribulation. God uses the nations of the world to judge other nations deserving punishment. The sovereign control of God in the affairs of human history is a constant theme throughout the Bible. God is not a passive observer to human events. He is working them all out for His glory. He is accomplishing His plan on His time schedule.

The People Affected by Babylon's Fall (18:9-19)

In the name of religion many have become prosperous. The lamenting and mourning of the people of earth over the fall of the harlot is indeed impressive. It tells us how vitally connected religion is to the economic systems of the world.

The Fall of Babylon the Great

The kings of the earth. The involvement of the kings of the earth with the harlot is clear (14:8; 17:2, 18; 18:3, 9, 23). They "weep and lament" over the woman's destruction, though they hated her (17:16). The words "alas, alas" describe a bitter anguish and cry, revealing a deep loss or a fearful expectation. These kings are aware that the day of God's wrath has come (6:15-17). They are also the ones the demons will summon to the battle of Armageddon, the great day of God Almighty (16:14). There they also will experience the wrath of Almighty God and be killed by the sword of the coming King of kings and Lord of lords (19:19- 21).

The merchants of the earth. The merchants weep and mourn over the loss of their customers, their standard of living, and available luxury items. This all comes as a great shock to the business world of tribulation times. The swiftness with which it happens is frightening indeed—"in one hour such great riches came to nothing." In the tribulation, the whole world will be affected by the destruction of the harlot with whom the merchants of the world have done business and become wealthy.

One is astonished to find among the items that will be lost to these merchants, the "bodies and souls of men" (18:13). Human life will be cheap, and people will be sold as merchandise. One cannot help but wonder if the prostitution and pornography enterprises of our world are not indicated by these words.

The harlot is corrupt for many reasons. One obvious one is the way she has deceived the people of the world about wealth. Religion has often been guilty of materialistic goals. It has deceived people into believing that material prosperity is a sign of God's approval. It has encouraged the "profit motive" and has seduced the nations of the world because of it.

The hunger for achievement and accumulation of wealth remains as the dominant factor of people's lifestyles and desires. The "fools" of this world are found daily in every marketplace and place of business (cf. Luke 12:13-21). But judgment day is coming! The merchants of the world, along with the kings of the earth, will mourn the sudden destruction of the woman who helped them become prosperous.

The shipmasters and sailors of the world. The prophet Ezekiel spoke graphically of God's coming judgment upon the ancient seaport city of Tyre (Ezekiel 27). His pronouncement of doom focuses on the reaction of the shipping industry to the fall of ancient Tyre, and it is remarkably similar to John's description of the fall of the harlot Babylon (Revelation 18).

Because of the strong emphasis on the shipping industry's relationship to this future Babylon, some have concluded it must be a major port city capable of handling much trade. There are many cities in the world that could become such a commercial center in tribulation days. We simply do not know how this will be fulfilled. Many Bible scholars have used this passage and others to conclude that the city of Rome must be intended, and that the harlot is, therefore, the Roman Catholic Church. While it is possible, we cannot draw such a dogmatic conclusion without further insights than we presently possess.

The Praise of the Believers (18:20)

Further details will be given in chapter 19 concerning this praise proclamation. It is the answer to the question of the martyrs of Revelation 6:10. The long-standing question about the suffering of the righteous and prosperity of the wicked is now settled. God's judgment on the harlot, in whose name and under whose influence multitudes of believers have suffered and died, will cause rejoicing in the hearts of all true believers. The kings, merchants, and mariners of this world will mourn and lament, but heaven will rejoice!

The Pronouncement of Babylon's Fall (18:21-24)

This is the third time a "mighty angel" has made an appearance (5:2; 10:1; 18:21). It could be Gabriel ("strength of God") or Michael the archangel. We simply do not know.

A violent catastrophe is announced. Jeremiah's pronouncement of judgment on ancient Babylon closely parallels the angel's pronouncement in Revelation 18:

> "Now it shall be, when you have finished reading this book, that you shall tie a stone to it and throw it out into the Euphrates. Then you shall say, 'Thus Babylon shall sink and not rise from the catastrophe that I will bring upon her. And they shall be weary'" (Jeremiah 51:63-64).

The stone in Revelation 18 is "like a great millstone" and it is thrown "into the sea," not the Euphrates River. The similarities between the two passages, however, are obvious. Just as ancient Babylon was destroyed, so the mysterious Babylon, the harlot of past and future history, will be destroyed. It will be sudden and violent, and the result will be amazing—the great Babylon "shall not be found anymore." It will be wiped off the face of the earth with one fatal blow from the hand of Almighty God!

Several consequences are described. The repeated word "anymore" reiterates the tragic consequences of the fall of Babylon. Neither music nor manufacturing nor marriage will be found in Babylon anymore. The removal of any sign of activity is summarized by the statement "and the light of a lamp shall not shine in you anymore." God will put the lights of Babylon out for good.

A basic cause is given. The reason given for the violent overthrow of Babylon the Great is her sorcery of all the nations and her murders of God's people. Her "sorcery" deceived the nations to carry out her wicked plans to eliminate the people of God. She has used the governments of the world to accomplish her purposes. Furthermore, she is inspired by Satan himself who works all kinds of miracles through her world leaders, the false prophet and the Antichrist. Enough is enough! God will bring her to an end. She "shall not be found anymore."

Chapter 26

The Lamb and His Wife

(19:1-10)

The apostle John begins the chapter with his familiar phrase "after these things." It is with a great sense of relief and triumph that this phrase is now seen. Babylon is destroyed and the time of the Lord's return to earth has arrived!

We were introduced in Revelation 5 to the beautiful description of our coming King and Savior, Jesus Christ our Lord, as *the Lamb of God*. That depiction of Him appears twenty-eight times in the book. In this chapter we are introduced to the Lamb's wife.

The Lamb and His Wife
(19:1-10)

¹*After these things I heard a loud voice of a great multitude in heaven, saying, "Alleluia! Salvation and glory and honor and power to the Lord our God! ²For true and righteous are His judgments, because He has judged the great harlot who corrupted the earth with her fornication; and He has avenged on her the blood of His servants shed by her." ³Again they said, "Alleluia! And her smoke rises up forever and ever!" ⁴And the twenty-four elders and the four living creatures fell down and worshiped God who sat on the throne, saying, "Amen! Alleluia!" ⁵Then a voice came from the throne, saying, "Praise our God, all you His servants and those who fear Him, both small and great!" ⁶And I heard, as it were, the voice of a great multitude, as the sound of many waters and as the sound of mighty thunderings, saying, "Alleluia! For the Lord God*

> *omnipotent reigns!* [7]*Let us be glad and rejoice and give Him glory, for the marriage of the Lamb has come, and His wife has made herself ready."* [8]*And to her was granted to be arrayed in fine linen, clean and bright, for the fine linen is the righteous acts of the saints.* [9]*Then he said to me, "Write: 'Blessed are those who are called to the marriage supper of the Lamb!'" And he said to me, "These are the true sayings of God."* [10]*And I fell at his feet to worship him. But he said to me, "See that you do not do that! I am your fellow servant, and of your brethren who have the testimony of Jesus. Worship God! For the testimony of Jesus is the spirit of prophecy."*

The Praise of God is Proclaimed (19:1-6)

After reading these words, one feels the need to listen to the famous "Hallelujah Chorus" from Handel's *Messiah*. What wonderful music that is, but it will not compare to the music and praise which heaven will give to our God!

The multitude who give this praise to God. This gigantic praise gathering in heaven is composed of several groups who bring continual praise to God:

1. A great multitude. Verse 1 speaks of "a great multitude," reminding us of the great multitude of Revelation 7:9. This is a reference to the tribulation believers who have been martyred. When believers die, they are immediately "with the Lord" (2 Corinthians 5:8). What wonderful assurance for those whose believing loved ones have died. When the tribulation believers are killed, they are immediately ushered into the presence of the Lord, awaiting the resurrection of their bodies when the Lord Jesus Christ returns to this earth in power and great glory (cf. Daniel 12:1-3). Thus they will join with all Old Testament believers in the promised resurrection of the body.

2. The twenty-four elders. We believe the twenty-four elders described in verse 4 represent the church of Jesus Christ from the day of Pentecost (Acts 2) until the rapture of the church before the tribulation period begins (see the earlier discussion about these elders in Revelation 4). Their presence in heaven during the tribulation is a strong argument in favor of the church being raptured to heaven before the tribulation begins.

3. The four living creatures. These cherubim are the worship leaders of heaven (4:6-9). When they initiate an act or word of worship, the twenty-four elders follow.

4. All His servants and those who fear Him, both small and great. This may simply be a reference to all who comprise the great multitude of martyrs in heaven. Revelation 6:11 describes the martyrs of the past as "fellow servants" with those who would be killed in the tribulation period. Perhaps the best view is that these "servants" include all the Old Testament believers and martyrs of past history as well as all the tribulation believers who have been killed.

Naturally, all believers in Jesus Christ would respond to this admonition to praise the Lord. Those of us who are alive and waiting for the coming of Jesus Christ find our hearts agreeing with all that the heavenly multitude does in giving praise to our God.

The motivation for the heavenly multitude's praise. The reason for this outburst of praise is obvious. We have just finished a description of the judgments God will bring upon this world during the tribulation period and the destruction of the harlot with whom all the kings and nations of the world have been involved and seduced. Babylon the great has fallen, and God is to be praised:

1. Because His character is revealed in these judgments. Verse 2 declares, "For true and righteous are His judgments" (cf. 15:3). They are "true" is the sense of being faithful to what He promised to do. They are "just" because they are deserved. God does not judge unfairly (Romans 2:1-16). The martyrs of Revelation 6:10 appealed to this aspect of God's character when they addressed Him as "O Lord, holy and true."

2. Because Babylon's conquest is fulfilled. God "has judged the great harlot who corrupted the earth with her fornication; and He has avenged on her the blood of His servants shed by her" (v. 2). That "her smoke rises up forever and ever" (v. 3) is no doubt a reference to the eternal punishment of hell itself upon all unbelievers (cf. 14:11).

3. Because God's earthly kingdom is coming. The Lord's sovereign rule over all things has continued from the beginning and is never once challenged or set aside. But the earthly establishment of the rule of God will come with the return of Jesus Christ to this planet. God's kingdom will be set up on earth, never to be removed, although it will manifest itself initially with a thousand years of peace and justice.

The message of praise the multitude brings. "Alleluia" is the same in all languages—"praise the Lord!" This is not a quiet expression of praise to God. Verse 1 says it was a "loud voice," and verse 6 adds, "the voice of a great multitude, as the sound of many waters and as the sound of mighty thunderings." Evidently God will change the ability of our eardrums to endure loud sounds. The music and praise of heaven is turned full volume!

A summary of what the multitude says is captured in the opening verse: "Salvation and glory and honor and power to the Lord our God!"

Salvation—they praise Him for His deliverance and reward to all who trust Him to fulfill His promises and plan.

Glory—they praise Him for His attributes and character, recognizing that He alone deserves to be praised.

Honor—they praise Him for His exalted position above all authority, recognizing His sovereignty in ruling over all the events of human history.

Power—they praise Him for His greatness; no one can do what He can do, an ability marvelously made manifest during the tribulation period.

This offering of praise to our God is to be a continual act on our part—"keep on praising God" (v. 5).

The Preparation of the Bride Is Announced (19:7-9)

The instruction to all. The admonition to "be glad and rejoice and give Him glory" is really a continuation of the praise of the preceding verses. All the believers of heaven are urged to get excited about the marriage of the Lamb and his wife.

There are three phases to a Jewish wedding in Bible times. One deals with the marriage contract and payment of a dowry. When the contract was finished, the couple was legally married though they were not to have sexual relations during the period of betrothal or engagement (usually one year). The second phase deals with a formal occasion when the bridegroom takes the bride to his home (cf. Matthew 25:1-13). The final phase is the actual marriage supper when the bridegroom comes to the bride's home (cf. wedding feast in John 2).

These three phases beautifully illustrate the relationship of Jesus Christ to His Church. The wedding contract would correspond to salvation, the rapture of the church to taking the bride to the bridegroom's home (heaven), and the marriage supper to the beginning event of the millennial kingdom of Jesus Christ as He comes to the bride's home.

Every wedding is a time for rejoicing. John the Baptist said that he would be a part of those at the marriage supper and would rejoice greatly when he hears "the bridegroom's voice" (John 3:29). In the coming marriage supper of the Lamb, the chief attraction will be the Bridegroom, our Lord and Savior Jesus Christ. Jesus indicated that believing Gentiles and Jews will sit down together at this celebration in the kingdom of heaven (Matthew 8:11).

The importance of the Bride's apparel. The problem of identifying the wife "arrayed in fine linen, clean and bright," is indeed difficult. Israel is called the "wife" of Jehovah. However, if the details of this symbolism are followed carefully, we would have to eliminate Israel from this picture. Israel has no need of becoming the wife of the Lord at a formal ceremony—she already is His wife. She is rebuked for her unfaithfulness, but the Old Testament never suggests that she is not the wife of the Lord.

This "wife" in Revelation 19 is the church of Jesus Christ. Ephesians 5:22-33 is a wonderful passage describing the roles and responsibilities of husbands and wives in marriage. Verse 32 states: "This is a great mystery, but I speak concerning Christ and the church." There is no doubt about it—the church is the wife of Jesus Christ, though the consummation of the marriage is yet future. Ephesians 5:27 says, "that He might present it to Himself a glorious church, not having spot or wrinkle or any such thing, but that it should be holy and without blemish." The church will appear in all her glory when the marriage supper of the Lamb takes place.

The importance of the wedding apparel is clearly presented in the parables of our Lord. In Matthew 22:1-14 the kingdom of heaven is likened to a marriage supper which a certain king gave for his son. Invitations were sent out, but the people did not respond. After destroying those who murdered the king's servants who came with the invitations, the king sent his servants into the "highways" and invited whoever would come. But the people were required to have a wedding garment for the occasion. Verses 11-14 contain these penetrating and enlightening words:

> "But when the king came in to see the guests, he saw a man there who did not have on a wedding garment. So he said to him, 'Friend, how did you come in here without a wedding garment?' And he was speechless. Then the king said to the servants, 'Bind him hand and foot, take him away, and cast him into outer darkness; there will be weeping and gnashing of teeth.' For many are called, but few are chosen."

Without the proper wedding apparel, one cannot attend the wedding supper. The consequences are those used to describe hell itself: "outer darkness . . . weeping and gnashing of teeth."

The wedding apparel of the bride in Revelation 19:8 is "the righteous acts of the saints." It is possible that this fine linen, clean and bright, is the result of the rewards the Lord will give to church-age believers at the judgment seat of Christ, which apparently will take place in heaven during the tribulation period on earth.

The righteousness of Jesus Christ makes our righteousness possible. The Bridegroom, our lovely Lord, signed the marriage contract in His own blood and paid the price for our redemption and salvation. We owe everything to Him Who "loved the church and gave Himself for it" (Ephesians 5:25). We have been declared righteous by faith in Him (Romans 3:28; 5:1,9), not because of our works (Galatians 2:16). Yet our works reveal that we have been justified by faith. Saving faith always manifests good works, produced by the Holy Spirit in the life of every believer.

The invitation to the marriage supper. "Blessed are those who are called to the marriage supper of the Lamb." This is the fourth beatitude of the book of Revelation (1:3; 14:13; 16:15). It is a wonderful blessing indeed to be invited to the marriage supper of the Lamb. Notice carefully that those invited are "called" to this marriage supper. It is the call of the Lord Himself that results in our salvation (1 Corinthians 1:9; Romans 1:6; Ephesians 4:1).

The invitation was powerfully given to the church in Laodicea: "Behold, I stand at the door and knock. If anyone hears My voice and opens the door, I will come in to him and dine with him, and he with Me" (Revelation 3:20). While the moment of our salvation grants us the privilege of intimate fellowship with our Lord, it is only at the marriage supper of the Lamb that the importance of the words "dine with him" will hit us. What anticipation should fill the hearts of true believers!

The impact of these words upon the believer. The message just given is hard to believe. We want to believe it, but will it really happen? That "these are the true sayings of God" reemphasizes the reality of that coming day and assures us that God's Word can be relied upon without any hesitation.

The Purpose of the Believer Is Revealed (19:10)

If ever a passage of Scripture proved beyond doubt that Jesus Christ is not merely an angel but the eternal God in human flesh, this is it. The apostle John is so excited over what he has just seen about the coming marriage supper of the Lamb, he falls at the feet of this angel who communicates God's message and starts to worship him. The angel immediately rebukes him. We are to worship God only (cf. 22:9)!

In contrast, when God "brings the firstborn [Jesus] into the world, He says: 'Let all the angels of God worship Him'" (Hebrews 1:6). The Father wants all the angels to worship His Son. The deity of Jesus Christ is the indisputable teaching of the Bible.

The purpose of the believer is clearly stated in this verse: we are to worship the Lord. The worship of God alone should be the primary objective of every believer (4:9-11). He alone is worthy!

The last phrase of verse 10 is most enlightening: "For the testimony of Jesus is the spirit of prophecy." Prophecy is intended to glorify Jesus Christ. He is the central feature of it, and any teaching of prophecy that takes our minds and hearts away from Him is not being properly communicated. The name of this book is "the revelation of Jesus Christ." It unveils the character and glory of God's Son, our Lord Jesus Christ.

Chapter 27

The Second Coming of Jesus Christ

(19:11-21)

In one sense, the whole book has been building up to this one dramatic moment of prophecy—the return of Jesus Christ our Lord to this earth. In the first chapter we read, "Behold, He is coming with clouds, and every eye will see Him" (1:7). The moment has arrived!

The Spectacular Description of the Coming Glory
(19:11-16)

¹¹ *Then I saw heaven opened, and behold, a white horse. And He who sat on him was called Faithful and True, and in righteousness He judges and makes war.* ¹² *His eyes were like a flame of fire, and on His head were many crowns. He had a name written that no one knew except Himself.* ¹³ *He was clothed with a robe dipped in blood, and His name is called The Word of God.* ¹⁴ *And the armies in heaven, clothed in fine linen, white and clean, followed Him on white horses.* ¹⁵ *Now out of His mouth goes a sharp sword, that with it He should strike the nations. And He Himself will rule them with a rod of iron. He Himself treads the winepress of the fierceness and wrath of Almighty God.* ¹⁶ *And He has on His robe and on His thigh a name written:*

> *KING OF KINGS*
> *AND LORD OF LORDS.*

His Names Identify Him Clearly
(19:11-13, 16)

Though many names are used in the Bible to describe the person and work of Jesus Christ, this one passage describing His return to earth focuses on four characteristics of His name. The strong emphasis upon His name is obvious, clearly identifying Him for us all. When we refer to the "name" of the Lord we are describing His character and nature.

The reliability of His name. The adjectives "Faithful and True" clearly identify Him, for Jesus Christ is called the "faithful witness" in Revelation 1:5 and the "Faithful and True Witness" in 3:14. Because He is *faithful*, many wonderful blessings are ours:

1. He makes good on His promises (Deuteronomy 7:9; Hebrews 10:23). Because Jesus Christ is "faithful" all of His promises will come true—including His promise to come again (John 14:3).

2. He helps us in our temptations (1 Corinthians 10:13).

3. He protects us from Satan (2 Thessalonians 3:3).

4. He will never forsake us (2 Timothy 2:13). God's faithfulness makes it impossible for Him to turn His back on us or His promises. Salvation depends upon God's character, not our performance.

5. He will forgive our sins (1 John 1:9). Our forgiveness is rooted in the faithful character of God.

Because He is *true* and not a counterfeit, we can be confident that He is genuine and, therefore, totally reliable. Jesus Christ is "the *true* God," meaning that He is the real thing (1 John 5:20). Furthermore, He does not lie; there is no dishonesty in Him (John 7:18). Finally, we can rely upon His ways and judgments, for they are just and true (Revelation 15:3; 19:2).

The recognition of His name. When we read that "He had a name written that no one knew except Himself," we realize there is much about our Lord we simply cannot recognize or know. We are told His name is "wonderful" (Judges 13:18; Isaiah 9:6), meaning it is incomprehensible, too difficult for us to understand. The knowledge of the Lord is described in that way in Psalm 139:1-6. There is so much about our Lord we simply do not know. But He knows! His self-realization is powerfully revealed when Revelation 19:12 says "no one knew except Himself."

The revelation of His name. Verse 13 says, "and His name is called The Word of God." This name clearly identifies Him as Jesus Christ. John penned these words in his Gospel:

> In the beginning was the Word, and the Word was with God, and the Word was God.
>
> And the Word became flesh and dwelt among us, and we beheld His glory, the glory as of the only begotten of the Father, full of grace and truth (John 1:1, 14).

In his first epistle John called Him "the Word of life" that was "manifested to us" (1:1-2). Jesus put God on display. He was God in human flesh, sent to reveal the eternal God to the creatures He Himself had created.

The royalty of His name. Our coming King will rule the nations of the world. He is described as having a name written on His robe and on His thigh:

KING OF KINGS
AND LORD OF LORDS.

This unique title of our wonderful Lord reveals His sovereignty over all. No leader, nation, or world empire of the past, present, or future, deserves to be mentioned in the same sentence with our glorious King. He is King and Lord of them all!

His Nature Describes Him Powerfully (19:11-13)

The character and nature of our coming Lord is dramatically described in this passage by at least four statements in addition to His names:

His justice. Verse 11 makes it clear that what He does when He comes again is done "in righteousness." There will be no charge of injustice when He "makes war." The nations of the world have already been described as a withered and over-ripe harvest (14:14-20) that needs to be reaped by the justice and vengeance of Almighty God. That is a consistent theme throughout Scripture.

His knowledge. His eyes not only see everything, but describing them as "like a flame of fire" (cf. 1:14 and 2:18) implies that because He sees everything, we cannot get away from Him and His judgment of our sin. Hebrews 4:13 reminds us that "there is no creature hidden from His sight, but all things are naked and open to the eyes of Him to whom we must give account."

His authority. The crowns on His head are not the crowns of reward but the crowns ("diadems") of royalty and majesty. Because His head is adorned with "many" of these diadems, we must acknowledge His authority over all (Ephesians 1:21). His authority exceeds that of all human and angelic authority.

His authority in relation to the "armies of heaven" is also presented in verse 14 when it says they "followed Him" on their white horses. *Who are the "armies of heaven"?* Their clothing ("fine linen, white and clean") is the clothing of the Lamb's wife (19:8), and thus the church of Jesus Christ must be a part of the "armies of heaven." They could also include Old Testament believers and tribulation believers who have died previous to this great moment, now resurrected and clothed in the apparel which pictures the righteousness of God. The resurrection of Old Testament believers and tribulation martyrs will occur at the end of the tribulation when the Lord returns to the earth (cf. Daniel 12:1-3).

Since the Bible teaches that Jesus Christ will return to this earth with "all the holy angels with Him" (Matthew 25:31), some Bible teachers include the angels in the "armies of heaven." They do not restrict the clothing to what only redeemed people could wear, but emphasize that angels also at times appear in "white robes."

His wrath. That His robe is dipped in blood is not speaking about the cross and the blood of Jesus Christ that was shed there. That event was completed, and God's work of redemption is over. The picture of the resurrected Lord in chapter 1 made no mention of a robe "dipped in blood" (1:13).

Isaiah 63 tells us where the blood comes from and what it represents—what a remarkable description it gives us of the coming Messiah! His robes are stained with the blood of those He has destroyed. This is the same bloodbath described in Revelation 14:20. The emphasis is on His anger, His fury, His vengeance. The righteous anger of Jesus Christ will be poured out against this world—"the great day of His wrath has come, and who is able to stand?" (6:17).

The Nations Will Obey Him Completely (19:15-16)

One of the truly remarkable verses about Jesus Christ is Revelation 19:15. Three actions of our Lord are described in this one verse. He "strikes" the nations with the sword of His mouth, He "rules" the nations with a rod of iron, and He "treads" the nations in the winepress of God's wrath.

He strikes the nations. The "sharp sword" refers to a long and heavy sword used by the Thracians. It can also describe a sword long enough to throw as a spear or javelin. The Word of God is described as a "sword" in Hebrews 4:12, though the word there refers to the two-edged hand weapon popularized by the Romans.

It is His Word that strikes the nations. He merely speaks the word and His judgments are executed swiftly. This blow of destruction upon the nations is described in Psalm 2:9 and Isaiah 11:4 as well.

He shepherds the nations. When verse 15 states, "He Himself will rule them with a rod of iron," it uses the Greek word for "shepherd." The shepherd's rod is used for correction. Paul speaks about this in 1 Corinthians 4:21 when he says, "Shall I come to you with a rod, or in love and a spirit of gentleness?" Jesus is called "that great Shepherd of the sheep" (Hebrews 13:20), "the good shepherd" (John 10:11), and "the Chief Shepherd" (1 Peter 5:4), all of which express warm encouragement to believers. Even the Shepherd's rod can be a "comfort" to the believer according to Psalm 23:4.

However the rod the Shepherd of the nations will use is "a rod of iron." The point is not to be taken lightly. It is a rod that will bring order and justice to this world. The nations will be shepherded with sovereign authority. Jesus Christ and His believers will rule the nations of the world when His kingdom is set up on earth.

He stomps the nations. The last phrase of verse 15 states, "He Himself treads the winepress of the fierceness and wrath of Almighty God," describing the trampling of the nations in the winepress of God's wrath (Isaiah 63:1-6; Joel 3:13; Revelation 14:14-20). It is the day of the Lord, a day of God's wrath poured out upon the unbelieving nations of the world.

The Terrible Destruction that Will Come
(19:17-21)

[17] *Then I saw an angel standing in the sun; and he cried with a loud voice, saying to all the birds that fly in the midst of heaven, "Come and gather together for the supper of the great God,* [18] *that you may eat the flesh of kings, the flesh of captains, the flesh of mighty men, the flesh of horses and of those who sit on them, and the flesh of all people, free and slave, both small and great."* [19] *And I saw the beast, the kings of the earth, and their armies, gathered together to make war against Him who sat on the horse and against His army.* [20] *Then the beast was captured, and with him the false prophet who worked signs in his presence,*

> *by which he deceived those who received the mark of the*
> *beast and those who worshiped his image. These two were*
> *cast alive into the lake of fire burning with brimstone.*
> *²¹ And the rest were killed with the sword which proceeded*
> *from the mouth of Him who sat on the horse. And all the*
> *birds were filled with their flesh.*

Armageddon has arrived! That feared day when the final war of humanity takes place is now before us. Human history as we know it will come to a dramatic close. God's day of vengeance and wrath will explode upon the world scene in a spectacular display of His power and glory. The whole world will know that Jesus Christ is King of kings and Lord of lords!

The Coming of All Birds to the
Supper of the Great God (19:17-18)

In the destruction of the king of the north, the battle of Gog and Magog (Ezekiel 38-39), a similar scene is pictured of the birds of heaven being invited to devour the flesh of those conquered. This gruesome event will occur twice in the last days of human history. When the invasion of the king of the north occurs (possibly before the tribulation period even begins), the vultures of the earth will gather for this feast Ezekiel describes, devouring the flesh and blood of the invaders. At the end of the tribulation period (Armageddon) this event will occur again as all the kings of the earth become the supper upon which the birds of heaven feast.

Notice three things about the coming of these birds:

The position of the angel. The picture of "an angel standing in the sun" is dramatic indeed, revealing the glory of God and the fulfillment of His purposes upon planet earth. Joel 2:31 says that "the sun shall be turned into darkness." Perhaps the position of the angel begins that process by which people on earth will know that judgment day has arrived.

The proclamation to the birds. The sound of a loud voice has occurred on six previous occasions in this book (6:10; 7:2, 10; 10:3; 14:15; 18:2). It always introduces some important message or event affecting the vengeance and victory of God.

The purpose of this gathering of birds. Matthew 24:27-28 speaks of this carnage at the return of Jesus Christ: "For as the lightning comes from the east and flashes to the west, so also will the coming of the Son of Man be. For wherever the carcass is, there the eagles will be gathered together." A variety of viewpoints concerning this "carcass" and the "eagles" have been expressed throughout church history.

The most logical explanation of this prophecy of Jesus is the event described in Revelation 19:17-21. The "carcass" depicts the nations of the world who have gathered against the Lord and His people. The "eagles" represent all the birds of heaven who will literally feed on the flesh of those armies destroyed by the coming of Jesus Christ.

The Final Conflict of the Tribulation (19:19)

The beast (Antichrist) is the most powerful leader on earth at the end of the tribulation period. He and his associate, the false prophet, have deceived the nations of the world. They have now assembled "the kings of the earth" for the battle of that "great day of God Almighty" (16:14).

The interesting fact of verse 19 is that the beast and the kings of the earth have come together "to make war against Him who sat on the horse and against His army." They may have gathered initially for other reasons, but when the battle begins, they are fully aware of the One against Whom they will be fighting—Jesus Christ our Lord! The battle quickly becomes "no contest" (2 Thessalonians 1:7-10).

The Capture of the Beast and the False Prophet (19:20)

The reason for the capture is implied. The beast is captured because he has been the object of the world's worship, and the false prophet is captured because he has persuaded the peoples of the world to worship the beast. Such idolatry cannot be tolerated any longer. These two receive special attention in the description of the final judgment due to their significant roles of deception and wickedness toward the people of God who have suffered greatly at their hands. God's vengeance will be poured out on them for it.

The result is a dramatic reminder to all unbelievers of their final destiny. The fact that they are "cast alive" into hell might indicate that their torment and suffering will be greater than others who will inhabit that awful place. They will experience the horrors of eternal punishment for a thousand years before the rest of unbelievers (cf. 20:15).

The Consequence the Nations Will Face (19:21)

From the information given in Matthew 25:31-46, there will be survivors among the nations of the world who will stand before the Lord and receive either commendation for their kindness to the people of Israel during the tribulation period or eternal condemnation for their rebellion and indifference to the people of God. This judgment of the nations will occur at the end of the tribulation when Jesus Christ returns to the earth. (It is possible this is the event described in Daniel 12 and Joel 3.)

According to Daniel 12:1-3, the righteous dead will be resurrected as well to go into the millennial kingdom of our Lord. This group would include all Old Testament believers as well as tribulation believers who have been martyred. Believers from the church age, represented by the twenty-four elders in heaven, will have been resurrected at the rapture of the church before the tribulation period begins.

While at times we have difficulty understanding the sequence of events and the meaning of many prophetic statements, certain facts are clear. The Bible teaches:

1. The return of Jesus Christ our Lord to this earth;
2. The defeat and destruction of unbelieving nations;
3. The eternal punishment of the wicked;
4. The bodily resurrection and eternal life of all who believe in the Messiah, our Lord Jesus Christ.

Chapter 28

The Millennial Reign of Christ

(20:1-15)

After the devastation of Armageddon, several matters must be resolved in our prophetic understanding. What is going to happen to planet earth now that the political, religious, and economic systems of the world have been destroyed? What will happen to Satan? Will he still be free to exercise his diabolical schemes? Other questions involve the righteous dead, and those who are still alive at the end of the tribulation period. What about unbelievers? What happens to them? These questions become the key issues of Revelation 20.

What Is the Millennium?

Millennium is the Latin word for a thousand years. This is the only passage in the Bible that refers to this thousand-year period of time. We are told the following things in this passage:

1. Satan cannot deceive the nations until the thousand years are over (v. 3);

2. Tribulation martyrs will live and reign with Christ for a thousand years (v. 4);

3. Other dead will not live again until the thousand years are over (v. 5);

4. Those who are a part of the first resurrection will reign with Christ for a thousand years (v. 6);

5. After the thousand years are over, Satan will be released (v. 7).

The Millennial Reign of Christ

Several views about the meaning of the thousand years have been put forth throughout church history. They include the following:

View one. It is not a literal thousand years but a symbolic term for the preaching of the gospel and the control of Satan's power between the first and second comings of Jesus Christ. Some hold that it represents the reign of believers in heaven during the present course of church history. There are many variations of this view, but it is basically known as *amillennialism* (no literal thousand years). Most of the adherents of this view based their ideas upon Augustine's work, *The City of God*.

View two. It is a literal thousand years that immediately precedes the second coming of Jesus Christ. This viewpoint argues for the triumph of the gospel during the last thousand years of church history before Jesus Christ returns. It is known as *postmillennialism* (Jesus Christ returns *after* the thousand years).

View three. It is a literal thousand years that will come immediately after the return of Jesus Christ to this earth and the tribulation period is ended. This view is known as *premillennialism* (Jesus Christ comes *before* the thousand years). Although there are varying views among premillennialists about the timing of the rapture of the church, they agree that Jesus Christ will reign for a thousand years after He returns to this earth. It will be a fulfillment of many Bible prophecies that refer to a visible manifestation of the kingdom of God upon earth in which righteousness and justice will be provided for all.

The Binding of Satan during the Thousand Years
(20:1-3)

> [1] *Then I saw an angel coming down from heaven, having the key to the bottomless pit and a great chain in his hand.* [2] *He laid hold of the dragon, that serpent of old, who is the Devil and Satan, and bound him for a thousand years;* [3] *and he cast him into the bottomless pit, and shut him up, and set a seal on him, so that he should deceive the nations no more till the thousand years were finished. But after these things he must be released for a little while.*

Those who believe that Satan is presently bound and that the thousand years indicates present church history are hard-pressed to prove their point. First Peter 5:8 warns: "Be sober, be vigilant; because your adversary the devil walks about like a roaring lion, seeking whom he may devour." Other passages speak of his blinding of unbelievers and attempts to deceive or hinder believers (2 Corinthians 4:3-4; 11:13-15; Ephesians 2:2; 1 Thessalonians 2:18; 2 Timothy 2:26). Doesn't sound like he's under control, does it? When Satan is cast into hell (20:10), he joins the beast and the false prophet who are already there and who do not appear on the scene of history until the tribulation period. Therefore, Satan's binding during and release after the thousand years must have occurred after the tribulation.

The Revelation of Satan's Destiny (20:1)

Three possible viewpoints exist about the identity of the angel who comes down from heaven with the key to the bottomless pit and the great chain in his hand:

It is Jesus Christ Himself. This view connects the "key to the bottomless pit" with Revelation 1:18 where we were told that Jesus Christ has "the keys to Hades and of Death." However, that text does not say that He has the key to the bottomless pit, unless one were to argue that it is the same as Hades, the abode of the wicked dead, the place of torment for unbelievers. The bottomless pit (the abyss) was mentioned in Revelation 9 and apparently is the abode of demons, the evil angels of Satan himself, who is called "the angel of the bottomless pit" (9:11).

It is Michael the Archangel. Michael and his angels fought with the devil and his angels and Michael won (12:7-9). The thought is that the angel who would officially bind Satan would most likely be the one who was victorious over him.

It is one of God's unnamed angels. The text does not reveal the name of the angel. It simply says that "an angel" had "the key to the bottomless pit and a great chain in his hand." It is best to leave the text alone and simply state that we do not know the name of the angel. The verse merely indicates that the destiny of Satan during the thousand years is to be chained in the bottomless pit where other demons exist.

The Recognition of Satan's Activity during the Tribulation (20:2)

When the angel lays hold of Satan, we learn three things about him which remind us of his activity during the tribulation period:

He controls the political system. In Revelation 12:3 the "great fiery red dragon" was pictured with "seven heads and ten horns," the terrible beast of 13:1 and 17:7-18. It is the dragon who gives the beast "his power, his throne, and great authority" (13:2).

He deceives the nations. In Revelation 12:9 the dragon was called "that serpent of old" and was described as the one "who deceives the whole world" (cf. 20:3, 8). Paul likewise wrote about Satan's deceptive activities (2 Corinthians 11:3, 13-15).

He accuses the believers. The names "the Devil and Satan" identify him as a slanderer. Revelation 12:10 says he is the "accuser of our brethren, who accused them before our God day and night."

The Result Satan Will Experience for a Thousand Years (20:2-3)

The angel does four things to Satan: (1) He binds him (with the chain) for a thousand years, (2) he casts him into the bottomless pit, (3) he shuts him up, and (4) he sets a seal on him. Other passages speak of God's imprisonment of demonic beings. Second Peter 2:4 says "the angels who sinned" are delivered "into chains of darkness, to be reserved for judgment." Jude 6 says the same thing about "the angels who did not keep their proper domain, but left their own habitation." These evil angels are "reserved in everlasting chains under darkness for the judgment of the great day."

The Reason for This Binding of Satan (20:3)

Verse 3 states clearly the reason: "so that he should deceive the nations no more till the thousand years were finished." It does not say that he is prevented from deceiving believers which he does presently. In their glorified state, it would be impossible for Satan to deceive believers anymore. The reference to "nations" reveals that the battle of Armageddon does not destroy all the nations of the world, only the kings and their armies. Zechariah 14:16 makes it clear that nations will exist during the coming kingdom of God on earth: "And it shall come to pass that everyone who is left of all the nations which came against Jerusalem shall go up from year to year to worship the King, the LORD of hosts, and to keep the Feast of Tabernacles."

The Release of Satan after the Thousand Years (20:3)

Satan will be released from his prison "for a little while" after the thousand years have expired. God allows us to see what happens when

Satan is given the opportunity to deceive the nations of the world once again. Satan makes one last attempt to overthrow the people and purposes of God, and God brings him to a swift end, casting him into the lake of fire to be tormented forever and ever. (More on the release of Satan when we come to Revelation 20:7-10.)

The Blessings Believers Will Experience
(20:4-6)

[4] And I saw thrones, and they sat on them, and judgment was committed to them. And I saw the souls of those who had been beheaded for their witness to Jesus and for the word of God, who had not worshiped the beast or his image, and had not received his mark on their foreheads or on their hands. And they lived and reigned with Christ for a thousand years. [5] But the rest of the dead did not live again until the thousand years were finished. This is the first resurrection. [6] Blessed and holy is he who has part in the first resurrection. Over such the second death has no power, but they shall be priests of God and of Christ, and shall reign with Him a thousand years.

The Responsibility for Judgment (20:4)

The ones who sit on thrones are the twenty-four elders of Revelation 4:4, representing the completed church in heaven. Jesus said in Matthew 19:28, "Assuredly I say to you, that in the regeneration, when the Son of Man sits on the throne of His glory, you who have followed Me will also sit on twelve thrones, judging the twelve tribes of Israel."

The judgment of Israel is described in Ezekiel 20:33-38 as the casting out of rebels. The apparent focus of the judgment in Revelation 20 is the giving of rewards. Those Jewish believers of the past who are resurrected at the end of the tribulation period (Daniel 12:1-3) and all the tribulation believers are at this time given their rewards. Those making the judgments are the ones who sit on the thrones, the twenty-four elders.

The Resurrection of Believers (20:4)

The "first resurrection" consists only of believers. It includes the resurrection of Jesus Christ as the "firstfruits of those who have fallen asleep" and "afterward those who are Christ's at His coming" (1 Corinthians 15:20, 23). Church-age believers will be resurrected at the rapture, before the tribulation begins (1 Thessalonians 4:16-17), and all Old Testament believers, along with tribulation martyrs, will be resurrected at the end of the tribulation. The special emphasis of these verses is upon those martyrs of the tribulation period who did not worship the beast or his image or receive his mark.

All who have a part in the first resurrection are described as "blessed and holy (v. 6a)." They not only are resurrected but they will never die again ("over such the second death has no power"). This is an eternal and physical resurrection promised to all believers (John 11:25-26).

The Resurrection of Unbelievers (20:5)

It is clear from these verses that a period of a thousand years separates the resurrection of believers from the resurrection of unbelievers. Later in this chapter we shall see the awesome scene of the great white throne judgment of God and what happens to all the wicked dead who are resurrected to stand before God.

The Reward of Believers (20:6)

The reward includes political ("reign") and religious ("priests") responsibilities during the thousand years. We shall reign with Jesus Christ as "kings and priests" (Revelation 1:6; 5:10; 2 Timothy 2:12).

There will be religious festivals during the thousand-year reign of Jesus Christ (cf. Zechariah 14:16) and a temple (Ezekiel 40-48) where continual religious ceremonies and worship services will be held, all in praise and honor to our Lord! Revelation 22 describes the glory of the eternal state and the heavenly city, where "His servants shall serve Him," and "they shall reign forever and ever" (22:3, 5).

The Battle at the End of the Thousand Years
(20:7-10)

7Now when the thousand years have expired, Satan will be released from his prison 8and will go out to deceive the nations which are in the four corners of the earth, Gog and Magog, to gather them together to battle, whose number is as the sand of the sea. ⁹They went up on the breadth of the earth and surrounded the camp of the saints and the beloved city. And fire came down from God out of heaven and devoured them. ¹⁰And the devil, who deceived them, was cast into the lake of fire and brimstone where the beast and the false prophet are. And they will be tormented day and night forever and ever.

The Deception of the Nations (20:8)

Satan is the deceiver, and in spite of being imprisoned for a thousand years and being totally unable to affect anyone on earth, he immediately acts in accordance with his nature. He cannot do otherwise.

But why does God allow Satan this last effort? The text does not say, but several possibilities immediately come to mind. For one thing, God demonstrates by this one final event that even under the best conditions, mankind's problem is in the heart. Left to himself, man chooses to rebel. Another possibility is that God is demonstrating that Satan's depravity cannot be cured, even with his thousand-year binding. Another possible reason behind this final rebellion is to clearly demonstrate to all God's justification in exacting eternal punishment.

The "nations" deceived by Satan must come from the children born to those who enter the millennial kingdom in their natural bodies. While outward obedience and submission is required during the millennial reign of Jesus Christ, inward faith and commitment is another question. The final rebellion proves the biblical teaching of the total depravity of mankind.

What about "Gog and Magog"? One of the fascinating facts of this section is the mention of Gog and Magog. These names are used in Ezekiel 38 and 39 to identify the northern confederacy that invades the nation of Israel, an event that will probably precede the beginning of the tribulation period. The battle of Revelation 20 is not the same battle; here, the names are used symbolically to depict the nations Satan has deceived to come and do battle against God and His people. The number of the people is "as the sand of the sea." The population has exploded during the thousand years.

The Destruction of the Rebellious Nations (20:9)

God allows these nations to surround the camp of the believers and "the beloved city," which refers to Jerusalem, the capital of the millennial reign of Jesus Christ. God's love for the city of Jerusalem is clearly established by biblical teaching (cf. Psalm 78:68; 87:2).

The actual judgment God uses to destroy this rebellion is different from that in Ezekiel 38 or Revelation 19. It is the same judgment He used on Sodom and Gomorrah—"fire came down from God out of heaven and devoured them." In one dramatic display, God brings to an end the final rebellion of mankind!

The Final Destiny of Satan (20:10)

No prophetic message would be complete without a word about Satan's final destiny. The archenemy of our souls, the deceiver, the slanderer, the father of lies, the murderer, the one who blinds the minds of unbelievers, the god of this age, the evil spirit working in the sons of disobedience, the prince of the power of the air, the angel of the bottomless pit . . . will be "*cast into the lake of fire and brimstone.*"

Satan will be in hell forever, along with the beast and false prophet who were put there a thousand years earlier. This unholy satanic trinity "*will be tormented day and night forever and ever.*" Those who are cast into hell are not annihilated as some religious groups teach. They experience torment forever and ever; it is an everlasting fire into which they are cast. Satan deserves it, and the justice of God demands it (cf. Matthew 25:41)!

The Books that Judge the Dead
(20:11-15)

¹¹ *Then I saw a great white throne and Him who sat on it, from whose face the earth and the heaven fled away. And there was found no place for them.* ¹²*And I saw the dead, small and great, standing before God, and books were opened. And another book was opened, which is the Book of Life. And the dead were judged according to their works, by the things which were written in the books.* ¹³*The sea gave up the dead who were in it, and Death and Hades delivered up the dead who were in them. And they were judged, each one according to his works.* ¹⁴*Then Death and Hades were cast into the lake of fire. This is the second death.* ¹⁵*And anyone not found written in the Book of Life was cast into the lake of fire.*

No passage of the Bible is more important or more awesome in its statements.

The Description of the One Who Judges (20:11)

The word *throne* appears forty-five times in Revelation, but only sixteen times in the rest of the New Testament. The One sitting on the throne in chapter 4 is God the Father, but the throne is not called "the great white throne." This throne in chapter 20 appears to be a special place where the judgment of unbelievers is to take place. The word *great* might refer to the issues involved rather than the throne's physical size, and the word *white* pictures the purity and righteousness of the One Who is the Judge of all men. It is quite probable that the One Who sits on this throne is none other than Jesus Christ our Lord. Jesus Christ is the Judge before whom believers as well as unbelievers will stand (cf. John 5:22, 27; 2 Corinthians 5:10).

The awesome presence of the One Who sits on this throne is evident from the statement "from whose face the earth and the heaven fled away. And there was found no place for them." The old order must be replaced (cf. Revelation 21:1; 2 Peter 3:10-13 Matthew 24:35; Isaiah 65:17). Some Bible teachers place the renovation of the heavens and the earth at the end of the tribulation; others place it at the end of the millennium. If a chronological sequence is being pictured in Revelation 20, it would obviously be placed at the end of the thousand years. This would seem logical in the light of the final rebellion of Satan and the nations at the end of the thousand years.

The Dead Who Are Judged (20:12-13)

Some Bible teachers believe there is only one general judgment of all persons, believers and unbelievers. However, such a view does not fit the facts. The resurrection of believers occurs before the millennium while the resurrection of unbelievers occurs after the thousand years (20:4-6). The only judgment that takes place after the thousand years is the judgment of unbelievers. Two things need to be stated about the dead who are resurrected for their final judgment:

Their position in life is not a factor at the day of judgment. Those to be judged come from all walks of life, and their achievements and status on earth will have no bearing upon the judgment they will receive. Many people have been led to believe otherwise, but the facts of the Bible still stand.

The dead are described as "standing before God," indicating that they are to be sentenced. A verdict is to be rendered by the Judge of all the earth.

The place from which they come reveals their identity. Mentioning the "sea" shows that the method of burial has nothing to do with God's power to raise them up for this day of judgment. No one escapes regardless of the method of burial. The fact that "Death" delivers them to the throne of judgment indicates that the resurrection has taken place, which would confirm the earlier statement of verse 5—"but the rest of the dead did not live again until the thousand years were finished."

The mention of "Hades," the abode of the wicked dead, clarifies that the dead who stand before the great white throne are unbelievers. When Jesus told the story of the rich man and Lazarus, He said the rich man was "in torments in Hades" (Luke 16:23). The word *Hades* is used eleven times in the New Testament and is to be distinguished from the word *Gehenna,* which refers to the final Hell, the lake of fire. Hades is certainly like Hell, a place of terrible torment, but it is the temporary abode of the wicked dead who await the great white throne judgment and their final sentencing.

How the Dead Are to Be Judged (20:12-13)

The "works" of believers are judged (1 Corinthians 3:11-15; 2 Corinthians 5:10) and the issue is rewards. The "works" of the wicked are also evaluated and judgment is given "according to their works." Just as there are degrees of reward for believers, we are compelled to argue degrees of punishment for unbelievers. That God will render to every man according to his works is a truth that appears over forty times in the Bible. This concept of degrees of punishment for the wicked is clearly revealed in the teaching of Jesus Christ (Matthew 11:20-24). To whom much is given, much will be required.

It is obvious that one book is of critical importance—"the Book of Life." This is the book into which the names of true believers are written. Your name must be written in that book in order for you to escape the judgment of hell and to live forever with the Lord. Names cannot be erased from that book (3:5) and they are written in the book "from the foundation of the world" (13:8; 17:8). While this causes great misunderstanding and accusations against the wisdom, justice, and sovereignty of God, the Bible urges us to "rejoice because your names are written in heaven" (Luke 10:20). The question believers often ask is "Why me?" While we know the sovereign grace of God is behind our salvation and that we were chosen before the foundation of the world so that we would praise the glory of His grace (Ephesians 1:3-6), we still find it difficult to understand. Our task is to praise and worship the Lord, even though we do not have the answers to all our questions.

The Destiny of Those Who Are Judged (20:14-15)

When Death and Hades are "cast into the lake of fire," we realize what Revelation 21:4 says, "there shall be no more death." Jesus said of those who are cast into hell, "their worm does not die and the fire is not quenched" (Mark 9:44). No one will ever die again! That is a tragic reality for the unbeliever who must face an eternity in hell without God and without hope. Hades, the temporary abode of the wicked, will be cast into the eternal fire, and all who dwell there will find themselves lost forever in eternal torment and punishment.

The final judgment and destiny of unbelievers is described as being the "second death." The first death involves the separation of the body from the soul and spirit. The second death involves the separation of the person from God forever. Spiritual death is the separation of physically-alive people from a relationship with God because of sin (cf. Isaiah 59:1-2; Ephesians 2:1).

Into this lake of fire all unbelievers will be thrown. They join the beast and false prophet (19:20) and Satan himself (20:10). No verse in the Bible should cause us to flee to the grace and forgiveness of our Lord Jesus Christ as much as this one statement in Revelation 20:15: "And anyone not found written in the book of life was cast into the lake of fire." The Bible has warned of this place of terrible judgment many times and challenged us all to flee the wrath of God, repent of our sin, and believe in the gospel of our Lord and Savior Jesus Christ. Have you committed your life and future to Him?

Chapter 29

The New Jerusalem

(21:1-22:5)

The book of Revelation is an unveiling of Jesus Christ in all of His glory. Earlier we gave a threefold outline of the book as it relates to Jesus Christ:

The Lord of the Churches (1:1-3:22)
The Lion over the Nations (4:1-20:15)
The Lamb among the Believers (21:1-22:21)

The word *lamb* appears twenty-eight times in this book. It now takes on special meaning to all who have come to put their trust in Jesus Christ as Lord and Savior. We are now introduced to "the Lamb's wife" (21:10), a spectacular description of the heavenly city, the New Jerusalem, which is the eternal home for believers.

Is Heaven a Real Place?

Within the culture and history of the human race, there is a great deal of evidence pointing to our longing for a better life, our hope for a perfect society where every desire and need is fulfilled. While we may often question the reality of a place called "heaven," in our hearts we hope it exists and that we will be a part of it.

The word *heaven* appears over seven hundred times in the Bible. The Bible indicates there are actually three heavens:

First heaven: earth's atmosphere
Second heaven: outer space (including stars, planets, and galaxies)
Third heaven: where God dwells

The apostle Paul describes in 2 Corinthians 12:2 his experience of being "caught up to the third heaven." Verse 4 calls it "Paradise," the place believers will go "to eat from the tree of life, which is in the midst of the Paradise of God" (Revelation 2:7). Apparently "Paradise" and "the new Jerusalem" are the same place, a city being prepared by God.

Old Testament believers longed for their eternal home. Hebrews 11 speaks of believers such as Abel, Enoch, Noah, Abraham, Isaac, and Jacob desiring a heavenly home, not simply an earthly dwelling. Verse 16 says God "has prepared a city for them."

There is a real "place" God is preparing for believers (John 14:1-3). It is called "the city which has foundations, whose builder and maker is God" (Hebrews 11:10). It is called "the heavenly Jerusalem," and it is the place where the true church is being assembled (Hebrews 12:22-24). Written on the overcomers (believers) is the name of "the city of My God, the New Jerusalem, which comes down out of heaven from My God" (Revelation 3:12). Technically the heavenly city comes down to earth out of the third heaven where it is being prepared at the present time. But since the city is called "the heavenly city," it is certainly valid to refer to it as heaven.

The Introduction to the New Jerusalem
(21:1-8)

¹And I saw a new heaven and a new earth, for the first heaven and the first earth had passed away. Also there was no more sea. ²Then I, John, saw the holy city, New Jerusalem, coming down out of heaven from God, prepared as a bride adorned for her husband. ³And I heard a loud voice from heaven saying, "Behold, the tabernacle of God is with men, and He will dwell with them, and they shall be His people, and God Himself will be with them and be their God. ⁴And God will wipe away every tear from their eyes; there shall be no more death, nor sorrow, nor crying; and there shall be no more pain, for the former things have passed away." ⁵Then He who sat on the throne said, "Behold, I make all things new." And He said to me, "Write, for these words are true and faithful." ⁶And He said to me, "It is done! I am the Alpha and the Omega, the Beginning and the End. I will give of the fountain of the water of life freely to him who thirsts. ⁷He

*who overcomes shall inherit all things, and I will be his
God and he shall be My son. [8]But the cowardly, unbelieving, abominable, murderers, sexually immoral, sorcerers,
idolaters, and all liars shall have their part in the lake
which burns with fire and brimstone, which is the second
death."*

The apostle John says "I saw" (vv. 1 and 2), suggesting two distinct
visions. The word "then" which begins verse 2 indicates a sequence.
First, the change in the present physical system we now see; second,
the coming of the New Jerusalem out of heaven from God.

The Pattern of Things in the Universe Will Be Changed (21:1)

Three things are brought to our attention about this future day:
Our physical surroundings will be new. Our surroundings will be new
in kind and quality, not simply new from the standpoint of time. The
prophet Isaiah spoke of this over twenty-seven hundred years ago
(Isaiah 65:17; 66:22). The apostle Peter spoke of it as the believer's
hope (2 Peter 3:13).

We are in need of a change. This globe has been polluted in a
multitude of ways by the technology and selfishness of mankind. We
are in ecological crises, but we'd rather not talk about it much less do
anything about it. We have apparently decided to leave this task to
future generations. One day, a total change will take place; everything
will be made *new*.

Our present physical environment will pass away. The verse reads "for
the first heaven and the first earth had passed away." Peter describes
the catastrophe using terms that picture a nuclear nightmare (2 Peter
3:10-12). Peter speaks of the "heavens" being dissolved, along with the
earth. Perhaps the stellar heavens will explode.

Our future environment will be different. The phrase "there was no more
sea" tells us our new environment will be much different from what
we presently know. Some believe this verse is not teaching the permanent removal of water from the planet, for in fact the heavenly city
has a river. However, all of the passages speaking about the sea and
water in the future kingdom of God deal with the millennial period,
not the eternal state described in the last two chapters of Revelation.
Outside of the river in the New Jerusalem (22:1), there is no mention
of the sea or bodies of water in the eternal state.

The Presence of a New City Will Be the
Main Attraction in Eternity (21:2)

We are told several wonderful things in this single verse:

The character of the city. Finally, a city that is cleaned up. No more sin, crime, and pollution—no unbelievers will be present (21:8, 27; 22:3, 15). It is a *holy* city!

The contrast of the city. The New Jerusalem is unlike the earthly one. Revelation 11:8 called the earthly city where our Lord was crucified and risen again, "spiritually . . . Sodom and Egypt."

The coming of the city. The New Jerusalem "comes down out of heaven from My God" (3:12). The source is God Himself Who has been designing and preparing this city for His people; He is its Builder and Maker (Hebrews 11:10). Though the specific site is not revealed, the Bible makes it clear that the new city will sit *on the earth.*

The comparison of the city. The beauty of the city is described "as a bride." According to verse 9, it is "the bride, the Lamb's wife" that is depicted. The city is identified with its inhabitants. We are beautiful to God and we are the bride of His Son, Jesus Christ our Lord, the blessed Lamb of God Who has taken away the sin of us all. Since both Israel and the church are "a bride" of the Messiah, we conclude that all believers of all ages will share the joys and blessings of living forever in the New Jerusalem.

The Purpose of God Will Be Fulfilled (21:3)

God's presence with us was a reality when Jesus Christ came into this world. As John wrote in his Gospel, He "tabernacled" among us "and we beheld His glory" (John 1:14, 18). Colossians 2:9 says that in Jesus Christ "dwells all the fullness of the Godhead bodily."

After Jesus' ascension the Holy Spirit takes up His residency in the hearts of all believers. God's presence is made real to us by the Spirit, but since we cannot see Him, the full force of God's presence is not experienced. One day things will be different. The psalmist declared (Psalm 16:11):

> In Your presence is fullness of joy;
> At Your right hand are pleasures forevermore.

What a wonderful day is coming when God will be among us forever!

The Past Will Be Removed (21:4)

Few passages could bring as much comfort and joy as this one. This life is full of sorrow, suffering, pain, and death. All of that will be removed by God forever. He will wipe away *every* tear—what a demonstration of His compassion and love. God knows about our tears (Psalm 56:8), and one day He will wipe them away forever! These are not tears shed in heaven, but the tears of this present life. There will be no tears in heaven—"the former things have passed away."

The Promises of God Will Be Realized (21:5-8)

The One Who speaks is the One Who "sat on the throne." This is a reference to God the Father. He is called "the Alpha and the Omega, the Beginning and the End," a designation also used for the Son (1:8). This portion of God's Word strongly emphasizes that God's promises to us will be realized—we can count on it. His promises are based on several things:

Based on His ability to do it. He made the heavens and the earth in the beginning (Genesis 1:1), so it should not be too difficult to change it all and make it brand new. He has the power to do it, which should help us depend upon what He says.

Based on the accuracy of His word. John was instructed to write down, "these words are true and faithful." Jesus Christ is the "Faithful and True Witness" (3:14); His Word is completely trustworthy (Luke 21:29-33).

Based on His authority to do it. Alpha is the first letter in the Greek alphabet and Omega is the last one. God is the first and last word; He is the beginning and end of all things. Everything exists because of Him and His divine purpose. No other authority makes it possible and no other authority can be called upon to execute it.

Based on the assurance He gives. The phrases "to him who thirsts" and "he who overcomes" are all we need to know. If you come to Him for a drink, you will receive it. Do you have a taste for the water of life? Jesus said, "If anyone thirsts, let him come to Me and drink. He who believes in Me, as the Scripture has said, out of his heart will flow rivers of living water" (John 7:37-38; cf. 4:13-14).

The Bible establishes the entrance requirement to the New Jerusalem so that no one will misunderstand or make a false conclusion. Only those who believe in Jesus Christ as Savior and Lord (drink the water of life) will have eternal life and share in the blessings of the heavenly city. If you have believed in Jesus Christ as your Lord and Savior, you will be a citizen of heaven (Philippians 3:20-21). What wonderful assurance!

A solemn reminder. Verse 8 reminds us of the consequences of sin. If we continue to reject God's salvation through Jesus Christ, the consequences are awesome indeed—"shall have their part in the lake which burns with fire and brimstone, which is the second death." So the theme upon which chapter 20 ended is once again emphasized in chapter 21. Make no mistake about it, there is a hell to shun.

When we continue in sinful practices without repentance, we manifest that we have never been born again (Galatians 5:19-21; Ephesians 5:5-6). Our only hope is the work of Jesus Christ Who died for our sins and rose again that we might live forever with Him. Without His atoning work, there is no hope for any of us.

The New Jerusalem
(21:9-21)

⁹*Then one of the seven angels who had the seven bowls filled with the seven last plagues came to me and talked with me, saying, "Come, I will show you the bride, the Lamb's wife."* ¹⁰*And he carried me away in the Spirit to a great and high mountain, and showed me the great city, the holy Jerusalem, descending out of heaven from God,* ¹¹*having the glory of God. And her light was like a most precious stone, like a jasper stone, clear as crystal.* ¹²*Also she had a great and high wall with twelve gates, and twelve angels at the gates, and names written on them, which are the names of the twelve tribes of the children of Israel:* ¹³ *three gates on the east, three gates on the north, three gates on the south, and three gates on the west.* ¹⁴*Now the wall of the city had twelve foundations, and on them were the names of the twelve apostles of the Lamb.* ¹⁵*And he who talked with me had a gold reed to measure the city, its gates, and its wall.* ¹⁶*And the city is laid out as a square, and its length is as great as its breadth. And he measured the city with the reed: twelve thousand furlongs. Its length, breadth, and height are equal.* ¹⁷*Then he measured its wall: one hundred and forty-four cubits, according to the measure of a man, that is, of an angel.* ¹⁸*And the construc-*

tion of its wall was of jasper; and the city was pure gold, like clear glass. [19]*And the foundations of the wall of the city were adorned with all kinds of precious stones: the first foundation was jasper, the second sapphire, the third chalcedony, the fourth emerald,* [20]*the fifth sardonyx, the sixth sardius, the seventh chrysolite, the eighth beryl, the ninth topaz, the tenth chrysoprase, the eleventh jacinth, and the twelfth amethyst.* [21]*And the twelve gates were twelve pearls: each individual gate was of one pearl. And the street of the city was pure gold, like transparent glass.*

The Invitation to See the New Jerusalem (21:9-11a)

The announcement of the angel. I find it interesting that one of the seven angels who poured out the seven bowls of wrath, the seven last plagues, is the one who invites John to see the holy city. The blending of God's wrath and judgment with God's promise of eternal blessing is a reminder of His character; He manifests both attributes throughout all His dealings with humanity.

The angel is described in verse 15 as "he who talked with me" and is the one before whom John falls down and receives a rebuke for that attempted act of worship, which belongs only to God (22:8-9).

The ability of John to see it. In chapter 17 John was carried away in the Spirit to the wilderness; here he is taken to "a great and high mountain." The contrasting locations properly fit what John saw in each vision. The holy city is far more wonderful than the sight of the harlot on the beast with seven heads and ten horns.

As we indicated in Revelation 1:10, John was being transported into the future in the realm of the spirit, rather than the flesh. John is transferred in time to the actual events of the day of the Lord and the future. He is an eyewitness of those events and tries to describe them in the language of his day. What an incredible experience this first-century apostle must have had.

The overall appearance of the city. One simple statement summarizes John's first look at the holy city—"having the glory of God." The New Jerusalem reflects all that God is. His incomparable attributes are all contained in the expression "the glory of God." The city is a wonderful manifestation of the glory and character of Almighty God. God prepared and designed a city that would truly reveal the wonder of His nature and would cause us all to worship Him forever.

The Impact of This City on John (21:11b-21)

Words are so inadequate at times, and John must have felt overawed by what he saw. He is obviously stunned by the beauty and majesty of this heavenly city. What excitement must have filled his heart as he realized this is the eternal home of all believers! The details of this city are indeed incredible and wonderful to contemplate. It is a city that comes from God and has been prepared by Him for our enjoyment and blessing throughout eternity.

The shining of its light. The light was like that which comes from the most expensive gem imaginable ("most precious stone"). It is difficult to accurately identify the "jasper stone." It could be a diamond or something like a chalcedony, which is a translucent form of quartz. The jasper stone is mentioned in connection with the wall (v. 18) and with the first foundation of the wall of the city (v. 19).

The structure of the city. Three items are brought to our attention: the wall, the gates, and the foundations. The wall is "a great and high wall," which may emphasize that it keeps out what is not wanted. It is an impossible barrier to cross if you are not invited to enter the gates of the city. Verse 17 says the wall is 144 cubits, but it does not say whether this refers to its width or its height. A wall 200 feet high—or 200 feet thick—would be impressive.

There are twelve gates with twelve angels at the gates. On the gates are written the names of the twelve tribes of Israel. Special mention is made of Israel and the church by the twelve gates and twelve foundations containing the respective names of the tribes and the apostles. This confirms our view that the heavenly city is intended for all believers in all history.

The foundations of the city could be stacked on top of each other, with each foundation covering the entire base of the city. Another possibility, and perhaps the more likely choice, is that one foundation sits under each gate, so that there are three foundations per side. We simply do not know. What we do know is that the names of the twelve apostles are written on these foundations. Ephesians 2:20 speaks of the church being built on the foundation of the apostles and prophets.

The size of the city. We are told that the angel used "a gold reed" to measure the city, its gates, and its wall. Normally, a reed of measurement was about ten feet long, but could be longer. It is gold to match the majesty and royalty of what is being measured.

The city is laid out "as a square." The length and width are equal, each side measuring twelve thousand furlongs. Since a furlong is approximately six hundred feet, each side measures roughly fourteen hundred miles, making it considerably larger than the city Ezekiel spoke about during the time of the millennium (cf. Ezekiel 48:9-20).

Since the height of the city is the same as its length and width, some have suggested the city is a cube; others say it is a pyramid. Frankly, there's no way to prove either view.

The stones of the city. What an amazing array of precious stones. This city is a jeweler's fantasy. With its gigantic stones through which an enormous supply of light will pass, this city will be a stunning sight indeed! There are not enough words to express the impact of such beauty upon the human eye.

1. The wall of jasper. As we acknowledged earlier, we simply do not know what a "jasper" is. Verse 11 referred to "a jasper stone," describing it as "clear as crystal." It is possible this entire city is encased in a crystal-clear wall 200 feet thick through which the light of God will be diffused. What a sight!

2. The gates of pearl. Imagine—a gate made of one solid pearl!

3. The street of gold. This is not 24-carat gold, this is 100 percent pure. You can see right through it.

4. The city of gold. The whole city has the appearance of wealth and royalty. The city is not "like gold," but is made of "pure gold." The worth alone is impossible to calculate.

5. The foundations adorned with precious stones. There are twelve foundations, each one about five hundred miles long, or fifteen hundred miles on each side if the foundations are stacked on top of each other. Can you conceive of what a precious stone would look like that was hundreds of miles long and wide?

The Glory of the New Jerusalem
(21:22-22:5)

[22]But I saw no temple in it, for the Lord God Almighty and the Lamb are its temple. [23]And the city had no need of the sun or of the moon to shine in it, for the glory of God illuminated it, and the Lamb is its light. [24]And the nations of those who are saved shall walk in its light, and the kings of the earth bring their glory and honor into it. [25]Its gates shall not be shut at all by day (there shall be no night there). [26]And they shall bring the glory and the honor of the nations into it. [27]But there shall by no means enter it anything that defiles, or causes an abomination or a lie, but only those who are written in the Lamb's Book of Life.

> ^{1}*And he showed me a pure river of water of life, clear as crystal, proceeding from the throne of God and of the Lamb. ^{2}In the middle of its street, and on either side of the river, was the tree of life, which bore twelve fruits, each tree yielding its fruit every month. And the leaves of the tree were for the healing of the nations. ^{3}And there shall be no more curse, but the throne of God and of the Lamb shall be in it, and His servants shall serve Him. ^{4}They shall see His face, and His name shall be on their foreheads. ^{5}And there shall be no night there: They need no lamp nor light of the sun, for the Lord God gives them light. And they shall reign forever and ever.*

The Ingredients that Make This City So Wonderful (21:22-22:2)

Looking at the city is indeed a dazzling sight, but more needs to be said about the blessing this heavenly city will be in comparison to what we know now.

The place of worship will be the Lord Himself. There is no temple in the eternal state. There is no building or structure in the heavenly city to which we must come for worship. The millennial reign of Jesus Christ will have a temple, but not the eternal city. The Lord God Almighty and the Lamb are the only temple we will need. They are the fulfillment of all we have symbolized by our worship; they are the objects of our praise.

All symbols that help us focus on the Lord will be rendered useless by the glory of God's presence, a reminder to us not to place too much importance on present symbolism, structures, and order of worship. May God help us not to worship a building, a program, or even a way of doing things. We must worship the Lord! What makes the New Jerusalem so special is that we will finally be "with the Lord" forever and ever (1 Thessalonians 4:17; John 14:3; Philippians 1:23). He is the only temple we will need in the eternal state.

The presence of the Lord will eliminate the need for the sun and the moon. This is another point that distinguishes the eternal state from the millennial reign of Christ. The New Jerusalem appears to be unique by what is missing: No more death, sorrow, crying, or pain (21:4); no temple (21:22); no need of the sun or moon or lamp (21:23; 22:5); no night (21:25; 22:5); no defilement, abomination, or lie (21:27); and no more curse (22:3). What a wonderful place it will be with all of these things gone forever.

Verse 23 tells us "the glory of God illuminated it, and the Lamb is its light" (cf. Isaiah 60:19). In his first epistle, John tells us that "God is light, and in Him is no darkness at all" (1:5). Jesus claimed to be "the light of the world" (John 8:12). Apparently His light is not simply a metaphor for physical and spiritual life, it is real illumination that makes everything daylight in eternity. God spoke light into existence before He created the sun, moon, and stars. No problem to God. His own glory provides all the illumination we need in the eternal state.

The purpose of God for all nations will be fulfilled. God's original purpose for all His creation was stated back in Revelation 4:11:

> "You are worthy, O Lord,
>   To receive glory and honor and power;
>   For You created all things,
>   And by Your will they exist and were created."

God's original purpose is that all the nations will worship Him. His plan during this present age is to bring people to Himself out of every nation, tribe, tongue, and people (Psalm 66:4; Isaiah 66:23; 1 Peter 2:9).

Verses 24-26 tell us a few things about the eternal state that we have not seen in previous passages:

1. There will be nations and kings on the earth who are saved. How encouraging to note that not all were destroyed when the nations came to do battle against Jerusalem and the Lord Himself. There will also be "kings of the earth" who will be a part of the eternal state.

2. The nations and kings on earth come into the heavenly city. The way verses 24 and 26 are worded ("bring their glory and honor into it)" suggests there will be multitudes of people on earth in the eternal state who have access to the heavenly city but are not its primary residents. Who are these nations and kings? Probably those who come out of the tribulation period, those described as "sheep" in Matthew 25:31-46, and those born during the millennium who do not rebel against the Messiah, are all a part of the "nations" on earth in the eternal state.

3. Access to the heavenly city is provided for all. The "gates" of the heavenly city are never shut. There is no night in eternity, only daylight. People are free to go in and out of that beautiful city without restriction. In describing the future blessings of the nation of Israel, Isaiah predicted that this day would come:

> "Therefore your gates shall be open continually;
>   They shall not be shut day or night,

> That men may bring to you the wealth of the
>   Gentiles,
> And their kings in procession."
>
> (Isaiah 60:11)

4. All the glory and honor which kings and nations received will now be brought into the heavenly city. God's ultimate purpose is achieved. Whatever honor or glory nations and kings have received in this life, it will all be turned toward the Lord Himself in the eternal state. No one will ever struggle for fame, power, position, and greatness again. What a delightful world that will be! *All* the glory will be given to the Lord.

The protection of this city will eliminate all evil. Israel, the church, the tribulation saints, the "sheep," those saved in the millennium, "are written in the Lamb's Book of Life." They are the only ones who can ever enter the heavenly city. All unbelievers will be in the lake of fire (20:15). There will be no more lying or defiling. No act or word of humanity will ever again be an abomination to God and His purposes. Sin will be gone forever, and the devil and his angels will be in hell. What a glorious existence the eternal state will be.

The picture of eternal life will be portrayed by a river and a tree. Notice several things about this river and tree:

1. The purity of the river. The words "clear as crystal" obviously indicate there is no pollution in this water. It is pure life. Drinking the water of life is equal to believing on Jesus Christ as your Lord Savior (cf. John 4:13-14; 7:37-39). In Revelation 22:17 we read "and whoever desires, let him take the water of life freely." Salvation is being portrayed by the river of life; eternal life is symbolized by the purity of the river.

2. The place from which the river comes. The source of eternal life is God Himself. When we become believers in Jesus Christ, we are born of the Holy Spirit (John 3:1-8), we are born of God (John 1:12-13). When Jesus spoke of salvation as "rivers of living water" flowing out of a person's heart, the apostle John explains, "But this He spoke concerning the Spirit, whom those believing in Him would receive" (John 7:38-39).

3. The position of the river and the tree. The reference to "its" street refers us back to the city. The street of the city, described earlier as "pure gold, like transparent glass" (21:21), seems to be divided down the middle by the river. The tree of life is located on both sides of the river, perhaps a continuous hedgelike appearance on either side of the river, possibly implying a row of trees rather than a single tree.

4. The productivity of the tree of life. Ezekiel 47 speaks of the millennial kingdom and the tree-lined river that flows from the temple to the sea. Since God created trees and fruit and called it "very good," we should not be surprised to find evidence of His original creation in the eternal state. This is especially true in the case of the "tree of life," representing eternal life. This tree was found in the Garden of Eden, and was one Adam and Eve could partake of freely until they sinned (Genesis 2:9; 3:22).

It is difficult to ascertain the meaning of the river and the tree. Is there to be literal fruit on the tree from which we may freely eat, or is this to be taken symbolically? Was there not literal fruit on a literal tree in the Garden of Eden, the Paradise of God, before Adam and Eve sinned? Why twelve kinds of fruit? Is that not symbolic in that the tree yields every month, and there are twelve months in a year?

The questions are easier than the answers. Eating and drinking are common symbols portraying faith in and communion with the Lord. It is possible that such actions will continue forever as a constant reminder of the ground upon which we will enjoy the blessings of eternity. We are saved by faith alone in the person and work of the Messiah, Jesus our Lord.

5. The purpose of the leaves of the tree. The "leaves" of the tree symbolize the eternal life and salvation all peoples have received if they have come to the Lord. That they are for "the healing of the nations" means the tree of life is the key to the perpetual health of all peoples who find themselves in the eternal state. It is hard to conceive of the need for healing in the eternal state when all pain and death has been removed forever. What ills would exist that would need to be healed? It is better to think of the tree as the symbol of life, bringing health and eternal life to all who believe in the Lord.

The Involvement of Believers in the Eternal State (22:3-5)

We will not be sitting on clouds doing nothing; heaven will not be boring. There will be constant activity and "joy inexpressible and full of glory" (1 Peter 1:8).

We shall struggle no more. The "curse" was a result of humanity's fall into sin (Genesis 3:14-19). It has caused much blood, sweat, and tears. In the eternal state, the curse and its effects are done away. Our bodies will be brand new, fashioned like the resurrected body of Jesus Christ, without the limitations we presently know. No more dust, no more decay—the curse is gone forever (Romans 8:18-25)!

We shall serve Him. One of the most frequent words describing the role and responsibility of a child of God is that of "servant." Our Lord was a "servant" (Philippians 2:5-8), and the one who will be the greatest in the kingdom of God will be the "slave of all" (Mark 10:42-45). We need to recognize now what our servanthood will be like in eternity: we will serve *Him.* It is not ultimately other people that we serve, though in fact we do minister to others out of love and concern for them. We are really serving the Lord (Colossians 3:23-24).

We shall see His face. No words are more meaningful to the believer in love with Jesus Christ! Imagine—we will actually see the face of Him Who loved us and gave Himself for us (1 John 3:2). We will serve Him and see His face—what a summary of the blessing of heaven and our involvement in the eternal state.

We shall see without lamp or sun. The Lord is all the light we need. There will be no darkness, no need of public utility companies. The sun's light is no longer needed. We will see as we have never seen before, everything made clear by the light of the Lord God Himself (21:23).

We shall supervise the universe in our Lord's behalf . The role and responsibility of believers in reigning with Jesus Christ is a frequent topic of the Bible. Revelation 3:21 is a promise to believers that they will sit with Christ on His throne. The twenty-four elders of chapter 4 are sitting on thrones with crowns of gold on their heads. Revelation 5:10 says believers "shall reign on the earth." Paul wrote in 2 Timothy 2:12 that "we shall reign with Him." The tribulation martyrs, along with all those who have a part in the first resurrection, are described as those who will "reign with Him a thousand years" (Revelation 20:4, 6).

Our responsibilities are not detailed for us, but we have the clear statement that we "shall reign forever and ever" (22:5). Our responsibilities in the millennial reign of Christ will be completed at the end of the thousand years, but that does not mean we shall not continue to reign with the Lord forever and ever. Only eternity will reveal what marvelous opportunities and responsibilities we shall have. What a wonderful life it will be!

Chapter 30

Jesus Christ Is Coming Soon!

(22:6-21)

Three times in these sixteen verses we read the words of our Lord Jesus Christ that capture His final message to us:

"I am coming quickly!"

He had said before that He would come quickly, but those were warnings that He would come to judge the churches of Ephesus (2:5), Pergamos (2:16), and Sardis (3:3) if they did not repent. However, in His message to the church in Philadelphia He did refer to His second coming when He said, "Behold, I come quickly!" (3:11).

That His coming will be sudden when it does happen is obvious. First Corinthians 15:52 speaks of His coming as being "in a moment, in the twinkling of an eye." The emphasis of the word *quickly* in Revelation 22 is more like the word *soon* than *suddenly,* though both are true.

Jesus Is Coming
(22:6-21)

⁶*Then he said to me, "These words are faithful and true." And the Lord God of the holy prophets sent His angel to show His servants the things which must shortly take place.* ⁷*"Behold, I am coming quickly! Blessed is he who keeps the words of the prophecy of this book."* ⁸*Now I, John, saw and heard these things. And when I heard and saw, I fell down to worship before the feet of the angel who showed me these things.* ⁹*Then he said to me, "See that you do not do that. For I am your fellow servant, and of your brethren the prophets, and of those who keep the*

words of this book. Worship God." [10]*And he said to me, "Do not seal the words of the prophecy of this book, for the time is at hand.* [11]*He who is unjust, let him be unjust still; he who is filthy, let him be filthy still; he who is righteous, let him be righteous still; he who is holy, let him be holy still."*

[12]*"And behold, I am coming quickly, and My reward is with Me, to give to every one according to his work.* [13]*I am the Alpha and the Omega, the Beginning and the End, the First and the Last."* [14]*Blessed are those who do His commandments, that they may have the right to the tree of life, and may enter through the gates into the city.* [15]*But outside are dogs and sorcerers and sexually immoral and murderers and idolaters, and whoever loves and practices a lie.* [16]*"I, Jesus, have sent My angel to testify to you these things in the churches. I am the Root and the Offspring of David, the Bright and Morning Star."* [17]*And the Spirit and the bride say, "Come!" And let him who hears say, "Come!" And let him who thirsts come. And whoever desires, let him take the water of life freely.*

[18]*For I testify to everyone who hears the words of the prophecy of this book: If anyone adds to these things, God will add to him the plagues that are written in this book;* [19]*and if anyone takes away from the words of the book of this prophecy, God shall take away his part from the Book of Life, from the holy city, and from the things which are written in this book.*

[20]*He who testifies to these things says, "Surely I am coming quickly." Amen. Even so, come, Lord Jesus!* [21]*The grace of our Lord Jesus Christ be with you all. Amen.*

The Impact of This Book (22:6-9)

The reliability of its message. The message John received is "faithful and true." The same was said of the vision he was given of the eternal state (21:5). The promises of God found in this book will come to pass ("faithful") and all the visions and events recorded are genuine ("true") and therefore totally reliable.

The reminder of how the message was given. The source of this revelation is the Lord God Himself, Who used an angel to deliver it to His servant, the apostle John, as well as to all His servants. This reminder underscores what was said in the opening verse of the book. The message concerns the "things which must shortly take place."

The response we should give to its message. This sixth beatitude of the book—"Blessed is he who keeps the words of the prophecy of this book"—is similar to the first (1:3). The main intent of prophecy is to cause us to obey what God says and to apply what we learn. If our interest in prophecy is simply to develop an outline of the sequence of events or to hear the viewpoints of what all its symbols represent, then we have missed the point of prophecy. Prophecy is to have an effect on how we *live*. It should motivate us to a life of purity and faithful service to the Lord (1 John 3:3; Matthew 24:45-51; 25:14-30).

The reaction of John to this book. John fell at the feet of the wrong person, but his reaction is quite understandable. He had just received more information about the future than anyone had ever seen or known. No wonder he was overcome with awe.

The rebuke of the angel. The angel's admonition to John is based on his position: "I am your fellow servant." Angels are not to be worshiped. Jesus Christ, however, is so far superior to the angels that they are instructed to worship Him (Hebrews 1:1-14). Jesus Christ is God in human flesh or He cannot be our Savior from sin.

The Importance of the Book (22:10-15)

The Revelation presents to us the person and character of Jesus Christ like no other book. It gives added dimensions to the picture we see of Him in the Gospels. The book of Revelation tells us about our future like no other book, and presents clearly the consequences of the gospel.

It reveals the climax of God's plan of the ages. Daniel the prophet was told to seal up the vision he received (Daniel 12:8-10; cf. 8:26; 12:4):

> Although I heard, I did not understand. Then I said, "My lord, what shall be the end of these things?" And he said, "Go your way, Daniel, for the words are closed up and sealed till the time of the end. Many shall be purified, made white, and refined, but the wicked shall do wickedly; and none of the wicked shall understand, but the wise shall understand."

The book of Revelation is an answer to Daniel's question about understanding. The words of his prophecy are no longer sealed up now that "the Revelation of Jesus Christ" has been given to John. The

Lord intends that all should hear this message, "for the time is at hand." The closer we get to the fulfillment, the more imperative it is for us to study and understand the prophecies of this book.

Two things are brought out in verse 11 about the final destiny of humanity:

1. The impossibility of any changes in the eternal state of both believers and unbelievers. What we decide, we must decide *now*. There will be no opportunity to change our destiny after our death.

2. The enormous contrast between the final destiny of the believer and the unbeliever. A great gulf stands between the "unjust" and the "righteous," between the "filthy" and the "holy." The difference is between heaven and hell, the heavenly city forever or the lake of fire forever. What an awesome thought.

It reveals the coming of Jesus Christ. The importance of the book of Revelation to the hope of the believer cannot be overstated (cf. Titus 2:13). The rewards Christ brings at His coming are especially important to believers (22:12). God's justice will be clear to every believer when He rewards them "according to his work." The rewards will be certainly greater than the effort (Mark 10:29-30), but they will be distributed righteously, according to what we have done, not what someone else has done.

This judgment of believers for reward will occur at the judgment seat of Christ (1 Corinthians 3:11-15; 2 Corinthians 5:10). While we are not told exactly when this judgment will occur, it may happen in heaven during the tribulation on earth. The twenty-four elders of Revelation 4, who represent the completed church in heaven, have already been rewarded, since there are "crowns of gold" upon their heads.

The theme of reward occurs frequently in the Bible and applies to unbelievers as well as believers. We will all be rewarded for what we have done in this life (Romans 2:6-11; 14:12; 1 Corinthians 3:8).

It reveals the Divine character of Jesus Christ. That Jesus Christ is "the Alpha and the Omega, the Beginning and the End, the First and the Last," reveals His nature and character as it relates to God's plan of the ages and our prophetic future. Revelation 1 relates all three descriptive phrases to our Lord Jesus Christ (vv. 8, 17). These titles are used in Isaiah's prophecy to refer to the only God (41:4; 44:6; 46:9-10; 48:12). The Divine character of Jesus Christ is clearly revealed in the book of Revelation.

It reveals the consequences of the gospel. No fact underscores the importance of the book of Revelation as much as this one. The consequences of the gospel are clearly taught—the lake of fire for unbelievers, the heavenly city on earth for believers. Verse 14 contains the seventh beatitude of the book. No more "blessed" condition could be ours than the confidence that we shall enter the gates of the heavenly city and be with the Lord forever!

Two things are clear from these verses about the consequences of the gospel: (1) They describe how we may enter the heavenly city, and (2) they determine who is inside the city and who is outside the city. Three times in these two final chapters we find reference to what will *not* be found in the city (21:8; 21:27; 22:15). Outside the city are "dogs," a derogatory term for that which is to be despised (cf. Philippians 3:2); "sorcerers and sexually immoral and murderers and idolaters, and whoever loves and practices a lie." Those who are characterized by such sinful practices have no relationship to Jesus Christ our Lord and will be outside the city. Specifically, they will be in the lake of fire (20:15; 21:8).

The Final Invitation of the Book (22:16-21)

There are many invitations in the Bible. The Lord Jesus invited people to believe in Him and to come to Him. An invitation is an opportunity as well as a responsibility. We cannot remain indifferent or passive to the invitations in the Bible dealing with our eternal destiny.

The Person Who is the center and object of this invitation. The speaker identifies Himself clearly—"I, Jesus." He then identifies Himself further, making it clear that He is the Messiah, the promised King, and our Hope. The statement "I am the Root and the Offspring of David" identifies Him as the Messiah, the Son of David, the One Who will sit on the throne of David and rule the world (Isaiah 11:1-5; 2 Samuel 7:12-16; Psalm 132:11-12).

Jesus also identifies Himself as "the Bright and Morning Star," a phrase used in Revelation 2:28 as a promise to the overcomers in the church of Thyatira. Numbers 24:17 also identifies the Messiah as a "Star" from the line of Jacob and a "Scepter" from the line of Israel. The "Morning Star" implies that the dawning of a new day is at hand. Jesus Christ is our Hope of a new day. No matter how dark the night of present world history is, the "Bright and Morning Star" tells us that a better day is coming, a brand new world where all will be joy and peace forever.

The provision of this invitation. One simple word describes the heart of this invitation—*Come!* Jesus said in Matthew 11:28, "Come to Me, all you who labor and are heavy laden, and I will give you rest." Elsewhere He promised, "the one who comes to Me I will by no means cast out" (John 6:37).

1. The people who give the invitation. The Holy Spirit "will convict the world of sin, and of righteousness, and of judgment" (John 16:8). Jesus spoke about being "born of the Spirit" (John 3:5-6), and Titus 3:5 says our salvation comes "through the washing of regeneration and renewing of the Holy Spirit." The ministry of the Holy Spirit is to draw people to Jesus Christ; He extends the invitation, "Come!"

In cooperation with the Holy Spirit, the bride—the church of Jesus Christ—also extends the invitation. Here is a great challenge to all believers to be involved in evangelism, inviting people to put their faith and trust in Jesus Christ as Lord and Savior.

2. The prerequisite that must be faced. The "thirst" and "desire" must be there or no decision will be made. Sensing our own need for the gospel is so important. Without Jesus Christ as our Savior and Lord, we are headed for an eternity without God and without hope in a place called "the lake of fire."

3. The promise the invitation gives. The "water of life" refers to eternal life, being with the Lord forever in the heavenly city on earth. Jesus told the Samaritan woman that the water He gives would be "a fountain of water springing up into everlasting life" (John 4:14).

4. The price of this invitation. Though it cost Jesus Christ His own blood, His death on the cross for our sins, it does not cost us anything. Salvation is a free gift given by the grace of God (Ephesians 2:8-9). The gift of eternal life must be received (Romans 6:23); it cannot be earned or deserved by human performance.

The punishment for those who reject this invitation. Verses 18 and 19 are crucial when discussing the authority and finality of God's revelation in the Bible. The inspiration of the Bible (2 Timothy 3:16) refers to the reliability and accuracy of what is written. The writers were not inspired; they were controlled by the Holy Spirit so that what was written was not of any private interpretation, but exactly what God wanted to be said (2 Peter 1:19-21). Inspiration refers to the accuracy of what is written.

When we speak of the revelation of God, we are dealing with the issue of authority. The Bible *is* the Word of God, we don't make it the Word of God by how we interpret it or apply it. But does God continue to give additional information by direct revelation not found in the Bible? To that question, we answer a firm *no!*

According to Hebrews 1:1-2, "God, who at various times and in different ways spoke in time past to the fathers by the prophets, has in these last days spoken to us by His Son." What "days" are intended here? The days in which God revealed Himself in Jesus Christ and delivered to His apostles the information about His Son; that revelation is now found in the New Testament.

Revelation 22:18-19 completes our understanding. With the writing of this book of prophecy, which outlines events all the way into the eternal state, God's direct revelation ceased. No more is to be given. All that God wants to say, He has said to this generation. Anyone who claims to receive direct communication from God today is deceiving himself, and disobeying the clear teaching of the Bible.

Two consequences are listed: (1) The plagues of this book for anyone who tries to add to the words of this prophecy, and (2) the removal of his part from the Book of Life and from the holy city, and the things written in the book. These consequences can only apply to unbelievers. Those who reject the invitation of the book and do not respond to the Lord Jesus Christ, trusting Him for their eternal salvation, will be lost forever, separated from the promised blessings of this book because they have rejected its final invitation.

The prophecy that makes this invitation so important . It is an event that will happen soon—"Surely I am coming quickly." The return of Jesus Christ is a motivating factor in persuading people to respond to the invitation. It is the eager expectation of every true believer, as John himself expresses: "Amen. Even so, come, Lord Jesus!" Are you anticipating the return of Jesus Christ? Is it your hope?

A Final Word

John's last remark is very much like Paul's salutations: "The grace of our Lord Jesus Christ be with you all. Amen." How fitting to be reminded of our need of His grace. God's wonderful grace makes our salvation possible. It stands in sharp contrast to the wrath and judgment of God revealed in this book.

Have you responded to the grace of our Lord Jesus Christ? Grace gives you what you do not deserve. The apostle Paul wrote (Titus 2:11-14):

> For the *grace of God* that brings salvation has appeared to all men, teaching us that, denying ungodliness and worldly lusts, we should live soberly, righteously, and godly in the

present age, looking for the blessed hope and glorious appearing of our great God and Savior Jesus Christ, who gave Himself for us, that He might redeem us from every lawless deed and purify for Himself His own special people, zealous for good works.

Bibliography

Alford, Henry. *Word Studies in the New Testament*, vol. 4. Chicago: Moody Press, 1958.

Ames, A. H. *The Revelation of St. John the Divine*. New York: Eaton & Mains, 1897.

Atkinson, Benjamin F. *The Revelation of Jesus Christ* . Louisville: Herald Press, 1939.

Augustine. *The City of God. The Fathers of the Church*. Trans. Walsh and Monhan. New York: Fathers of the Church, Inc., 1952.

Barclay, William. *Letters to the Seven Churches*. London: S.C.M. Press Limited, 1957.

Barnes, Albert. *Notes, Explanatory and Practical, on the Book of Revelation*. New York: Harper & Brothers, 1851.

Barnhouse, Donald Grey. *Revelation*. Grand Rapids: Zondervan Publishing House, 1971.

Beechick, Allen. *The Pre-Tribulation Rapture*. Denver: Accent Books, 1980.

Bennett, Edward. *The Visions of John in Patmos*. London: A.S. Rouse, 1892.

Blackstone, William E. *Jesus Is Coming*. Old Tappan, N.J.: Fleming H. Revell Co., 1908.

Boettner, Loraine. *The Millennium*. Philadelphia: The Presbyterian and Reformed Publishing Co., 1958.

Buis, Harry. *The Book of Revelation*. Philadelphia: Presbyterian and Reformed Publishing Co., 1960.

Camping, Harold. *The Fig Tree*. Oakland: Family Stations, Inc., 1983.

Chafer, L.S. *Systematic Theology*. Dallas: Dallas Seminary Press, 1947.

Clouse, Robert G., ed. *The Meaning of the Millennium* . Downers Grove, Ill.: InterVarsity Press, 1977.

Bibliography

Corbin, Bruce. *The Book of Revelation*. Grand Rapids: Zondervan Publishing House, 1938.

Cox, Clyde C. *Apocalyptic Commentary*. Cleveland, Tenn: Pathway Press, 1959.

Criswell, W. A. *Expository Sermons on Revelation*. Grand Rapids: Zondervan Publishing House, 1962.

Culver, Robert. *Daniel and the Latter Days*. Old Tappan, N.J.: Fleming H. Revell, Co., 1954.

Darby, J. N. *Notes on the Apocalypse*. London: G. Morrish, 1842.

Davis, George W. *The Patmos Vision*. Los Angeles: McBride Printing Co., 1915.

Evans, William. *Christ's Last Message to His Church*. Old Tappan, N.J.: Fleming H. Revell Co., 1926.

Ford, Desmond. *The Abomination of Desolation in Biblical Eschatology*. Washington, D.C.: University Press of America, Inc., 1979.

Fruchtenbaum, Arnold G. *The Footsteps of the Messiah*. San Antonio: Ariel Press, 1982.

Gaebelein, Arno C. *The Revelation*. New York: Our Hope Publication Office, 1915.

Gager, LeRoy. *The Second Exodus*. Burnaby, B.C.: Second Exodus Publications Society, 1981.

Graham, Billy. *Approaching Hoofbeats: The Four Horsemen of the Apocalypse*. Waco, Tex.: Word Publishing Co., 1983.

Grant, F. W. *The Revelation of Jesus Christ*. New York: Loizeaux Brothers, n.d.

Gromacki, Robert Glenn. *Are These the Last Days?* Schaumburg, Ill.: Regular Baptist Press, 1970.

Haldeman, I. M. *A Synopsis of the Book of Revelation* . Published in a booklet series by the author, n.d.

Harrison, Norman B. *The End*. Minneapolis: The Harrison Service, 1941.

Hastings, J. *The Great Texts of the Bible—Revelation* . New York: Charles Scribner's Sons, 1915.

Hislop, Alexander. *The Two Babylons*. 3d edition. New York: Loizeaux Brothers, 1943.

Hoyt, Herman A. *The End Times*. Chicago: Moody Press, 1969.

Ironside, H. A. *Lectures on the Book of Revelation*. New York: Loizeaux Brothers, 1930.

Jamieson, Robert, A. R. Faussett, and David Brown. *A Commentary Critical, Experimental, and Practical on the Old and New Testaments*. 6 vols. Grand Rapids: Wm. B. Eerdmans Publishing Co., 1945.

Jennings, F. C. *Studies in Revelation*. New York: Loizeaux Brothers, 1937.

Kelly, William. *Lectures on the Book of Revelation*. London: W. H. Broom, 1874.

Kirban, Salem, and Gary C. Cohen. *Revelation Visualized*. Salem Kirban Inc., 1971.

_____. *How the World Will End*. Wheaton, Ill.: Tyndale House Publishers, 1968.

Kuyper, Abraham. *The Revelation of St. John*. Trans. John Hendrik de Vries. Grand Rapids: Wm. B. Eerdmans Publishing Co., 1935.

Ladd, George E. *A Commentary on the Revelation of John*. Grand Rapids: Wm. B. Eerdmans Publishing Co., 1972.

LaHaye, Tim F. *Revelation Illustrated and Made Plain* . La Verne, Calif.: El Camino Press, 1973.

Larkin, Clarence. *The Book of Revelation*. Philadelphia: Rev. Clarence Larkin Estate, 1919.

_____. *Dispensational Truth*. Publisher and date unknown.

Laymon, Charles M. *The Book of Revelation*. Nashville: Abingdon Press, 1960.

Lenski, R. C. H. *The Interpretation of St. John's Revelation*. Columbus: Lutheran Book Concern, 1935.

Lindsay, Hal. *The Late Great Planet Earth*. Grand Rapids: Zondervan Publishing House, 1970.

_____. *There's a New World Coming*. Santa Ana: Vision House Publishers, 1973.

MacArthur, Jack. *Expositional Commentary on Revelation*. Eugene, Ore.: Certain Sound Publishing Co., 1973.

McCarrell, William. *Christ's Seven Letters to His Church*. Findlay: Dunham Publishing Co., 1936.

McClain, Alva J. *The Greatness of the Kingdom*. Chicago: Moody Press, 1968.

McGee, J Vernon. *Reveling Through Revelation*. 2 vols. Los Angeles: Church of the Open Door, n.d.

Morgan, G. Campbell. *A First Century Message to Twentieth Century Christians*. Old Tappan, N.J.: Fleming H. Revell Co., 1902.

_____. *The Letters of Our Lord*. Old Tappan, N.J.: Fleming H. Revell Co., n.d.

Newell, William R. *The Book of Revelation*. Chicago: Moody Press, 1935.

Pache, Rene. *The Return of Jesus Christ*. Chicago: Moody Press, 1955.

Peake, Arthur S. *The Revelation of John*. London: Primitive Methodist Publishing House, 1919.

Pentecost, J. Dwight. *Things to Come*. Grand Rapids: Zondervan Publishing House, 1958.

Bibliography

Pettingill, William L. *The Unveiling of Jesus Christ* . Findlay: Fundamental Truth Publishers, 1939.

Pink, Arthur W. *The Antichrist*. Swengel: Bible Truth Depot, 1923.

Ramsay, W. M. *The Letters to the Seven Churches of Asia*. London: Hodder & Stoughton, 1904.

Robertson, A. T. *Word Pictures in the New Testament*, vol. 4. New York: Harper & Brothers, Publishers, 1933.

Ryrie, Charles Caldwell. *Revelation*. Chicago: Moody Press, 1968.

Scott, C. Anderson. *The Book of Revelation*. London: Hodder & Stoughton, 1905.

Scott, Walter. *Exposition of the Revelation of Jesus Christ*. London: Pickering and Inglis Ltd., n.d.

Scroggie, W. G. *The Book of Revelation*. Edinburgh: The Book Stall, 1920.

Seiss, Joseph A. *The Apocalypse*. Grand Rapids: Zondervan Publishing House, 1957.

_____. *Letters to the Seven Churches*. Grand Rapids: Baker Book House, 1956.

Sibley, Julian Scales. *The Climax of Revelation*. Old Tappan, N.J.: Fleming H. Revell Co., 1932.

Smith, J. B. *A Revelation of Jesus Christ*. Scottdale, Penn.: Herald Press, 1961.

Smith, Wilbur. "Revelation." In *Wycliffe Bible Commentary*. Ed. Pfeiffer and Harrison. Chicago: Moody Press, 1962.

Snowden, James H. *The Coming of the Lord*. New York: The Macmillan Co., 1919.

Strauss, Lehman. *The Book of Revelation*. Neptune: Loizeaux Brothers, 1964.

Swete, B. H. *The Apocalypse of St. John*. Grand Rapids: Wm. B. Eerdmans Publishing Co., n.d.

Talbot, Louis T. *The Revelation of Jesus Christ*. Los Angeles: Church of the Open Door, 1937.

Tan, Paul Lee. *The Interpretation of Prophecy*. Winona Lake, Ind.: BMH Books, Inc., 1974.

Tenney, Merrill C. *The Book of Revelation*. Grand Rapids: Baker Book House, 1963.

_____. *Interpreting Revelation*. Grand Rapids: Wm. B. Eerdmans Publishing Co., 1957.

Torrance, Thomas F. *The Apocalypse Today*. Grand Rapids: Wm. B. Eerdmans Publishing Co., 1959.

Trench, Richard Chenevix. *Commentary on the Epistles to the Seven Churches in Asia*. New York: Charles Scribner & Co., 1872.

Tucker, Leon. *Studies in Revelation*. Binghamton: John Young Publisher, 1935.

Van Ryn, August. *Notes on the Book of Revelation*. Kansas City: Walterick Publishing Co., 1960.

Vaughan, C. J. *Lectures on the Revelation of John*. London: Macmillan and Co., 1870.

Walvoord, John F. *The Millennial Kingdom*. Grand Rapids: Zondervan Publishing House, 1959.

_____. *The Blessed Hope and the Tribulation*. Grand Rapids: Zondervan Publishing House, 1976.

_____.*The Revelation of Jesus Christ*. Chicago: Moody Press, 1966.

_____. *The Nations in Prophecy*. Grand Rapids: Zondervan Publishing House, 1967.

_____. *The Church in Prophecy*. Grand Rapids: Zondervan Publishing House, 1964.

West, Nathaniel. *The Thousand Years*. Fincastle: Scripture Truth Book Co., n.d.

White, John Wesley. *Re-Entry*. Grand Rapids: Zondervan Publishing House, 1970.

Wuest, Kenneth S. *Prophetic Light in the Present Darkness*. Grand Rapids: Wm. B. Eerdmans Publishing Co., 1955.